SELDOM RIGHT
BUT NEVER IN DOUBT

Essays, Journalism, and Social Commentary, 1997-2012

By Joseph Dobrian
With a foreword by Dorothy Parker

SELDOM RIGHT
BUT NEVER IN DOUBT

By Joseph Dobrian

Rex Imperator, New York, N.Y.

ISBN-10: 0983557225
ISBN-13: 978-0983557227
Library of Congress Control Number
Rex Imperator, U.S.A.

This is a work of non-fiction. However, the names of some people have been changed, to protect their privacy.

To the women I've tried to court or otherwise impress with my writing, over the past 50 years or so. My thanks to all yall.

TABLE OF CONTENTS

Death

FOREWORD
By Dorothy Parker

Last night reminded me of the type of date in which I find myself imprisoned, oftener and oftener these days, as my birthdays approach the fatal "30" mark: an endless dinner with a man who knows everything, and simply will not entertain the quaint little notion that he might occasionally be mistaken – with the exception that when I am literally being dined by such a gentleman, he will usually see to it that my dainty glass of sherry remains at least half-full.

In this instance, though, I had to content myself with an apple and Joseph Dobrian's new book, *Seldom Right But Never In Doubt* – the very heft of which suggests that Mr. Dobrian is rather more than half-full of himself. Or full of something, at any rate. Some may find his confessionals and declarations enlightening. I'm much more fascinated by the pathology.

Oh, dear, there I go again, being perfectly cruel to someone I'm sure is a very nice young man. Actually I could have stomped my little slippers on the hearthrug for joy when I discovered that this journalist, novelist, and political gnat had finally gotten his pontifications – which have been published in various venues over the past 15 years – organized in book form. It's difficult to support any argument that Mr. Dobrian is a great writer, or even a very good one, but he has at any rate mastered the art of verbal ecdysiasm.

That is no mean feat. However, the question of whether he has exposed anything worth seeing is left to you, dear reader. At least, the question might be debated if anyone took Mr. Dobrian one-tenth as seriously as he evidently likes to pretend he's being taken.

It's clear that Mr. Dobrian is one of those people who cannot go through life without seeing himself playing himself in a high-budget movie, doing whatever he is doing at the moment. In his rare moments of idleness, no doubt, he's the sort who poses for formal portraits in his dressing-room mirror.

In many of his essays, Mr. Dobrian is clearly trying to be a wit; in others, he tries to shock; at times, he's a pedagogue; at other times, a mere purveyor of opinions; occasionally a story-teller. Always and above all, though, ostentation is his racket.

One finds it difficult to escape the conclusion that Mr. Dobrian is, in most of his essays, a little less interested in stating his case than he is in impressing the reader with his style or (dare I suggest that it exists?) his charm. But let it never be suspicioned, rumored or otherwise bruited about that we are dealing with a stylist here. Mr. Dobrian has an adequate knowledge of the English language, as befits anyone who makes his living as a ghost-writer and trade journalist, and thus his prose is readable. It does not, however, cause one by its magnificence to leap from one's chair to dance a joyous tango with one's French poodle.

Once or perhaps twice, in reading these essays, you notice that some merciful pixie (of a literary bent) has whispered a memorable epigram into Mr. Dobrian's ear. "All of us dream of being God; none of us would be a saint" is one I don't think I'd heard before, and therefore I must give Mr. Dobrian the benefit of the doubt and assume that he invented it. You can just about see Mr. Dobrian tucking himself into bed with a coprophagous grin, on the night he thought of that little gem, secure in the knowledge that it would one day find a home in the pages of *Bartlett's*.

We might also point to the occasional instance of genuine humor, as when Mr. Dobrian describes an attack of gout in "A Most Romantic Illness." At other times, he can be enlightening – if you happen to be interested in the somewhat esoteric subjects on which he chooses to attempt to enlighten us. I, for one, do not know how I ever got along without knowing all about the evolution of the word "nimrod" as a common noun. But now, thanks to "A Nimrod In Search Of Daffisms," I plan to dine out on this precious knowledge, oh, ever so often!

At first blush, one occasionally will get the impression that Mr. Dobrian adopts positions not because he believes them but because he knows they will shock. But close reading of many of these essays will leave one convinced that however naughty, perverse, or just plain batty our young Sparky might be, he at least means every word he says. Whether or not his arguments are defensible, never let it be said that Mr. Dobrian ever takes the majority view without adopting a variant of it that the majority of his readers will find insufferable.

In rare, dramatic instances, the dear man is actually *right*, as in his various rants on political correctness and criminal justice – but on those occasions, he states his point in a manner clearly calculated to induce rages and massive strokes, rather than conversions, amongst those who take the opposite view.

Mr. Dobrian conscientiously makes himself dislikable, at times, with all the fervor of one who wants no more than unequivocal adoration – from everybody.

Seldom Right But Never In Doubt

Being A Writer

When people ask me how I came to be a writer (and I get that question a lot), I usually reply, "Because I'm not good at anything else." That's not meant to be funny, although I'm usually smiling when I say it. I've always enjoyed writing fiction, poetry, and essays. Before I was literate I would dictate stories to my mother or grandmother. I've been deliberately developing my language skills since I could talk.

I recently had an epiphany, following a brief conversation with a stranger: I realized that I actually talk in blank verse. That is to say that when I craft a sentence to be spoken, I pay attention to elements like meter, scansion, and assonance, probably more than does anyone I know. I now understand why my youngest sister, when she was about five years old, observed, "Joseph, you talk funny!"

Words are my racket; always have been. I never thought of making writing my profession, though, till I was about 20 years old. I'd wanted to be an actor, but I realized that the chances of success in that field were slim. I wanted, also, to be a lawyer, and maybe go into politics, till I realized that I was too lazy and unfocused to take that direction. Then when I was a junior at the University of Iowa, one of my professors handed me back a term paper on which she'd scribbled, "You must not go on to law school. Stay in this vale of tears and keep writing!"

So, I did. I cranked out a preposterously bad novel, over the next year. A couple of years after that, I produced another. Neither was published, but one copy of each still exists in someone else's possession, and I don't know where she's hidden them. She could blackmail me with them.

Through my mid-20s, I drifted from one job to another, to unemployment, to an aimless period of post-graduate study, during which I wrote for recreation but with no effort to improve the quality of my work. Then, at 26, I came to New York City and found a situation as a trade journalist.

I was, at last, writing for my living, and I discovered that professional writers have to sweat the small stuff. It was drudgery, writing about personal care products, giftware, and seasonal merchandise – but if it was akin to painting a barn, at least I learned how to paint a barn really well.

At 29, the magazine for which I worked went out of existence, and I had to choose between looking for another, similar job, or going freelance. I chose the latter, and I've been getting along as a freelancer ever since. I've had to learn how to satisfy lots of clients instead of just one, and that means constant attention to detail, constant attention to the mechanics of researching and writing.

The more I wrote for money, the more I wrote for fun in my spare time. The more I developed my talent for commercial writing, the better my recreational writing got. The more I wrote, the more I thought about what it means to be a writer.

I'm not talking, here, about "the writer's life." All writers take different approaches to writing in relation to the other parts of their lives. Some writers really do live the stereotype, locking themselves in a crummy apartment and skipping meals because all they can think about is writing. Others behave more or less like normal people – having families, playing golf, joining Rotary, and so on – so that you'd hardly know that they were writers at all.

What I'm talking about is one's obligation, as a writer, to one's clients, one's readers, and oneself. Being a writer means behaving in a professionally ethical manner – which means being as intellectually honest as you know how to be, at all times. It means checking your facts; it means judging fairly if you're judging at all; it means producing a quality product.

It goes without saying that you have to give your best when you're working for a paying client. But even if you're just writing for yourself, working on a speculative project that will bring you very little money if any, you can't let yourself down.

It's said that works of art are never finished; they're merely abandoned. That's probably true. But to my mind, the difference between bad art and good is whether the artist said, "Oh, I've spent enough time on this project; it's good enough," or "I've made it as good as I know how to make it."

To be a good writer, you need to develop honesty. That sounds odd: Most people would probably say that either you're honest or you're not; it's not a quality you develop. That may be, if you're using "honesty" in the moralistic/ethical sense. But I'm talking about being an honest writer. Many people who are as decent and trustworthy and moral as can be, are not honest writers.

We know dishonest non-fiction when we see it – if the writer has been unfairly tendentious, or careless in his research, or has employed logical fallacies, or relied too heavily on emotion, or thought out his position insufficiently. It's harder to spot dishonesty in fiction – after all, fiction is false by its nature – but you'll identify it every time you encounter an unbelievable character, a ham-fisted plot device, or dialogue that doesn't sound like the way people talk.

If you want to write well, you have to not only write good English, but write honestly. If you do that, you may find that you have to abandon some of the ideas that you brought to the project. You might discover facts, or lines of reasoning, that force you to re-examine your premises and change your position. Or, by making the plot of a fictional story more plausible, you might have to take the story in a different direction from the one you'd intended. To me, that is part of the fun of writing well, even if writing honestly can be frustrating and disconcerting at times.

We can't draw a plain distinction between a commercial writer and an artistic writer. I am both, and sometimes my work has a foot in both camps. But even at my most venal, I'm finicky about my style. In my opinion, you develop an æsthetically pleasing style only when you write with purpose. You might write to make a political point; you might write to illustrate the moral of a story; you might write to persuade someone to love something that you love. Whatever your purpose, if you know what it is, you'll write better.

If your purpose is merely to write beautifully, you'll write meaningless sentences, and passages as purple as regurgitated Kool-Aid – and you'll look like a self-dramatizing little shit who needs to be taught the fundamentals. I can say it no plainer.

*

Aside from the question of why I am a writer, the question remains: Why did I ever start, and why continue? The answer to that is much the same as it was when I was five or so: I can't help it.

I've been a loner all my life, partly because I learned very early on that I must trust nobody, and partly because I developed unpleasant traits that made me difficult to get along with. Since I often played alone, I would develop stories in my head, and sometimes act them out, aloud, speaking to imaginary people or soliloquizing to myself.

Possibly as a result of this, people started writing books about me. So to speak. I began to imagine, when I was four or five, that everything I did or experienced was being chronicled, in narrative form, by invisible men who haunted me, wherever I went, and wrote my actions down as fast as I could perform them.

"What's for supper?" Joe asked his mother as he walked into the kitchen.

Like that. I would imagine the words being produced, in my head. It would be particularly noticeable, and maddening, if I were stressed-out, such as if I'd just had a disagreement with my parents or been frustrated when trying to perform a task. Sometimes I'd be crying, in response to one of the countless humiliations that one suffers as a child, and my imaginary authors would be writing about that, too, describing it in detail that was even more embarrassing than whatever had induced the tears in the first place.

At that point, I would sometimes shout, *"They're writing books about me!"* and my poor parents could not figure out what I meant, nor could I explain it very well. I soon learned to control that reaction – I believe that that was a phase that lasted only a matter of weeks – but I didn't outgrow the fantasy till I'd reached adolescence.

At around that time – at age 12 or so – I began, occasionally, writing to impress other people. I think my desire to write was initially spurred by my desire to develop those childish fantasies of mine, and perhaps to explain myself to myself. But I started – if very slowly – to become a competent writer when I decided that I wanted people to read my writing and say, "He's worthy of my attention."

It was a little later – when I was about 15 – that I started trying to impress girls with my writing. I tried it on my first serious crush (a girl I should have known was unattainable), thinking that she might fall in love with either my beautiful English, or my ideas. She didn't. But that didn't stop me from trying the same thing, on other girls and women, for the next 40-plus years.

Many's the woman I've wooed with letters, or with essays and fiction that I let her see before anyone else saw them. Perhaps it's a reflection on the quality of my writing that it seldom worked – or maybe it's just not an effective method for anyone. *Cyrano de Bergérac* was only a play, after all.

You won't impress other people with your writing unless you write with a purpose to which your style is subordinate. I became (I hope) a pretty good writer when I decided that I wanted people to read my writing and say, "I'm convinced." Much of my writing has at its base a desire to persuade people to move in a certain direction: if not to change society altogether, at least bring people to my way of thinking on one issue or another, and make them want to do something about it.

I'm a writer because I'm self-absorbed and egotistical. I want to impress people. I want people to think I'm both wise and clever. I want to be talked about: preferably in a way that's favorable to me, but better that I create unfavorable buzz than no buzz at all. Most writers write for the sake of their egos, above all else. Airing personal grievances is frequently another strong motivator. People who do that, orally, call it "venting." That's what a lot of artistic writing is, be it fiction or non-fiction.

"All writers are vain, selfish, and lazy," George Orwell wrote, and I have to agree with him. He also asserted that in this respect, writers are quite different from most people – except for the sort of people generally considered the most successful.

"The great mass of human beings are not acutely selfish," Orwell wrote. "After the age of about thirty they almost abandon the sense of being individuals at all – and live chiefly for others, or are simply smothered under drudgery. But there is also the minority of gifted, willful people who are determined to live their own lives to the end, and writers belong in this class."

Just so.

I write commercially partly because I don't know how to

make a living any other way. But not only do I make money by writing commercially; I also write commercially the better to write artistically. Writing commercially, I sharpen my style, and force myself to think through a given issue. If I've had any success as an artistic writer, it's mainly because of the years I've spent writing about conduit lenders or merchandising techniques.

That success, for whatever it's worth, may also be due to the fact that I never got over my frustration at not being able to win over that girl, back in high school, with my words. I will never concede that that approach does not work. I will keep trying it.

I believe that's what folks call "crazy."

Politeness And Political Correctness

Idol-Worshipping

Throughout life, when we have a mission to fulfill – get a better job, get famous, attract a lover, excel at a game or sport, improve our personalities – we tend to choose role models on whom to pattern ourselves. This can be useful – but it can also be a pain in the ass.

We can't avoid choosing, as role models, people who stand higher than we do in terms of talent and accomplishment. Being a writer, I naturally tend to have other writers as role models, at least to some extent. It would be preposterous for me to admire a successful writer whose work I don't respect, or a talented writer who can't or won't get published. But to look with awe upon a giant can be, on the whole, counter-productive.

H.L. Mencken, George Orwell, A.J. Liebling, and Mark Twain are probably the four writers whose works I admire the most, and to some extent I look to such men for guidance on how to write and how to conduct my career. But I can't say that I made a conscious decision to admire and emulate these men. To the contrary, to examine their lives and accomplishments makes me uncomfortable. Each of the four, by the time he had reached the age of 40 or so, was appreciably more successful than I was at 40 (okay, Orwell was making a lot less money than I, but he was more famous, and was making a living writing what he wanted to write), and was a better writer than I.

Their greatness daunts and intimidates, more than it inspires. If I had a dollar for every time I've said to myself, "Stop wasting your time, Dobrian; you're never going to be *that* good," I could afford to have these very essays published in book form at my own expense, then buy copies myself, by the thousands, so as to turn the book into a best-seller.

And then, if I were widely enough read, and my name widely enough known, I *would* be one of the best writers in the English language – not because I was that talented, but because the numbers showed that I was the best!

Much more useful as role models are people whose fields of proficiency are nothing like one's own. If ever I had a personal hero, it was a man with a tested IQ of 76, who could barely read and write, who composed dreadful verse, professed hatred for my race, and made his living by hitting people. I find it utterly impossible to explain to my own satisfaction why I have always worshipped Muhammad Ali, but I always have and always will. He was and is a god – in the style of the Greek gods, with flaws and limitations.

If you're not a boxer yourself, you can look up to Ali without feeling inferior to him. I'm not trying to be the best heavyweight in the world, and I can do plenty of things that Muhammad Ali could never think about doing. Still, when I'm doing the things I do well, I can imagine how Ali would do them if he could, and I can try to bring some of his élan to my own efforts. (And it doesn't hurt a bit, when meeting a new client or going on a first date, to hear Ali's voice in my mind, whispering, "I am the greatest! Of *awwwwwwwwl tiiiiiiiime!*")

To pattern yourself after an utterly distant hero – someone long dead, or so famous that intimate friendship would be out of the question – is probably preferable to taking a close relative or friend as a role model. It's easy to concentrate on a distant hero's virtues, and overlook the faults. If you're too close to your role model, you will see his or her faults a little too well, and since you're looking at that person with loving eyes, those faults will be distorted into virtues.

That's why your five-year-old son comes home with a bunch of newly acquired naughty words that he refuses to stop repeating in front of Grandma: After all, he so loves and admires his slightly older and much more mischievous friend, who taught him those words! And how many happily married couples must unwittingly encourage each other's worst faults, by giving each other constant, unquestioning approval?

For most of us, the most satisfying role models are, indeed, those who have serious flaws. Muhammad Ali would sadistically torture opponents who displeased him. Mark Twain fought on both sides in the Late Unpleasantness. H.L. Mencken was more than slightly pro-Nazi, almost to the last.

To some extent, truly dreadful people – or even essentially worthless ones – can serve as positive role models. Adolf Hitler, for instance, was one of the finest public speakers of the 20th century. Any orator would benefit from studying his techniques. King Edward VIII of England (later the Duke of Windsor), was one of the shallowest, stupidest, most selfish men ever to blight a royal throne, but he sure knew how to dress. Madonna, whom some people consider a talentless, pretentious grotesque, must at least be admired for her drive and her tireless self-promotion.

Someone once remarked that if one wished to be a gentleman, one might do worse than to combine the qualities of certain Presidents of the United States: George Washington's sense of duty, Thomas Jefferson's intellect, Abraham Lincoln's geniality, Theodore Roosevelt's manliness, Woodrow Wilson's idealism, Harry Truman's integrity, John F. Kennedy's charm, and Jimmy Carter's compassion.

This is a fine suggestion. But however much we might admire some or all of those men, we still must consider Washington's haughtiness, Jefferson's hypocrisy, Lincoln's deviousness, Roosevelt's megalomania, Wilson's self-righteousness, Truman's narrow-mindedness, Kennedy's irresponsibility, and Carter's sanctimony.

And it's entirely healthy that we do consider those flaws. All of us dream of being God; none of us would be a saint.

Manners Change, Assholery Remains

It's not quite fair to say that people in general are less polite today than they were a generation or two ago. We hear that complaint, sure enough, but we've been hearing it for thousands of years, mainly from old folks, and if it were invariably true, we would have no time to do anything but spit in each other's eyes, stomp on each other's feet, and exchange hair-curling insults, in order to live up to our parents' and grandparents' assessments of our behavior. It appears to be true, though, that the bounds of permissible social behavior do change somewhat, from one generation to the next, so that we become more polite in some ways, and less polite in others.

For one thing, we seem to be more polite, these days, in making remarks about a person's physical characteristics. Even in my young day, it would be not at all unusual for someone to comment (very much within a child's hearing), "She's not very pretty, is she?" I was a rather fat kid, and I am still hoping that every adult who "good-naturedly" poked me in the belly ended up dying of some sort of slow-acting poison that caused them to literally rot to death. Today, such behavior would not be tolerated; back then, adults were positively astonished if a child took offense at such abuse.

Not long ago, children were often instructed to ignore people with obvious physical handicaps, to neither look at them nor speak to them unless it were absolutely necessary. Blind, crippled, or otherwise disabled people – children or adults – were frequently treated as though they were feeble-minded as well. (For instance, in a restaurant, a waitress might expect a wheelchair-bound person's escort to order for him.) Today, we've been pretty well conditioned to treat everyone as a "normal" person, whatever our private prejudices.

Our manners have disimproved, though, in this respect: We mind each other's business in a way that would have been unthinkable a generation ago.

Today, you can hardly eat anything in public without some busybody pointing out to you that you shouldn't be eating it. Just the other day, I was sitting at the bar of a local bistro, tucking into a nearly raw hamburger, and the person sitting next to me thought it appropriate to ask me, "Aren't you worried about the bacteria?"

What could have been the purpose of that question, other than to diminish my enjoyment of that burger?

In effect, a question of that sort is a form of bullying. Lots of people take pleasure in throwing punches at folks they know can't or won't hit back. (In this case, the questioner was a woman, who knew she wouldn't get a sock on the nose. A man would not have asked me that question, because such assurance would not have been in play.) In that sense, nothing has changed. Hassling a stranger about his food (or about smoking, or the wearing of fur) is a substitute for poking a fat little kid in the belly: both satisfy a subconscious sadistic urge to give discomfort to someone who is powerless to retaliate.

Every so often, though, you *do* get a chance to hit back, and it's at those moments when an impeccably well-mannered, sweet-natured, non-disputatious fellow such as myself gets to feel the thrill of swift reprisal.

Recently, a co-worker came into the office wearing an attractive fur coat. Another co-worker (this time a man who felt he could hassle a woman) said, "Nice fur. Is it faux?" She admitted that it was real, and he prissily snapped, "Then I don't like it any-more."

I demanded – rather abruptly, and loudly enough for all bystanders to hear – "What's on your feet, dude?" He looked down at his leather shoes, went a bit red, and started going "hummina, hummina, hummina…" The frisson of victory was identical to the one you feel when you physically punch the crap out of someone who richly deserves it.

Our TV-driven culture is a contributor to this shift in people's behavior. The various daytime talk shows, on which people are encouraged to be both judgemental and obstreperous, have taught us that it's socially acceptable to gratuitously badger other people. These talk shows have also, I suspect, also taught us to resort to *ad hominem* attacks in a debate, much more quickly than we used to. Of course, we've always used *ad hominem* remarks such as, "Oh, you're very young. Maybe when you're older, you'll understand my viewpoint." These tactics are verbal knees in the nuts: They dismiss not your arguments, but you as a person, in a manner that leaves with you no defense but to squeal, "I am *not* too young!" which of course makes you sound too young.

Nowadays, on TV talk shows, you'll hear one guest end an argument with another by loudly announcing, "Your breath stinks, you know that?" That sure by God settles it: How could a person with halitosis possibly have any merit in his arguments? Trouble is, such tactics are effective, because if I know that someone is an unhygenic slob, he'll have no credibility with me!

Probably, our manners would improve if it were considered socially acceptable to kill anyone who uses you rudely. After all, people who have been in prison – where such is the case – often say that society behind bars is far more genteel than any they've encountered in freedom.

In ordinary civilian life, though, it's tough to win a public debate purely on the merits of your case, even if you're a skilled

arguer – and even if you are, beyond doubt, on the side of the an-
gels. You had better be prepared to fight dirty, because your adversary almost certainly will.

Several fine weapons are at the disposal of any rhetorician,
each of which the namby-pambies might classify as unethical, but
which range in effectiveness from "very strong" to "unbeatable."

Plain old personal attacks, totally irrelevant to the issue at
hand, are often effective. For example, if A is trying to hide his
balditude with a comb-over, B could bring him to his knees by
saying, "Oh, by the way, you're not fooling anyone, ya bald-
headed hump!" From then on, the audience will not be able to get
A's comb-over (and the deliciously emphatic "bald-headed
hump") out of its collective mind, and though A might have every
fact and every syllogism on his side, he will come out of the fray
permanently injured.

The single most reliable attack of this type (as I suggested
above) is to say, in a kindly tone, "I have a feeling you won't have
that opinion when you're a little older." At worst, your adversary
will not be the same for the rest of the fight. More usually, he'll be
flat on his back, twitching, for the full count.

Simple name-calling is a much-underrated weapon, if the
nasty name's an impressive one. For example, in an argument between me and another person, witnessed by some dozens of people, my adversary referred to me as "typically right-wing crypto-
fascist." It doesn't much matter that the actual definition of
"crypto-fascist" is "one who secretly supports a governmental system of one-party dictatorship, forcible suppression of political
opposition, and private economic enterprise under centralized
governmental control." Nor does it matter that since our little
squabble had nothing to do with either government or economics,
and my interlocutor had no acquaintance with my views on same,
he most likely had no idea what "crypto-fascist" meant – other
than, "someone who disagrees with me, and who is therefore

evil." Still, the term has so much mojo that you can hurl it at any-one and expect it to impress at least one or two spectators.

Embellishment is a helpful weapon, as well. I draw the distinction between embellishment – in which the arguer uses distortions which he hopes his audience will not notice are exactly that – and mere hyperbole, which is exaggeration for dramatic effect, clearly not meant to be taken seriously.

For example, if A says something about "certain shrill, hysterical members of the radical feminist movement," B might accuse him of "using a hateful stereotype to characterize any woman who strives for social and political equality." And that sounds so impressive that a lot of listeners might believe that A really did do what B said he did.

Or, similarly, if A refers to B as "ignorant of the facts," B can deflect the audience's attention from his own ignorance by countering, "Oh, so anyone who disagrees with you is an ignoramus? Doesn't it ever occur to you that *you* might have your facts wrong? If you won't listen to any opposing opinions, if all you can do is name-call, then what is to be done with you?"

To associate one person or organization with another, far less socially acceptable person or organization, is a clever and popular trick. I once heard the right-wing columnist Cal Thomas, debating the late author Tom Braden (who had once had an article published in *Oui* magazine) refer to Mr. Braden as "this writer for pornographic magazines." This was one of the most exquisite cheap shots I've ever seen. Thomas was careful not to say "this writer of pornography," but the implication was clearly there, and was so outrageously misleading that Braden could only sputter.

Braden's article for *Oui* had had nothing to do with sex, and whether a magazine as tame as *Oui* could be called pornography is debatable at best, but that didn't matter. Braden couldn't explain the facts without sounding defensive; he was too old to knock Thomas' block off (and it would have been taken as proof that Thomas had been right, if he'd done so). Finally, Braden was reduced to demanding an apology, and walking off the stage when none was offered, leaving Mr. Thomas in command of the field.

A correspondent of mine tried this tactic in writing, the other day, referring to "the RepubliKKKan party" – implying that anyone who belongs to that party (and I guess that includes Abraham Lincoln) is also a member of the Ku Klux Klan or reliably sympathetic to it. However, this was an ineffective ploy, because it was hyperbole, rather than embellishment, and merely made him sound shrill, stupid, juvenile, and perhaps daft.

Which leads me to another fine weapon: suggesting that your adversary is not quite right in the head. You won't get anywhere by just rolling your eyes and saying, "This guy's nuts!" But if you do it with more sorrow than anger, using characterizations like "sad," "pathetic," "sick," and so forth, plus the indispensable phrase, uttered oh, so gently, "I feel so sorry for you," you have delivered a punch that'll be hard to shake off.

The ultimate weapon, though, is tenacity. As long as you can be the last one to say "Am not!" or "Are so!" you'll win, because if your adversary gets tired and says something to the effect of, "This is getting nowhere; I don't care to continue," you can cry, "*Ha!* You're giving up because you know I'm right and can't stand to admit it!" and the poor guy can either let you get away with it, or submit to another few hours of "Am not" and "Are so."

Sometimes, of course, you'll come up with a crusher – long after the fact. The French call it *l'esprit de l'escalier.* The Germans call it *Treppenwitz.* Either way, it means "staircase wit": the snappy comeback that you think of when you're on the staircase, leaving the encounter, and it's too late to use it.

One of the most memorable of those occurrences, for me, took place in 2009 while I was out campaigning for Mayor of New York City. I was handing out leaflets and buttons in Union Square

Park, and was getting friendly responses from most people. At one point, I approached two young people who were sitting on the steps at the south end of the park, where lots of people congregate. The young woman was hanging on the man very affectionately, and I didn't get a good look at her except to register that she was attractive. The man was apparently 20 or not much more, and he looked like what politically incorrect New Yorkers call a "shvugarican": an Hispanic of color. A tall, remarkably handsome man, well groomed, in impeccable and quite tasteful "business casual" attire: brown suit, beige shirt, tan hat, no tie.

I made eye contact with him, as I always do when I'm fixing to introduce myself to someone and offer a flyer, but before I could get a word out of my mouth, this guy gave me that hateful gangsta fish-eye – and the finger.

I just smiled a little and said, "You're a nice fellow, aren't you?" before moving on. And five seconds later it occurred to me that I should have added, graciously, "I'm sure your mother is proud of you." He could have taken that in any number of ways.

Several questions occurred to me. First, why the behavior? What did he get out of it, behaving aggressively and insultingly to someone he'd only laid eyes on a few seconds before, and never spoken to? I was genuinely puzzled.

Second, why is that behavior apparently restricted to a certain demographic? That wasn't the first time I've met young men who act like that, in New York City, and I report it as a matter of fact, not of prejudice, that these people have invariably been Hispanic, or apparently so. Is it something to do with their culture? Don't their parents teach them better? Again, I ask not rhetorically, but because I don't know.

Third, what does any woman see in a guy like him? Sure, he was good-looking, and dressed well, but one would think that any exposure to his personality would send her running in a matter of seconds. Yet this woman was hanging on him in obvious adoration. Her face was buried in his sleeve, so I don't know how she reacted to his gesture; indeed, I would guess that she never saw it. But he must behave like that at other times when she can observe it, and I can't imagine that the same disrespect and hostility isn't occasionally turned on her.

Finally, why would anyone make a point of establishing, in the minds of other people, that he is garbage? I just don't get that.

It's all too much of a mystery for me. I'd be most gratified to be enlightened.

I seriously doubt that this guy was trying to provoke me to violence. I suspect that he was showing off for his girl, and trying to reassure himself – because a guy like that usually does realize, on some level, that he *is* garbage.

Do I mean to imply that I'm never guilty of rudeness? Certainly not. Sometimes I can't resist the temptation to be a flaming asshole. But at least I sometimes feel guilty, and even on rare occasions ashamed, when I engage in assholery. Consequently (I hope) I continue to do it a little less, and a little less.

My worst behavior invariably takes place on social networking sites like Facebook and MySpace. There, it seems, it's considered socially permissible to engage in expressions of disdain, personal denigration, insult, and baiting – in situations where, in face-to-face conversation, polite dissent or correction might have been used. Often, in these situations, the argument is won not by whichever side has the better facts and reason, but by whichever side acts nastier.

If one person objects to the tone of the other, quite often the offending party will exclaim triumphantly, "If you've changed the argument to make it about my tone, it means you're wrong." It's analogous to the old saying, "The first one to mention Hitler, loses."

But let's examine the implications of that statement. It means, I suppose, that you can place yourself at great advantage by behaving as offensively as possible. Your adversary can either fight back in kind, or place himself at an even greater disadvantage by having to fight his own temper while still trying to play nice – or he can refuse to play, in which case you "win," since he's left the argument, allowing you to do a little victory dance and sing "Nyah, nyah!" If you do that, loudly enough, it'll be widely believed that your position has prevailed, regardless of the merits of your case, regardless of whether your conduct was correct.

To repeat, I've done this myself, and I'm ashamed. It's not decent behavior. It's simple bullying. And it's applauded by a large part of our society, perhaps more than it used to be. It seems that it's cute, now, to act trashy. To insult, to bully, to try to take away the other person's dignity. It's even admirable, to some people.

I hate to be one of these old farts who blames TV for everything, but, yes, we sure as hell have learned that attitude from the way people behave on TV. This is a trend that's been going on for a good 45 years, anyway. This behavior doesn't just happen on mid-day talk shows, like *Jerry Springer*. It also happens on quasi-official shows, like *Judge Judy*, where a woman wearing judicial robes routinely browbeats people, shouts them down, insults them, and comes up with new ways to disrespect them almost every day. This gives the people who watch her show the idea that this is how it's okay for a jurist to behave on the bench – and that therefore it must be okay to behave that way as a private person.

I don't blame the medium for somehow high-handedly providing this programming to people who'd rather be watching something else. TV is a business, and apparently to attract viewers (and advertising revenue), you have to appeal to the most brutal desires in all of us. Unfortunately the behavior of people like Judge Judy is attractive to a large percentage of the population.

People will agree in the abstract that bullying is bad, but when they're called on their own conduct they'll rationalize it. "Yabbut, I'm right, and he doesn't deserve courtesy." "Yabbut, he's stupid and ignorant." "Yabbut, his opinion is evil." "What, the little crybaby can't take it?"

When you get into an argument – and this is human nature, almost universal – if your adversary disagrees with you or presumes to correct you in a courteous way, you'll almost certainly give fair consideration to what he's said. Indeed, you'll look for ways to concede certain points, or admit that there's room for debate, or even admit the possibility that you'd been misinformed. Unless you're a trashy person to begin with, in which case you'll respond insultingly to anyone.

But if your adversary starts out sneering, contemptuous, and personal – especially if, as often happens, your adversary is misrepresenting your position, or using fallacious reasoning, or attacking you *ad hominem* – you're going to be distracted by his conduct, and you won't think about talking the issue out politely. You'll be too busy wishing you could bury a mattick-blade in his shit-stuffed head.

You're not used to getting talked to like that, face-to-face, unless you move in a really low-class crowd. I suspect that you do get talked to like that, in cyberspace, because people are aware that they're in no danger of getting a fat lip if they take liberties. Since their postings are usually pseudonymous or anonymous, they don't even risk much in the way of social opprobrium.

When you get talked to like that, it's extremely difficult not to escalate – which is often just what your adversary wants you to do. Add to this the fact that you feel compelled to respond as quickly as possible, so as not to create the impression that you've run away. You're so busy typing an emotional response that you won't pause a moment, and think, and consider that perhaps some respect is due your adversary: the respect that you might accord him if you were talking to him face-to-face. Of course if he has just shown you total disrespect, without your having provoked him, that'll further disincite you to keep it pleasant.

I've no idea how to deal with, or reduce, this kind of behavior. When someone else's insolence has blinded you with rage, it's extremely difficult to come up with the retort courteous, or the quip modest. All you can do is resolve not to start with anyone, yourself. If he's said something you can't go along with, but has not actually taken a verbal swing at you, you may allow yourself a little time, before you publish your contradiction, to ask yourself, "Am I being polite?" And if you can't be polite, here's a nice cool glass of STFU. Drinky-drinky.

Apologizing

Possibly the most shameful thing I have ever said to anyone – and I said it two or three times, in my youth, before it dawned on me that I had to resolve never again to say it – is this:

"If I offended you, I apologize."

The indescribable repugnance of that sentence was driven home to me yet again the other day, when a friend of mine came to me, beside himself with pain and rage, and I found myself unable to console him.

He is, in some ways, like me. He's a solid, harmless, and obviously respectable citizen, but he is eccentric in his manner, and, like myself, is cursed with a somewhat demonic appearance.

He is a collector of *netsuke* – those old Japanese ivory carvings – and he owns some priceless specimens. The other day, so he told me, he was talking with a casual acquaintance (female), who is also interested in *netsuke*. In the course of the conversation, he said, "You're welcome to come over some time, and see my collection."

The acquaintance replied, "I don't know; you're so scary-looking; I'm afraid of what would happen if I set foot in your lair!"

My friend was mortified, but he does get reactions like that sometimes – he's aware of how he looks – so he held his temper and said, "For Pete's sake, bring a boyfriend along; he'd be welcome too!"

She responded, "I guess I have an over-active imagination or something, but you do have such an odd persona, and I think I'd better decline."

My friend, by this time, was almost dumbfounded. All he could think of to say was something like, "Too bad you feel that way," and then withdraw from the conversation.

Then, three or four days later, he ran into this acquaintance again, and was no more than icily civil to her. She asked him what the matter was, and he explained, very patiently, and in an even tone of voice (mind you, this is his version) that she had insulted him: by plain implication calling him an habitual practitioner of rape, murder, or false imprisonment, who clearly meant to make her a part of his hobby if only he could lure her to his apartment.

"Oh, that was a joke," she insisted, with a nervous giggle.

"*Joke?*" he echoed, raising his voice just a trifle. "*Funny joke?* Don't insult my intelligence! You meant it all the way, and the proof is, you saw that I was offended, and you stuck to it – even when I made it clear that I was inviting you to bring a chaperone. You as good as call me a murderer or whatever, and now I'm supposed to act like nothing happened? I don't goddam well think so."

In a voice dripping with condescension, the woman sighed, "All right. *If* I offended you, I apologize."

My friend was actually going purple as he recounted this story to me. By this time, he was raging, almost frothing, as he recalled her "apology." "As well steal someone's wallet," he roared at me, "and then say, 'I'm sorry if you felt you were inconvenienced.'"

"Did you explain to her that that wasn't an apology?" I asked.

"I used that very analogy," he insisted. "I told her, 'You can tell me that your conduct was disgraceful, and you can beg my pardon, or you can fuck off!' She told me that Hell would freeze over before she begged my pardon, so I walked away. I mean, if she'd been a man, I'd have been justified in smashing his face in. And the worst of it is, she will go through her whole life pretending that I'm just oversensitive! She fucking called me a murderer, or whatever else she was implying that I do to my guests!"

What could I tell this guy? Her implication *had* been clear. She obviously *had* meant it. If she truly believed that my friend was a serial killer and proposed to murder her and her chaperone, she would, indeed, have had little alternative but to insult him by refusing his invitation – but my intuition tells me that (a) she realizes that she was in the wrong, and (b) she will still convince herself that *he's* the bad guy, for having the gall to resent her behavior.

She will never apologize, never repent.

The only proper way to apologize, when you insult someone, is abjectly. Repentance involves humbling yourself. It involves eating dirt. It does not involve implying that the other person is to blame – for being so over-sensitive as to be offended, or so selfish as to demand that you humble yourself.

In this case, there was no "if" about it. My friend *was* offended, as offended as anyone would be by such an insult. As offended as you would be, if you offered to feed a neighbor's dog while he was out of town, and he told you, with a straight face, "Thanks, but you'd probably just try to have sex with it."

In any case, you don't apologize for what the other person might be feeling. You acknowledge that you did harm, and that your action was bad – and you beg forgiveness for it. That's right, you *beg*, because forgiveness is not something you're entitled to; it's something that might be granted if you truly repent, and make amends as best you can.

Once, when I was in high school, I made a joking remark to a fat girl about her weight. I immediately felt awful about it and told her, "I'm so sorry. That was a really lousy, rotten thing to say, and I hope you'll forgive me." I got the impression that she was more taken aback by the apology, than she had been insulted by the original jibe. She probably had never heard such an apology before.

Because people don't apologize. They just don't. Admission of wrongdoing might damage their self-esteem. Or leave them vulnerable to a lawsuit, I guess.

Weak Bullies

At an otherwise delightful concert that I attended recently, I was reminded that bullies aren't always sociopathic youngsters, and they don't always use threats or abuse as their weapons. The weakest of us can bully, too, and such people are usually the best at getting away with it.

It was a tiny incident. Only two people were involved, and I believe I was the only witness. The bully probably doesn't remember it, 24 hours later, and for all I know the victim has forgotten it too. I only remember it because I am so easily outraged, which is a characteristic I'd like to get rid of but it's as much a part of me as one of my bones. With normal people, it probably would not have struck a nerve at all.

Sitting directly in front of me was a very old woman, perhaps 90, shrunken, frail, and palsied. When I sat down, I stuffed my gear (cape, hat, gloves) under her seat, because the chairs in this auditorium are constructed something like those in an airplane cabin in that if you want to stow anything, it's much easier to put it under the seat in front of you, than under your own. I saw others doing the same, and assumed it was common practice.

To my left sat three young ladies, 20 or so, who I supposed were Chinese. The one immediately next to me did as I'd done: stashed her coat under the seat in front of her. (That seat was unoccupied, and remained so during the performance.) At once, the old lady sitting in front of me turned around and said to her, "You're going to have to put that under your own seat." Of course the young lady complied.

I said nothing, but my silence required some effort. Here's what I might have said to that old lady, if I'd been crazy enough to do it:

"Look here, you: I see exactly what you're up to. For some reason or other, you get your jollies from ordering people around, telling them what they 'have' to do. That's not your seat; her coat isn't interfering with you in the least. Moreover, *my* shit is under *your* seat, and you're not saying a damn thing about that, are you?

"The only reasons you could have for admonishing this young lady are two. First, there's your need to throw your weight around, to assert your dominance in whatever pathetic way is left to you. Second, your need to make a young person feel ill-at-ease because you resent her for being young.

"I'm sure you would have loved to start with me, too, but you didn't dare, because I'm a man and I'm older, and you proba-bly were afraid that I might not have taken kindly to it. Besides, I have no youth for you to resent. No, you chose your target care-fully. You saw this young Asian woman, and you figured Asian women are submissive and deferential to their elders – so you started with her not because her conduct was at all offensive, but because you knew she was a safe mark.

"You put this young lady in the wrong simply because it gave you pleasure to put her in the wrong. She wasn't, but you had to make like she was, and you knew she'd think it rude to gainsay you. I bet you make a hobby of that sort of conduct, too, because not much else amuses you at your age.

"But, listen, lady: It's never too late to reform. Either re-solve, here and now, to renounce this dickery for the rest of your life, or go quietly to your goddam ice floe."

Of course, if I'd done that – indeed, if I'd uttered even the mildest, most cheerful rebuke or correction – I'd have been the bully, and the young lady on whose behalf I'd interposed would not have thanked me for it. Indeed, she'd have remembered me with even less indulgence than she might remember her geriatric adversary. All I could do in that situation was to make allowances for the near-certainty that being so old and decrepit would make anyone act like a jerk at times – and just pretend I'd seen and heard nothing.

(Indeed, once it became obvious that nobody was going to sit in the seat on my right, I removed all my gear thereto, just to make sure the old bag would have no reason to say further.)

As I said: a tiny, insignificant incident. But I'll probably never forget it, now.

Negroes, African-Americans, And Colored People

I have read many books by American Negro authors, in which they use Negro as the standard descriptive term. I've heard many speeches by American Negro speakers, in which ditto. And yet a friend of mine (who has been twice married to Negro men) stated to me positively and categorically that that term was uniformly offensive and demeaning. A few years ago, in an essay of mine, I described a certain celebrity as an American Negro, and one of my readers sent me the following comments:

"...the accepted term in society today is 'African-American,' not 'American Negro.' I know for a small minority of people this is still a point to be argued, but for most African-Americans (as I am), that is the preferred term... . Next year it may change (if we choose to do so) but it too will be one chosen by African-Americans, not one chosen by the majority population."

While I understand that African-American is a current term, I choose not to use it.

For one thing, African-American is now ridiculously over-used, to denote *any* negroid person, regardless of nationality. I've heard a police forensics expert say, "We recovered some strands of African-American hair from inside the hat." How did he know the nationality of the hair? I've heard supermodel Naomi Campbell referred to as African-American, although she is English-born, of Jamaican heritage.

Furthermore, many Americans with negroid blood have Caribbean, West Indian or South American backgrounds, and identify themselves as Jamaican, Cuban, Brazilian, etc., not African. (I once had a girlfriend who was a Negro, born in Trinidad, raised in England, but an American citizen who had purposely acquired an American accent. She called herself West Indian.) And if African-Americans must be negroid, what do you call an American of Boer descent?

My main reason for not using the term goes right to the point that my correspondent brought up: that the "preferred term...may change (if we choose to do so) but it too will be one chosen by African-Americans, not one chosen by the majority population."

Just who is "we"? My correspondent and his friends? The Congressional Black Caucus (who call themselves "Black")? The NAACP (who call themselves "Colored")? A committee of Negro intellectuals? Whoever can shout the loudest? Or is there a huge Negro convention every 30 years or so, at which they vote on what they're going to insist on being called for the next 30?

As best I recall, the politically correct term for Americans with recognizable negroid blood – and invariably this is a term demanded by certain Negroes themselves, *not* imposed by Whitey – has changed according to the following rough chronology:

1900: Colored
1930: Negro
1965: Black (Afro-American had a brief vogue among "progressives," circa 1968)
1990: African-American

By my estimate, the next groundswell of American Negroes demanding to be called something new will occur around the year 2020.

Will there be an exploratory committee appointed a couple of years before that, to compose a list of possible new locutions? Will there be nationwide campaigns, prior to the convention, to whip up support for one name or another? (I can just imagine the buttons and bumper stickers: "Color Me Ebonic!" "Proud To Be An Ethiop!" "What Makes A Hottentot So Hot?" "Call Me Shvartzer, Sucka!")

This issue reminds me of small children who insist on being called by a different name every day. At first, you humor them; finally you get sick of it and say, "Ah, grow up!"

I'm mystified – and disturbed – by the herd mentality that's implied in the notion that "we" will change the preferred term whenever "we" want to. This groupthink, this notion that persons of similar racial or ethnic background ought to act, speak and ideate in lock-step, is a principle that many American Negroes proudly defend. Most non-negroid Americans would be deeply embarrassed and affronted by the suggestion that they could or would take a certain intellectual position because that's the way "we" think.

(Non-negroid Americans who ape the mannerisms and lifestyles of other races or ethnic groups are generally treated with amused toleration – with admiration if they do it artistically – but American Negroes often vehemently renounce people of their race whose tastes, opinions, and ways of speaking are deemed "white.")

I prefer the term "Negro" because it relates to the (admittedly vague) terms generally used by scientists to differentiate the three largest racial groups: caucasoid, mongoloid and negroid. I use "Negro" to denote any person who by appearance or declaration is most closely identified with the negroid race. I use "American Negro" if needed for specificity. ("Black" doesn't quite work, because many people of other races – Australian Aborigines,

Tamils, some Polynesians, some American Indians – are also very dark-skinned.)

"Negro" isn't a perfect term, I'll grant. Virtually no American Negro is pure negroid. Nearly all have caucasoid blood, and many have a lot of it. Many eagerly claim American Indian (mongoloid) blood, whether they have it or not. (So do many "white" Americans – and people like me, who can't possibly get away with it because we're so white we're practically blue, usually feel a pang of regret.)

Besides, what do we call a man like Tiger Woods, whose racial breakdown appears to be just over 50% mongoloid (he has a little American Indian blood), about 35% negroid, and perhaps just under 15% caucasoid? He calls himself "Cablinasian," which I guess is as good as anything. For people whose ancestry is so racially mixed that it's hard to break it down, I prefer the term "Heinz": 57 varieties!

In an ideal world, perhaps, one's racial extraction would be interesting only for the sake of anthropological research, and would have no political import. As it is, for now we'll just have to muddle through with a bunch of imprecise designations, favoring those that appear to us to be the least inaccurate. The individual speaker/writer must be the final judge of what terms to use, and I prefer to base my decisions on something other than the arbitrary whims of a few people who have unilaterally appointed themselves spokespeople for their race.

You're Here, You're Queer, Whatever

I continue to be amazed by the constant, sometimes shrill, insistence from some political activists and "gay advocates" that one is born either homosexual or heterosexual, and that there is no choice involved. I'm equally amazed by the fact that anyone who challenges that tenet, in whole or in part, is likely to arouse a vociferous reaction, as though he had somehow threatened the personal security of all homosexuals and those who love them.

My own position is that it doesn't matter, and I don't understand why it should matter. From what I've read, it's probably true that one's sexual preference is inborn, and that it is not a choice. But what if it were a choice? What if the flames of homo- and heterosexuality blazed equally high in each of us, and we each chose to fuel one flame and let the other wane? What would be so bad about that?

It seems to me that by taking such a great emotional stake in the question of whether one's sexuality is a matter of genetics or choice, one is tacitly admitting that there's something wrong with homosexuality – and that if it were a choice, it would be a wrong choice. The subtext appears to be, "Yes, we admit that homosexuality is deviant and arguably immoral and in bad taste – but it can't be helped, and therefore must be tolerated." This strikes me as a somewhat less liberal position than mine, which is, "I don't care whether or not it's a choice, and I don't see why it should be an issue, because as far as I'm concerned, your being gay or straight is about as important – and about as relevant to your personal decency – as whether you prefer Coke or Pepsi."

A point often missed is this: By asserting that homosexuality is a choice, one isn't necessarily saying it's a bad choice. A person who posits that homosexuality is a choice may be scientifically mistaken, but he is not thereby condemning homosexuality or revealing himself as a homophobe.

In terms of your thoughts and desires, your sexual orientation is not a choice. In the behavioral sense, however, it certainly is. Every time you have sex (unless you're raped), you *choose* to do it, and you could have chosen *not* to do it.

Many homosexuals, for whatever reasons, remain chaste all their lives. Many others live heterosexually, never revealing their true inclinations to anyone. While these aren't choices I would recommend, I would say that these people's reasons were their own, and I would consider it arrogant and impertinent in the extreme, to suggest that these were wrong choices. And yet I hear other people – most of whom like to pat themselves on the back for their tolerance and liberalism – insisting that such choices are terrible, and that our society would be better off if they were not even contemplated.

I've been accused of homophobia once or twice because I've dared to suggest that engaging in homosexual acts – as opposed to homosexual desires – is a choice. I don't see how that makes me homophobic. I've never added, "and therefore homosexuals should cease this infamous behavior." But apparently that doesn't matter. I've also had it suggested that since I appear to lack any close friends who are gay, it must be because I have something against homosexuals in general. It's impossible to disprove the charge, of course.

That brings us to the question, "Who is a homophobe?" Is it someone who does his best to minimize the visibility and influence of homosexuals – by preventing them from being teachers or scout leaders, for instance? Is it anyone who, on whatever grounds, is opposed to same-sex marriage? Is it someone who is chronically uncomfortable around homosexuals and secretly believes that homosexuality is wrong – and yet, despite his private feelings, always treats homosexuals with courtesy and even argues in favor of their right to practice their preferences openly and enter same-sex marriages?

According to some people, even the slightest reservations about homosexuality, homosexuals, and their behavior – even if those reservations are never expressed – are enough to qualify you as homophobic. And, strictly speaking, that might be true – in the sense that a person who has homosexual longings but never comes close to committing a homosexual act could still arguably be called homosexual. But to use the definition so broadly debases the currency, so to speak. It cheapens "homophobe" in the same way that "racist" has been cheapened over decades to mean anyone shy of a Black Nationalist. (And yes, I'm aware of the double meaning in that last phrase. Did it on purpose.)

There are as many types of homophobes, I daresay, as there are types of homosexuals, and it's just as foolish to lump all homophobes together, and assert that they all think and act alike, as it is to do the same to all homosexuals.

Almost nobody who disapproves of homosexuality is of the extremist stripe. The people who go about with "God Hates Fags" signs, or who support criminalization or suppression of homosexuality, are anomalies in modern civilized societies. (That is, societies that aren't based on group psychosis, like some Middle Eastern countries.) Equating thought to deed has always been behavior restricted to the most intolerant and unforgiving of people, and those who consider themselves "enlightened" and "progressive" ought to take note of that.

And they ought to respect other people's choices.

This brings me to the concept of Gay Pride. As an idea, it's a year-long thing for many people, but there's also a week's worth of celebration associated with it, in June of every year. Particularly in large cities with significant homosexual populations, the festival culminates with a flamboyant parade (which, it must be said, gay and straight people both enjoy).

These celebrations don't do anyone any harm. But some people ask this question: Why should Gay Pride be celebrated in any way? Why should anyone be particularly proud (or ashamed, for that matter) of being homosexual? Why should one's sexual preferences be any more socially significant than one's tastes in food and drink?

When you stop to think about it, you have to conclude that Gay Pride Week is not much different from any of hundreds of celebrations observed annually by certain localities or certain groups of people who have something in common. Just in the state of Iowa, where I grew up, we have Solon Beef Days, the Pella Tulip Festival, the Pork Festival (complete with a Pork Queen, who is *not* chosen for her porcinity), the [Des Moines] Register's Annual Great Bicycle Ride Across Iowa, Czech festivals, Scandinavian festivals, and so on. The rationale for any and all of these festivals can be boiled down to two-and-a-half words: "It's fun."

One's tastes, I guess, are a good enough excuse for having fun. Just as good an excuse as one's ethnicity, one's profession, or what the local farms produce. If people who liked potato salad were to form an organization for the awareness of the potato-salad-eating lifestyle, and have a weekend of celebration, culminating in a gala parade down Fifth Avenue, why should anyone object? Even people who aren't all that hipped on potato salad might be glad of the chance to party down.

(Just as I go to the Gay Pride Parade to ogle the topless lesbians, a person who is not a big eater of potato salad might go to the Potato Salad Pride Feast out of an affinity for celery or bits of hard-boiled egg.)

But why not take it further? Perhaps the potato salad culture could develop a colored-handkerchief code: A red hankie hanging out of your back pocket indicates that you like bits of pimiento in your potato salad; a brown one would mean that you preferred bacon; a light green hankie would denote celery; a dark green one, pickles (you wear the dark green hankie in your left or right pocket, to indicate your preference for sweet or sour pickles). A vomit-colored ribbon on the lapel expresses sympathy for those who were poisoned by tainted mayonnaise.

Beyond much doubt, the Gay Pride Parade is the most fun and picturesque of New York City's innumerable celebrations. I'll prefer a crowd of screaming queens and diesel dykes to those suburban thick-necks who gather here for St. Patrick's Day, any old time.

(The Irish claim that "everyone's Irish on St. Patrick's Day," and some folks who are not Irish at all will use the holiday as an excuse to get drunk and stomp each other to death, as the Irish do according to one of the more obnoxious stereotypes. At least nobody claims that everyone's queer during Pridefest, and straight folks don't use the celebration as an excuse to... oh, never mind.)

Other gay-driven gatherings are a little harder for me to understand. The Gay Games, for instance, are quite a concept. Why does there have to be a separate set of athletic contests for gay people? Are they somehow handicapped, so that they're at a disadvantage when competing against straight people? Or are there gay ways and straight ways of performing athletically?

(Okay, I daresay wrestling takes on a whole new significance at the Gay Games. And perhaps effeminate men have an advantage in the shot-put, because that's the one event in which you're *supposed* to throw like a girl. And maybe instead of walking races, they have sashaying races. I'm just guessing.)

I can hear some of my homosexual readers saying, at this point, "Why are you stereotyping us like this?"

That brings up one objection that some people might have to Gay Pride celebrations: They encourage those very stereotypes. We hear talk about a gay lifestyle, about specifically gay ways of dressing, talking, acting, and enjoying oneself. This must be stultifying for gay people themselves. And at a time when so many gay people are demanding to be treated as "just folks," particularly on issues such as same-sex marriages and adoption by gay couples, I wonder why so many gay people tend to hold up undesirable or bizarre behavior as particularly commendable.

I was struck by this during a recent Gay Pride Parade in New York City, when the parade's Grand Marshal passed by the reviewing stand in his limo, and the public-address announcer introduced him as an "'out,' HIV-positive City Councilman."

A few years ago, similarly, in a race for the City Council seat representing the heavily gay Greenwich Village constituency, candidate Tom Duane made his gaiety a campaign issue, implying that his being homosexual made him better qualified to represent the district. His main opponent, Liz Abzug, had theretofore said nothing about her own sexual preferences, but Mr. Duane's "coming out" had clearly given his campaign such a boost that she felt obliged to publicly state, "I'm gay, too!"

Ah, the Duane supporters countered, but our boy is HIV-positive! Top that! Ms. Abzug, having presumably had a less varied, more germ-free career than Mr. Duane, could not top it, and went down to a crushing defeat at the polls.

The implicit suggestion that a gay person who is HIV-positive is somehow more gay than someone who is not, or somehow deserves greater prestige because his private habits are unsanitary and reckless, is ridiculous. It amounts to praising a member of a minority group for reinforcing the worst stereotypes that attend that group. It's roughly equivalent to saying that a Negro who's illiterate and in prison is more of a Negro, and more deserving of recognition by the Negro community, than a Negro who's educated and law-abiding, or that an Irishman who has a drinking problem and 20 kids he can't feed is more Irish than some other Irishman who's soberly supporting a smaller family.

There's obvious pressure in the gay community to live up to certain stereotypes, and to toe the political line dictated by the most vocal. This is made clear when a tiny contingent of Log Cabin Republicans (a gay Republican organization) is routinely booed along the parade route by the more politically correct bystanders.

Clearly, too, there are certain uniforms that gay people are expected to wear, and certain mannerisms they're expected to affect. "Straight-acting" is a common descriptive term among gay people – sometimes value-neutral and sometimes denigrating, but never equivocal in its meaning.

Nothing will convince me that hundreds of thousands of gay men were genetically hard-wired to start talking like Richard Simmons as soon as they hit puberty, or that they really want to talk that way. They must have had to acquire that voice in order to fit in with their crowd. And I've heard lesbians complain that they always did love to wear dresses and makeup, but that it has only recently become politically correct for a lesbian to do so – and it's still not easy for them to eat meat, vote Republican, or proclaim that the New Age movement is bunk.

This is uncomfortably close to what we see in many Negro communities, where people who refuse to marginalize themselves – who study hard, get white-collar professional jobs, and speak standard English – are branded "Oreos" or "Uncle Toms." Likewise, certain Jewish cults, such as the Satmar and Lubavitcher sects, proselytize to other Jews – arguing, in effect, that you're insufficiently Jewish if you don't wear outlandish attire, live in a ghetto of your own making, and shut yourself off as much as possible from the outside world.

Still, most groups that behave that way are frankly separatist in their outlook. They might be hypocritical, if they still expect to reap the benefits provided by a society to which they refuse to contribute, but at least they don't pretend that they want to be accepted just like "everyone else."

Gays, on the other hand, *do* generally demand social acceptance, *do* strive to be considered part of mainstream society. In my own opinion, that is what they deserve. I don't think any sensible person would disagree that gay people deserve the same rights as anyone else to vote or hold office. They should not suffer discrimination in the workplace; they ought not to fear being beaten up on the street any more than straight people do; and aside from the fact that I'm personally uncomfortable with it, I can't see much objection to same-sex marriage.

The reality is, though, that if you go around dressed in a jockstrap and a policeman's hat, with chains strung through your nipples, doing Judy Garland imitations, most people will think you are weird, and will, to some extent, marginalize you, or at least treat you as distinctly *other*. If you are a quiet, solemn person who dresses conservatively and doesn't go out of his way to let everyone know what his sexual preferences are, you're likely to be treated much the same as any ordinary straight person.

I say, to the gay community, don't worry about being mainstream. You'll never be any good at it anyway, and the parade would get boring.

Now, am I homophobic, myself? Yes, I am, a little. I'm not proud of it, and I happily put my prejudice aside when I meet a homosexual who doesn't justify it. But the immediate suspicion, and mild discomfort and dislike, are always there when I first meet an obviously gay person of either sex.

I think a lot of gay people have the wrong idea about why so many straight folks are homophobic. I don't mind if people want to have sex with people of their own gender. I don't mind if they celebrate that preference in public. I don't mind men dressed in tutus, or women dressed as lumberjacks. None of that is obnoxious to me, nor do I consider it morally wrong. I don't even mind much if a gay guy comes on to me. (I'm perfectly capable of saying "No, thank you.") I'm also not afraid of "catching gay" from having gay people around me.

But here's why I am wary of homosexuals: because a noticeable proportion of them are obtrusive, hostile jerks who enjoy getting in your face, intentionally making you uncomfortable, and telling you how to behave.

I'm pretty sure that many people's homophobia has to do with this peculiar aggressive officiousness of many homosexuals. I never want to deck anyone for acting like a sissy. But I do want to deck a damn busybody who thinks he knows what's good for everyone else, who maybe plants an uninvited kiss on my cheek in order to raise my consciousness, or screams at me like a psychotic Ethel Merman.

Have you ever had a huge zit on your neck, which you can't cover up, so you have to take it out in public, and just pray to a merciful God to get you through the day? And has anyone, under that circumstance, said to you, "Gosh, that's quite a zit on your neck!" Was it an effeminate gay man who made that remark? Of course it was! A straight man would have bitten his own tongue out, sooner than let you know he'd seen anything.

A comparable incident: Once upon a time, I was peeing in the men's room, next to a rather fey co-worker, who, when I was done and starting out the door, lisped at me, "Tsk! Wash your hands!" Would a straight guy have said that?

(I replied that I'd been taught, in infancy, not to pee on my hands.)

I've observed analogous meddlesome, hostile tendencies among lesbians: analogous, not similar, since they tend to be more overtly hateful. Like the time I was at a meeting of people in the publishing industry – mostly women – and in the context of a discussion of editorial content, I mentioned a series of health-related articles then appearing in *Penthouse* magazine. Immediately, a masculine-looking woman, her face purple, leapt out of her chair and stormed over to me, hissing, "You've got a lot of damn nerve, mentioning *Penthouse* in a room full of women!"

Worse yet was an incident from my college days, when a girlfriend and I were both taking a class called "The Feminist Novel" (okay, I was crunchy back then). My friend, who was rather conservative, often made comments in the class discussions that varied from the politically correct feminist line. By God if one of the several openly lesbian classmates didn't take my friend aside one day, and inform her that "my group" felt that she was being detrimental to the class by expressing her views so frequently!

My first job, when I came to New York, was in a call center, making collection calls. I acquired the nickname "Joe the Butler" because I was chatty and courteous with the deadbeats I was trying to get money out of. My boss saw that my approach was as effective as anyone's, and never criticized it. My other co-workers just kidded me about it. But the obviously gay fellow who sat next to me, who'd plainly taken a dislike to me because I was a hick from Iowa, would hiss, "Don't chit-chat with these people, Joseph! They're not your friends!"

Because they act out their hostility in a way that causes discomfort and yet leaves no opportunity for retaliation, such people are cowards and bullies. Not long ago, I had to pass by a picket line of anti-fur demonstrators on my way into Macy's department store. There were maybe 10 or 12 demonstrators, all of them scrawny, grotesquely effeminate men, holding up disgusting pictures of flayed animals and suchlike inflammatory propaganda, chanting their anti-fur chants in their hissy-fit voices.

I felt furious almost to the point of wanting to do violence. Not because these guys were obviously gay; not because they were opposed to the wearing of fur (although I bitterly disagree with the "animal rights" crowd on that issue) – but because they were no better than the jerkoffs who behave similarly in front of abortion clinics.

Nothing will convince me that these idiots really cared about the issue. It was simply a matter of weak, un-manly men finding an outlet for their rage at their own ineffectuality.

A real man, if he can't help himself and needs to get rid of some rage, goes to a gym and finds a sparring partner or a heavy bag. These girly-boys in front of Macy's were looking for the same kind of endorphin release, but they had to do it by imposing themselves on passersby.

The gay community demands "tolerance," and a fair demand it is. And plenty of gay people set a good example. It's the vocal minorities, that perpetuate the stereotypes, that keep homophobia alive.

'I'm All For Free Speech, But...'

In a recent blog post, I asserted that in this country at least, the Left has a near-monopoly on the use of force to break up meetings or prevent certain viewpoints from being expressed publicly. I stand by that, but that is not to say that the Right is much more respectful of the concept of "freedom of speech." Contempt for that concept is common among Americans, and expression of that contempt is usually preceded by, "I'm all for free speech, but..."

It's useless to pretend that we have free speech or a free press in the U.S. Our Federal government allows greater freedom of expression than do most other national governments, but that freedom is steadily being chipped away, usually to the applause of a large percentage of the populace. Just about everybody opposes free speech somehow, whether they want to censor anything to do with sex or scatology, or ban "hate speech," or forbid criticism of a certain political party. Only a very few of us are free speech absolutists.

On the other hand, almost nobody who opposes freedom of speech is willing to say, "I oppose freedom of speech." To say so, in the minds of many who do in fact oppose free speech, would be as dangerous as saying, "I see nothing wrong with having sex with children."

I can understand why anyone would be afraid to make the latter assertion, even if he sincerely believed it. That position is so unpopular that if he said it, he would risk social ostracism, criminal investigation, and perhaps prosecution. But why are so many Americans afraid to say, "I oppose free speech," when that position is manifestly popular, and when many Canadians and Europeans make that very statement with impunity?

This question presented itself to me recently, when I got into a conversation with someone who said, in all seriousness, that criminal charges should be lodged against right-wing propagandists Glenn Beck, Rush Limbaugh, Sarah Palin, Michele Bachmann, and perhaps others, for "incitement to violence."

"Can you show me," I asked him, "where any of those people ever exhorted people to commit violent crimes? Much less, can you show me where someone, because he heard such an exhortation, went and committed a violent crime? Or are you in fact urging criminal prosecution for speech that you find offensive?"

"Like proving the existence of death panels and the lack of Obama's birth certificate, I don't need to prove anything," he said. "I just need to ask those questions. Like why do some of those callers into Beck's and Limbaugh's show feed off each other, to the point where a man infuriated by an Obama sticker rams repeatedly into an SUV with a little girl in it? Freedom of speech is one thing, but people advocating violence need to re-assess their roles in the current situation."

To this response, I had to point out that he was still evading my questions, and that he hadn't asked any of his own. Instead, he'd stated affirmatively that Beck, et al., should be prosecuted for their speech. I'd asked him to show me where they'd incited violence, and he would not.

"You're actually advocating prosecution of speech that you think is offensive or that might influence opinions in a direction that you don't like," I told him. "It's a simple question, and I'll ask it again: Did any of those people you list ever exhort people to commit violent crimes?"

"You never change a man's mind by arguing with him," he

replied, and I had to force back the urge to suggest that somebody wasn't acting much like a man.

Instead, I said, "I'm not arguing: just stating your position a little more honestly than you're willing to, yourself."

At this point my interlocutor said, "Done with ya, bro," and walked away from the conversation.

Here's what I found remarkable: He could have answered me. He could have said, "No, not in so many words, they didn't – and maybe I spoke hastily when I said they should be prosecuted; I didn't mean that." In that case, I'd not have thought the less of him; in fact I'd have respected him more. Or he could have said, "No, not in so many words, they didn't – but, yes: I favor criminalization of speech that might tend to inflame." In that case, I'd have had fun trying to get him to define his terms and propose his limits.

But, no. He kicked over the chessboard and ran like a mutt. It was his perception, correct or not, that he was going to lose face no matter how he answered my question.

We all hate to admit that we've said something wrong or stupid; I know I do. Even though we know deep down that admitting a mistake tends to minimize or prevent damage, we won't do it, because our pride's at stake. But I don't think that's what was going on here. I think this fellow really does oppose freedom of speech, really does think there should be prior restraint against certain types of speech, really does think that certain political speech should be criminalized.

So why wouldn't he say so? He wouldn't have faced social ostracism; plenty of people agree with him. What was he afraid of?

I think he was afraid of what he'd think of himself. If you come right out and say "I oppose free speech," you'll have to admit certain things about yourself, to yourself – and those admissions are not pleasant for most people.

The New Victorians

Shortly before advice columnist Ann Landers died, she published a letter from a woman who complained that a neighbor boy was using binoculars to spy on her while she sunbathed nude. Soon thereafter, Ms. Landers published a letter from another reader, stating that in some jurisdictions, at any rate, that behavior would constitute criminal trespassing.

"The offense [the letter stated] includes trespassing or surreptitiously invading the privacy of another, to spy or eavesdrop, with the purpose of sexually arousing or gratifying oneself. 'Trespass' is not confined to the physical boundaries of the victim's real estate. It includes the use of binoculars, telescopes, camcorders, tape recorders, stethoscopes and even a water glass held against a hotel wall.

"Behavioral specialists say that voyeurism is often a precursor to more dangerous and potentially violent forms of self-arousal. The boy needs professional counseling."

Ms. Landers, whom I always considered one of the biggest nincompoops ever to come out of the Hawkeye State, did not disappoint me. She replied, "Your suggestion of professional counseling is a good one."

Who needed counseling here? A boy who took advantage of an opportunity to look at a naked woman? Or the woman who expected people not to look at her when she's naked? Or people who claimed that the boy needed counseling because he had normal curiosity and a normal sex drive?

If someone is handing out free ice cream, do I need counseling because I accept it? And what's a counselor going to tell this kid? That it's not nice to look at a naked woman who is exposing herself in public? That there are more politically correct ways for him to get a boner?

This sunbathing woman is, in effect, walking through Bedford-Stuyvesant with a sign saying "I Hate Niggers," and then complaining when someone punches her in the nose.

In civil law, at least, there's a phenomenon known as an attractive nuisance. An unguarded construction site is a good example. There might be signs saying, "keep out," but we all know that children will want to play on the site, and will do, and might get hurt – in which case the construction company can be held liable for not posting guards or building a high fence around the site.

I'd call this a case of an attractive nuisance, even without knowing what the nude woman looks like. If this woman doesn't want people to see her nude, she can quit sunbathing, or build a high hedge around her house, or hire goons to beat up anyone they catch looking at her.

The idea that "voyeurism is often a precursor to more dangerous and potentially violent forms of self-arousal" is often trotted out by radical feminists, religious extremists, and other professional wowsers. And it's true, in the way that "Every junkie started on milk" is true – but in a practical sense it is a plain lie, put about by people who are afraid that someone, somewhere, might be having a good time.

We like to pretend that our society grows steadily more enlightened, more progressive, and less inhibited by irrational taboos, but that is simply not so. Our attitude toward nudity is a classic example. When I was living in Iowa, in my late teens and

20s, many people thought nothing of going to one or another of the local swimming holes to swim, sunbathe, and party nude on a summer afternoon – boys, girls, men, and women alike. I'd be surprised if very many of us, congregating in the same spot today, would doff our clothes – and not just because gravity has taken its inevitable toll.

I well recall a gorgeous afternoon at one of these oases, maybe 35 years ago, when I was soaking up the sun with three or four high-school girls, all of us in our birthday suits, when we became aware of someone spying on us from behind some foliage on a bluff overlooking our little beach. We just about fell apart laughing: Why, we wondered, didn't this guy just stroll on down and join us, and get a much closer look?

We never kidded ourselves that we were just enjoying our natural state with no hint of sex in the air. *Of course* we all got a bit titillated by seeing each other naked, and everyone knew it. It wasn't ever talked about. It was just generally understood that you could look all you wanted, so long as you were cool about it. None of us would have dreamed of being overtly lascivious, by word or deed, because there just wasn't any need for it, and it would have spoiled the fun, in any case, by making people self-conscious.

These days, in the men's locker room at my health club, I observe that few men walk to and from the showers without towels draped round their waists. I have even seen guys go into a shower stall with their shorts on, close the curtain, reach an arm out to hang their shorts on a nearby hook, take their shower, reach out for a towel, towel off behind the curtain, reach back out for the undershorts, and only then emerge from the stall.

If any boy in my high-school gym class had covered up with a towel in the locker room, he'd have been called every kind of sissy in the book! How did this happen?

In what were called "Victorian" times (an unfair epithet, since Queen Victoria herself was neither stuffy nor prudish), people put cloth covers over piano-legs to keep gentlemen from becoming aroused by the sight of them; invented various ridiculous euphemisms for bodily parts and functions; bound children's hands at night to prevent them from masturbating. Today, we recommend professional counseling, and perhaps criminal prosecution, for a kid who likes to look at nude women. Thus progresses Humankind down the path of enlightenment.

Working Dirty

If you're suffering from writer's block, you can always turn to one of the two oldest funny subjects in the world.

To prove it, there's the story of an elderly Southern Baptist preacher who, with an old friend of his, drove to Atlanta for a three-day visit, to take in some Braves-Dodgers games and generally enjoy the big city. It turns out that the hotel in which they were staying was hosting an open-to-all oratory contest, with a grand prize of $10,000. The preacher's friend says to him, "Hey, there's a chance for you to pick up some change!"

"Oh, I don't know," the old preacher says. "I might can give a decent sermon every Sunday, but that's because I have all week to work it up; I never was much good at talking spur-of-the-moment. Besides, what would I talk about?"

"Hell, anything," his pal replies. "Talk about screwing."

The old preacher is a good 150 miles from home, and he figures, "Who's going to know?" So he enters the contest that night, and delivers a true rip-snorter of an extemporaneous speech about screwing. It's ribald, it's witty, it's descriptive, it's persuasive, and it has the whole audience whooping with appreciation. The old preacher never thought he'd be able to shed his inhibitions and "work dirty," as it were, but by God he did it; you'd never have guessed that back home he was as prim and puritanical as anyone you'd ever want to meet. And, of course, he wins the grand prize of $10,000.

Back home, a day or two later, he hands his wife the cheque, explaining that he'd won it in an oratory contest.

"How wonderful!" she cries. "What did you speak about, dear?"

The minister blushes a bit, and replies, "Why, I spoke about sailing and yachting."

"Oh," says his wife, a bit perplexed.

Next day, she takes the cheque to the bank, and whom should she run into there but the preacher's old friend with whom he'd gone to Atlanta.

"Isn't it just the nicest thing, how my husband won that speaking contest?" she asks him.

"Why, yes, ma'am, it was a...ahem, well, a fine speech."

"Yes, I guess it must have been, but I'm astonished that he was able to find much to say on *that* topic!"

"Er...hrm..."

"You see, he's only done it twice, and the first time it made him sick, and the second time, his hat flew off!"

*

This brings up a question that revives itself every time an old-time comedian from vaudeville, radio, or TV kicks the bucket: Exactly what is so great, anyway, about "working clean"? Self-appointed connoisseurs of comedy said it about Lucille Ball, when she died a few years ago; they said it about George Burns a year later; they said it about Bob Hope, too, when he croaked: "You know, what was really admirable about her/him, was that s/he always worked clean, never felt the need to resort to filth."

This is, first of all, undeserved praise, because in the 1930s through the 1950s, when those folks flourished, it simply wasn't possible to work any other way than clean, unless – like, say, Sophie Tucker – one specifically chose to cultivate a raffish audience. What do you suppose the sponsors of *I Love Lucy* would have said if Miss Ball had suggested writing in a scene in which she fumblingly tries to insert a contraceptive diaphragm? Or what would have happened to Jack Benny if he'd said, "Oh, Rochester, call up Sophisticated Escort Service, will you, and ask them what five dollars will get me."

That's not to say, though, that if they'd been working in the past 25 years or so, they wouldn't have thought of doing scenes like that. What could have been funnier than Jack Benny haggling with a madam? And since Lucille Ball had a wonderful imagination and depended so much on physical clowning, there's no telling what she'd have come up with if sex had been one of the colors on her palette.

To compliment a comedian for not using humor that might be called raunchy, though, is like saying of Norman Rockwell, "He never resorted to cheap abstractions, or otherwise stooped to expressionism." Using sexual humor, or not, might be better regarded as a matter of personal style rather than of personal morality. Some comedians – Bill Cosby, for instance – simply don't seem to find sex an interesting topic on which to build their jokes. Richard Pryor, on the other hand, was a specialist in sexual humor, and only those who are determined not to laugh at his "disgusting" antics would suggest that he wasn't funny.

To my mind, an example of comedy that bordered on "resorting to filth" (although that is much, much too strong a term) was the classic 1970s sitcom, *All In The Family*. In that show, there were hardly any actual jokes about sex, elimination, or other naughty subjects; instead, Archie would say the word "toilet," or you'd hear the sound of that dread instrument being flushed off-camera, and that would get a laugh. It was embarrassing – like having a five-year-old boy tell you an utterly pointless story that he thinks is hilarious because it contains the word "poop."

Growing Up

Where's Mine?

Most children have to deal with being bullied or harassed, at least a little. But in elementary school in particular, in every class, there's going to be one kid who's at the very bottom of the pecking order: the one whom anyone can pick on who feels like indulging in a little cruelty for its own sake.

Know this; believe and understand this: *That kid is never blameless.*

The butt of the classroom won't be the crippled kid, the deformed kid, the mentally slow kid, or the kid who's the wrong ethnicity. Only the lowest of the low will harass someone for something he can't help, and such malefactors are usually disciplined or shunned by their peers. The butt of the classroom is a different animal.

There's always a reason why the butt of the classroom (it's usually a boy) gets picked on, and it's always something he could change. He might have a disagreeable personality. He might have an uncontrollable temper. He might have poor personal hygiene. He might be weak and ineffectual to a point where the other kids just lose patience with him. Whatever the reason, if he's the picked-on kid, it's going to be his own fault to some extent. We cannot deny this fact. It's critical that we face it.

During my years of elementary school, I was that kid. I still have nightmares about it. I was not just casually picked on in class. Invariably, four times a day, walking to or from school, I'd be accompanied by about half-a-dozen kids who'd torment me in various ways: usually just teasing or name-calling, but sometimes there'd be physical assaults as well. I remember being spat upon occasionally.

In my second-grade class, the most visually noticeable kid was a boy named John. All the boys wore jeans, including John, but John always had a clean, pressed, long-sleeved white shirt. He also wore polish in his hair, the way grown businessmen did in those days, and you sometimes saw older kids, high school kids, polishing their hair, but kids of seven or eight, no.

John carried himself in a slightly aristocratic way. He wasn't unfriendly, or stuck-up, but he was a little reserved, with a straighter posture than most kids, and maybe a more cultivated way of talking. I was not particularly friendly with John, but at least he never picked on me.

In the spring of my second grade, John's eighth birthday came up, and he invited all the boys in the class to his party. It was a typical Saturday afternoon kids' birthday party, but with this difference: At this party, quite a few of the boys thought to add to the fun they were having, by having a little fun with me. They'd surreptitiously punch me or poke me, or whisper little insults at me, and I can't remember the exact details, but they were bad enough that John's mother had to intervene a couple of times.

What was particularly painful was the knowledge that John's mother was being drawn away from the main business of administering the party, in order to attend to this little subplot – and I blamed myself, and was deeply ashamed of myself, for two reasons.

First, I should not have been the boy who attracted this kind of attention. If I was, it was my own fault. It was due to some flaw in myself – and I was sure that it was some flaw that I could have corrected if only I'd had the self-knowledge and the self-discipline to do it.

Second, why did I not take care of business? Why did I not turn myself into a dangerous person who could and would retaliate with devastating effect, if some other kid started with me? Why did I not learn how to just drive my fist into a kid's face so that his nose would come out the back of his skull?

I came home from that party feeling as low as I'd ever felt in my life up to then. And I'll repeat: my anger was not so much directed at the other boys. I understood that these were normal children. They were doing what boys their age will do.

It's *fun* to gang up on some other kid. It makes you feel like you're part of the community, and it's a way of reminding yourself, "At least I'm not that kid." Ganging up on someone is an important part of life, at that age, and I suppose it always will be, as long as there are children.

Now let's fast-forward a couple of years. John didn't host a party in the third grade, as I recollect, but he did in fourth grade.

It's not like I was thinking about it, let alone looking forward to it. But one afternoon, in school – it was right after lunch, and the kids were coming into the classroom but the teacher hadn't called us to order yet – John in his white shirt and polished hair was going around the room, handing out small white envelopes. Obviously party invitations; there was no way they could have been anything else. John handed an envelope to every boy. Except one.

As he was sitting down at his desk, I leaned over and asked him, "Hey, John, where's mine?" I asked him again, a little louder, "Hey, John, where's mine?" There's no way he didn't hear me, but he didn't even look in my direction.

What was obvious to me, was the reason why I was being publicly shunned. Almost certainly, it was because he and/or his mother had decided that the party would be considerably less enjoyable if I were included.

That was my fault, and mine alone. I accept that. If I'd been John, or his mother, I'd have wanted to exclude me, too.

But what in God's name were they thinking? John was a bright kid, and his mother was a cultured, sophisticated woman. Did it simply not occur to them that it wouldn't be quite the thing, to physically hand out formal invitations to a party to every single boy in the classroom with the exception of one? Really?

If you want to exclude one kid from your party, there are ways. There are telephones. There's a perfectly good postal service. Failing both of those, you have a car and two good legs, and you can deliver the invitations to every boy's home. But, no. For some reason, no.

Ever since then – and almost 50 years have now passed – that incident has stuck with me. And still, if I ever wanted to take revenge on anyone, for any wrong or slight that I've suffered in life, John and his mother would be at the top of my list.

Unfortunately, I never will, because I don't know whom to blame for it.

For example, could the mother have been completely innocent? Could she have written out an invitation for me, which John then decided not to pass along?

Or might John have been innocent? Maybe his mother said to him, "Honey, we just can't invite that boy again; he'll ruin the party for everyone because the other kids will be picking on him."

I want to be fair. I would not want to punish an innocent party. And that is why this little incident – this trivial incident, which a saner and more decent person than myself would have forgotten about long ago – will never be avenged.

But I will always wonder: Did John feel any pang of conscience, when I asked him, "John, where's mine?" Or did he feel that I deserved to be snubbed, and snubbed publicly, and did he take pleasure from doing so? Or – what is probably the most likely

– did he simply not think about it at all? Would he even remember it, today, if I were to see him and bring it to his attention?

He would probably just ask, "Gosh, why would you want to dwell on a thing like that?" And I daresay a lot of other people would ask the same question. I would be the bad guy, you see, for having carried this grievance around with me. And maybe I am.

Probably many other people have had a "Where's mine" experience, at some point in life. Perhaps one important step toward growing up is realizing that if you didn't get one, it's your own damn fault. Curing the fault, though: that's the killer.

'Unconditional Love' – And Corporal Punishment

Not long ago, I got into a conversation with a client of mine about my living arrangement. I had mentioned that I'm a life-long bachelor, and although I'm interested in women, I'd never come close to getting married. I told her that I agreed with Katharine Hepburn, that "a man and a woman should live separately and visit frequently."

My client was taken aback, as though she'd never heard this view expressed before. "But didn't you ever want kids?" she asked.

"Frankly," I replied, "I'd sooner have had a leg sawn off. I can see no good reasons to have children, and plenty not to. They're a crushing financial burden. When they're small, they take up every single second of your life. You never get a full night's sleep; your whole house will reek of sour milk and fæces; you'll never see the inside of a restaurant or a theatre. When they're a little older, they run around and break things. Every summer, you have to take them on vacations that are as much fun as two weeks in a Gestapo interrogation cellar. When they're teenagers, you go broke bailing your sons out of jail and paying for your daughters' abortions. Then you have to pay hundreds of thousands of dollars to send them to college even though you know perfectly well that college is a racket that serves only to waste four years of a person's life. Finally, the little bastards will hate you and resent you for the rest of their days, because no matter how well-intentioned you are, you're going to find some way to make them miserable.

"And why do adults all make their kids miserable, anyway? I swear, it's because people take stupid-pills when they become parents. How else do you explain the complacency with which they routinely destroy their children's self-confidence, self-sufficiency, and self-esteem; deliberately tell the kids preposterous lies about practically every subject under the sun; give them sexual hang-ups from which they'll never recover; and in many cases inflict brutal physical punishment in the guise of 'discipline'?

"And you're saying I should be in a hurry to make myself stupid and miserable, just for the sake of producing a few more profoundly unhappy people?"

My client, who has three children, was gracious enough to agree that my arguments were not entirely exaggerated. Even more gratifying, she refrained from giving the stock answer that people almost always give me when I make that little speech:

"But it's worth it, because with a child you have unconditional love."

If I could work my will, anyone who uses the phrase "unconditional love" should be immediately sterilized (although in most cases, it's too late). It has got to be one of the silliest, emptiest phrases ever inflicted on our language.

A child's love of a parent is never unconditional. Sure, when you're small and utterly helpless and entirely dependent on your parents, you will love them because whenever you see them you know you're going to get food, or a hug, or your diaper changed. But you'll love whoever takes care of you because they're taking care of you, not because they're your parents. This is not unconditional love; this is love based on your custodian's willingness to keep you alive. At this age, you love your parents the way you love breathing; you have no choice.

As your dependence wanes – and this can happen at a young age – your attitude toward your parents will depend on a great many factors other than their ability to tend to your basic needs. In very few cases can a kid older than four honestly say, "I love my parents and always will, no matter what they might do" – nor is it healthy for anyone to feel that way about anyone, in my opinion. Strap a large group of adults into polygraph machines and ask "Do you really and truly love your parents?" and I'd lay eight against your five that you wouldn't get more than 50 percent truthful affirmatives.

I have no children, but I do have a houseful of cats, and I have no doubt that they love me; they show it constantly. But this is not based on my tending to their minimal needs. The reason they're always in my lap or on my shoulder is because I'm forever giving them treats, petting them, playing with them, and telling them how pretty and clever they are. If all I ever did for them was fill their bowls and change their litter, would they pay me that much attention?

If you want children because you like children, or because you feel it's your moral duty to propagate, or because you could use a tax deduction, then by all means go ahead and have them. If you want something to love you, a pet is way cheaper, quieter, and possessed of a stronger psyche. Its love is more easily won, and more easily kept.

If you want *unconditional* love, get a doll.

*

Ditto, if you want something to spank.

Many child care professionals – psychologists and them kind of folks – condemn spanking as a parenting tool, despite common report that it's in use, at least occasionally, in 90% of American households with children, and despite the amazingly high percentage of people who were spanked as children and say they still approve of spanking in principle.

I'm pretty much a Neanderthal on most issues, according to some of my more liberal friends. I'm not 100% opposed to the death penalty (although pretty close). I strongly oppose gun control and affirmative action. I think civil rights legislation might have been a necessary evil but was not something to be desired for itself. My basic position on public assistance is, "Are there no prisons? Are there no workhouses?" But with regard to punishing children, I'm a bleeding-heart and proud of it.

For the life of me, I can't imagine how anyone who's ever had it done to them would think that spanking had done them any good. I was not spanked often, but in each instance, I felt, and still feel, that it was unjustified and utterly counterproductive, and served no purpose other than to cow me into submission.

In extreme circumstances, *hitting*, by way of instruction, as opposed to *spanking*, by way of punishment, might have merit. If you crack the kid a good one the first time he tries to stick his hand into the fireplace or run into traffic, it certainly reinforces the lesson. "No, no, Georgie, we don't go touching flames," will just make Georgie want to do that very thing again once your back is turned. A good hard slap on the ear and a "You dumb little turd, don't you *ever* do that!" will convince Georgie that we don't go touching flames.

However, that's reinforcement, not punishment.

In my own childhood, I was never spanked for doing something immoral or naughty. For such behavior I would be scolded or shamed but never physically chastised. I would, occasionally, be spanked for displaying anger, or for being insolent or willful. And while on the whole my parents did a pretty good job of bringing me up, those spankings remain on the debit side of the ledger.

In my observation, that's not unusual. A lot of parents never spank their kids unless the kid is being obstreperous or disrespectful, and then they'll spank just because they can't think of any other solution.

There's a well-known joke about a man hitting a woman, which is generally regarded as funny only in a horrifying way: "Why do men hit women?" "Because they just will not shut up!" But in effect, that is exactly why we beat children, and we admit as much with a perfectly straight face, as though it were nothing for us to be ashamed of.

I've heard parents say, "It clears the air." Damn right it does. If you've got someone four or five times your size coming at you with an instrument of torture, the wind will go out of your sails pretty fast.

What truly mystifies me is the parent who says, "I only spank my kids if they give me back-talk, if they're disrespectful." In effect, they're saying, "Respect me because if you don't, I'll hurt you." I can hardly think of a policy less likely to inspire respect. They might coerce the kid into a superficial show of respect, but smoldering resentment will fester beneath it, and will mature like a fine old wine, to be brought out and savored on special occasions.

As a child, when I was punished by scolding or shaming, I would usually, on consideration, admit that I'd behaved badly (even if I could not bring myself to admit it out loud), and resolve to reform. This, after all, is how we usually punish our adult friends and relatives if they misbehave, and it usually works. As adults, we don't throw temper tantrums in public places, not because we fear being spanked, but because we fear looking like a damn fool.

When I was punished physically, as a child, my reaction was always, "Okay, you've proven that you can hurt me any time you like, but that does not change the fact that I was justified in being angry and had a right to show it, and your resorting to brute force is an eloquent admission that deep down, you know I'm right." (And yes, I did kind of talk that way as a kid, which was one reason why people felt like inflicting physical punishment, no doubt.)

A friend of mine once told me that she put a permanent end to corporal punishment by telling her mother, "If you ever hit me again, I'm going to hit you back, and I'll probably hurt you, because I've had a certain amount of karate, and I will try." This tactic will work only if you're pretty sure you can back it up, but on the whole, I approve of it.

Recently, a teenaged friend of mine was complaining that her guardian beat her. I told her, "Next time she hits you, grab her by the ear and pull down, as hard as you can. She'll have to choose between going to her knees or losing the ear; either way, you'll have her right where you want her." I guess it never did come to that, but it would have been fun to watch.

We've all been taught that if you hurt someone smaller and weaker than you, you're a bully. If you inflict calculated physical punishment on someone who's unable to defend himself, you're a torturer. But if you do that to your own child, you're a normal parent. Honest to God, I don't understand the distinction.

*

In my observation – and according to a lot of people with whom I've discussed this subject – nothing will infuriate a parent, nor incite that parent to the infliction of a beating, faster than the assertion that "I didn't ask to be born."

That, of course, is the standard argument of last resort for many children and teenagers, when they object to performing certain household chores, excelling in school, going to church, or whatever else their parents are trying to force them to do. It's usually advanced after the child has been informed that he has certain inherent responsibilities, simply as a consequence of birth.

"I didn't ask to be born" has become such a cliché (hardly anyone who has ever been a child has not used it at least once) that the standard adult reaction is to simply laugh at it, or to reply, "You march in there and do your homework, young man/lady, with no more back-talk, or you won't see the outside of this house for a month!" And if that doesn't work, physical pain is imposed.

The reason parents don't have any patience with the "I didn't ask to be born" argument is that it makes them look foolish – because it is, in fact, unanswerable! It's quite correct to assert that the simple fact of having been born places you under no obligation to do any work, to go to school, or to behave in a particular way.

Parents generally argue that by imposing certain rules on children, they are preparing them to cope with the unpleasant realities of adulthood, when even more complicated rules will be imposed by irresistible forces such as police officers, employers, tax collectors, politicians, and one's spouse.

To some extent, this makes sense. As an adult, you have a responsibility not to break your neighbor's leg, intentionally or by accident. As a parent, if your children lack the judgement to fulfill this responsibility on their own, it's up to you to help them fulfill it – by coercion if necessary.

But does failure to get good grades in school fall under the heading of "breaking your neighbor's leg"? I think not. We all take pride in a job well done, and we often do things we love to do for the sheer joy of doing them. But when we do something we don't particularly want to do – barring emergencies such as giving mouth-to-mouth resuscitation – we do expect to be rewarded. If your boss at work told you, "I'm not going to pay you; doing the job well should be its own reward," wouldn't you just about tell the boss what to do with that job? School is a kid's job, as surely as it's an adult's job to tighten screws on the assembly line. You think kids go to school for the pleasure of it? Did *you*? (Okay, maybe you did if you were a girl.)

If kids are to excel in life (as most parents want their kids to do), they must learn that by excelling, they will gain something pleasant. This is one of the simplest principles in the world. If you want a dog to sit up and beg, you'd better have a biscuit ready and waiting. If you want your kids to be great athletes, you'd better convince them that they can make big bucks later if they put in the effort now.

Sure, if a kid really wants to get into Harvard, no tangible reward from the parent is necessary to the achievement of good grades. But if the kid has no great interest in academics, it makes no sense to expect the kid to excel in school without some kind of incentive. If, in effect, the kid is supposed to get straight "A's" to please *you*, then a few dollars per "A" per semester is a bargain, and the kid is entirely justified in exacting them.

*

Now, I must refer to another subject on which many parents are eloquent: the ingratitude of their children.

"I give them so much," a parent will say. "I give them things I never dreamed of having when I was their age. Do they appreciate it? Fat chance!"

Guess what, you old fart: Your kids don't have your frame of reference, okay? You can't understand that?

The final word on filial ingratitude must go to the culprit in a celebrated murder case that took place in Westchester County, New York, a few years ago. A teenaged boy shotgunned both his parents; on his arrest, he explained, "All they gave me to drive was a crummy old Lincoln."

Parents, be warned. Nobody ever said life was fair.

A Child's-Eye View Of The World

The first time I looked at a map of the world, at the age of six, I was astonished to observe that there were, apparently, two Indias, two Chinas, and so on. Just as amazing to me was to see that Greenland was considerably bigger than the United States – almost twice as big – and that the United States could fit several times into the Union of Soviet Socialist Republics (which we simply called "Russia"), and that Antarctica was bigger than all the other land masses in the world, all put together.

I hadn't been told, of course, that a Mercator projection map distorts the size of land masses, making them smaller at the equator and much, much larger at the poles. This fact was made clear to me not long after, when I was shown the world on a globe. But what really blew my mind was the idea that there were two Asias in the world.

This map that I was looking at was clearly produced for an American audience, for it placed the United States in the dead center, longitudinally speaking, with Europe to the right and Asia – or one of the two Asias, anyway – to the left. Because of this placement, there was some overlap. That is to say, parts of Asia showed up both on the extreme left side of the map, and the extreme right. But that idea was too much for my infantile mind to grasp – or perhaps it just pleased me to come up with a bizarre explanation. At any rate, I got the idea that there were in fact two Asias, two cities called Shanghai, two cities called Dacca, etc., and that they were existing in parallel. For all I knew, those double cities each had the same people living in them, in duplicate.

I also noticed that the country of India, in outline, looked like a fat woman dressed in veils, dancing on her toes.

The names of the countries, some of them, presented problems to me, because like a lot of children of that age I could read well enough, but pronunciation was sometimes beyond me. Thus, at one point, I looked up from the map and called to my mother, "Mom, if 'nigger' is such a bad word, how come there's a country called Nigger [Niger]?" It's a good thing my mother explained the difference in spelling and pronunciation before I looked at Niger's immediate neighbor, Nigeria. If I hadn't known better, I'd surely have pronounced it with a hard G, and the stress on the third syllable, as though Nigeria were a physical disorder that involved the copious and uncontrolled discharge of...never mind.

Once those various confusions were cleared up, it became wonderful to me how dramatically my interest in the world was changed just by looking at a picture of it. Once I'd spent a couple of hours poring over the map, I had a good general idea of where everything was in the world, and I started reading more than just the funny pages in the daily paper. I started reading the articles, and their datelines, and obtained a pretty good grasp of world politics and current events even before I'd finished the first grade.

One confusion that took a little time to clear up was the comparison of this map to other maps that I subsequently encountered in school. These maps were somewhat older, so instead of north-central Africa being divided up into various countries, on these maps that portion of Africa was represented as just one huge blob of green, called "French West Africa." It took a little research to find out why that was.

Not long after that, I was exposed to maps of Europe, as they appeared pre-World War II, and pre-World War I. It started to sink in that the world was not, after all, a stable place. It occurred to me also that if only the Habsburg Empire had managed to hold together, I would not have had to learn to spell Czechoslovakia.

And in any case I could not understand why any country that had the good luck to be ruled by an Emperor, in all his finery (such as Austria-Hungary, Russia, and Germany) would deliberately choose some other form of government. As far as I was concerned, if you didn't have a monarch wonderfully attired, and opulent coaches for him to ride in, and brightly uniformed troops to march alongside, you were a second-rate country indeed.

That's by the way. My point is that just a few minutes of looking at a map of the world, and asking a few questions, and subsequently conducting some independent research, turned out to be more educational than anything I ever did in a classroom. That's a lesson that gets reinforced over and over, in childhood.

Cowpersons And Native Americans

A graduate student in sociology could probably put together a good doctoral project on the subject of "the last children to play Cowboys and Indians."

My experience with children is limited, so I might be wrong about this, but I suspect that Cowboys and Indians is as dead as Old Norse. I haven't seen it played since I was, maybe, eight. The game was already going out when I was a kid; we more usually played World War II.

Today, dramatic games of this type have lost popularity for a number of reasons. First, ever since the assassinations of Martin Luther King and Robert Kennedy, in 1968, various professional busybodies in the media have convinced parents that any game that involves mock combat or other dramatized violence is politically incorrect and likely to breed real violence. Second, for the past 60 or so years, there has been a growing movement on the part of parents and teachers to organize children's time as much as possible, channeling kids into adult-supervised sports, music lessons, and other activities – quite conscientiously minimizing free-form play. Third, when kids do have time to themselves, they tend to prefer video or computer games, which were not available a couple of generations ago.

Still, you'd think grownups would play Cowboys and Indians. We have organizations like the Society for Creative Anachronism (SCA), for people who like to play Knights In Shining Armor; we have "survival games," for people who want to "play guns" (the generic name for mock-combat games in my neighborhood when I was a kid). But if there's a bunch of people of any age, today, who get together to play Cowboys and Indians, I haven't heard of it. Why is that?

It should be pointed out, by the way, that "Cowboys and Indians" is a misnomer. Since we were aware, even at age six or seven, that Indians and Cowboys never fought each other (and that, indeed, some cowboys were Indians), we either played Cowboys, or we played Indians. In either case, the game was just a stylized team version of hide-and-seek, in which we "shot" any "enemy" we could see, and the victim was on his honor to drop dead and stay that way for a decent interval. Nobody wins; you just keep killing each other till Mom calls you to dinner.

It was a good way to learn history, if you were so inclined, because no kid was ever just "a cowboy" or "an Indian." You had to pick an historical or fictional role – as we put it, "be somebody." Some kids were TV characters, like Marshal Dillon or Hoss Cartwright. I looked askance at the kids who portrayed TV heroes – partly because they were always "good guys," and partly because I felt they were passing up a chance to learn about a fascinating subject.

I, and most of the kids I liked best, were historical figures. In my neighborhood, Wyatt Earp and Wild Bill Hickok were the two most popular characters, with Bat Masterson a good third. I was usually Doc Holliday, but sometimes, for a change, I'd be Black Jack Ketchum.

Black Jack appealed to me because he looked like a cartoon outlaw, with that big black moustache, and because, when they hanged him, the excessive drop tore his head off – the coolest thing I'd ever heard of! Sometimes I'd be Harry Longbaugh (The Sundance Kid), Johnny Ringo, or John Wesley Hardin. Always a bad guy, you observe.

There'd usually be one or two girls in the game, and their menu was limited. There weren't many cowgirls, and none of them were good guys. Girls could be Belle Starr (the most popular choice, because she was by far the nastiest), Etta Place, Laura Bullion, or Eugenia Moore.

As an Indian, I was usually Crazy Horse; my other favorites were Geronimo, Roman Nose, Gall, Satanta, and Little Crow. Unfortunately, my playmates' knowledge of Indians didn't go as far as mine did, and in any case our weaponry was not well suited to playing Indians.

It seems to me that if grownups were to form a club, similar to SCA, for playing Cowboys and Indians, they'd run out of historical characters pretty quickly; therefore, they'd have to decree that each member invent a credible character for himself. This would encourage careful study of how cowboys and Indians actually lived, and would go a long way to de-bunking various myths that still surround many heroes of the Old West.

For instance, I used to get impatient with any kid who was "being" Bat Masterson with a trick walking stick that turned out to be a gun. The TV character based on Masterson had such a gun, but the historical Masterson did not. He carried a cane because he was lame. A cane/gun would have been impractical and ineffectual, in both functions.

Ah, but how would we arrange the combat? With cowboys, I suppose you could have your choice of various scenarios: range wars, attempted bank robberies, street showdowns, and I suppose paintball guns could be manufactured in the shape of a Colt Peacemaker or a Winchester. With Indians, the scenarios would be limited only by your imagination, but how would you handle the actual fighting, which usually featured bows and arrows, tomahawks, and knives, as well as guns? Merely "counting coup" on a foe might not satisfy our bloodlust. (Not to mention that many Indian tribes had an unfortunate tradition of torturing captives. That would be difficult to re-enact while staying within the law.)

Those are all matters to be ironed out by someone more dedicated to the cause than I am – if any such person exists. But it does strike me that I, as I am, would make an ideal Wild West character. I'm a good card player; I dress with a degree of style; I'm a dab hand with a revolver. And wouldn't you just think that in one free-wheeling boom town or another, you'd encounter an intense-looking eccentric who insisted that he was the rightful Holy Roman Emperor?

Mind you, I did recently meet a boy who gave me some hope.

Living in a big city, you tend to try to live down the fact that you live in such close proximity to so many people. You're expected to treat your neighbors courteously, but in most cases the greatest courtesy you can extend them is to leave them alone. In smaller towns, that is less the case. It's good form to at least make the acquaintance of your immediate neighbors, and even to organize events to encourage fraternization – such as block parties. The one I attended shortly after I relocated to Iowa City, Iowa in 2010 was an especially impressive one of its kind, with much goodwill all around, and entirely too much to eat. The only incident I found unsettling was when I met myself, minus about 45 years.

There were a lot of children at this party, mostly babies and toddlers. They were doing the normal kid stuff: splashing around in the wading pool, playing with hula hoops, jumping and dancing and running and falling down. One of the older kids – I'm guessing he was nine or 10, and kind of chubby – was behaving quite differently from the others. I didn't notice him at first, but then a woman of about my own age glanced over at him and clucked disapprovingly, and asked me (in a tone of obvious dismay), "Oh, my God, do you *see* that?"

I did. All the other children were in various states of undress, ranging from total nudity to swimming trunks and t-shirts,
but this kid was got up in jeans, a flannel shirt, and jackboots. On
his head was a Civil War-style képi (Union blue), and he carried a
toy rifle on his shoulder as he marched round and round the pe-
rimeter of the party.

In my day, the early 1960s, kids going "armed" was commonplace, but even back then, this kid's behavior would have
been considered a little unusual. I know, because I used to do the
same sort of thing. I was much attracted to weapons, and even
more attracted to interesting clothes, especially uniforms – and I
loved role-playing, even at an age when most kids had either out-
grown it, or had to do it in secret to avoid embarrassment.

After this young fellow had completed three or four cir-
cuits, I stopped him and asked him which regiment he belonged
to.

"Fifth Iowa," he told me. He still had a little boy's voice.
"I'm a re-enactor. I was at a camp last week." Then he added,
"You look kind of historical yourself."

I'm not quite sure what he meant by that except that I was
almost the only male present in long sleeves, long trousers, and
short hair, and I was wearing braces instead of a belt, which does
create an antique effect. But the way he spoke to me was about
the way I'd have spoken to an adult, at his age. I always preferred
the company of adults – unlike children, they could be counted on
not to be vicious – and I would usually speak frankly to them,
much more so than I would to another child. Anyway, we talked
briefly about our interest in role-playing, and I mentioned that my
favorite Civil War character was P.G.T. Beauregard, and he wondered aloud why so many Civil War Generals had odd-sounding
names, and that was that.

I did worry about the kid a little, and not for the reasons
most adults would. Today, many uptight yuppie parents would

find his interest in war and weaponry horrifying, and demand that the kid be forced into some sort of treatment, or even institution-alized, for his own good. That was clearly on the mind of the woman who'd called my attention to this kid in the first place. I thought his interest in the Civil War, or in warfare generally, was entirely normal, and I'm appalled that such interests are apparently being conditioned out of boys by many parents and teachers. But this boy's evident desire to stand out and be different from other kids is probably going to buy him some grief; probably already has bought him some. I just hope he has learned to deal with other people's reactions to his weirdnesses better than I did.

Seeing him, alongside all those other kids, also made me think a little about why I attire myself the way I do: a little more formally than most people, even in the most casual situations, and a lot more formally on business occasions. It occurred to me that I was always like that, even as a little shaver.

Seeing all those kids in various stages of undress reminded me that I often resented being in that condition. I always hated wearing shorts; I even hated wearing knit shirts that didn't button up the front. I resented those evening parties to which children are brought in their pajamas because they'll be going straight to bed when they get home. Many adults remember that sort of thing fondly. Not I. What I hated most about childhood was the indig-nity of it, and the attire (or non-attire) of childhood had a lot to do with that.

Anyway, I wish this kid well, and above all I hope he gets away with it.

Those Happy School Days

One of the consolations of adulthood comes when summer is going into its home stretch, and I can remind myself that whatever other horrors may lie in store for me, at least I never have to go back to school again.

I heartily agree with one of my former high school teachers, who used to say, "I get so impatient with people who tell kids, 'These are the best years of your life.' If that's so, why not just commit suicide when you graduate high school?"

Indeed, it was only the faint hope that those might actually be the *worst* years of my life that sustained me as I was going through them. I could not, for the sake of my sanity, imagine that all of life could be as horrible as one's school years.

When I was between the ages of about seven and 13, the end of summer vacation was literally terrifying, because of the torment I knew I would experience for the next nine months. (I'd been excited about going into first grade, had looked forward to it, but my illusions had been shattered, almost immediately.) I still have nightmares in which, as an adult, I'm obliged to return to school because of some obscure technicality; I invariably wake up gasping and thrashing about like a drowning man.

School, for me, was much the way some soldiers have described war: insufferable boredom, punctuated by interludes of indescribable terror.

For a lucky few, school is a great confidence-builder. For many of us, it's an excruciating builder of one's capacity for self-hatred. For a lucky few, it's where you learn to make friends, "play nice," and have a good time. For many of us, it's where we learn once and for all that people are stupid, wicked, and sadistic, and that they enjoy being so.

In adulthood, I have encountered several old schoolmates who told me, "I would have liked to have known you better then, but I always had the impression that you didn't like me much." I had to explain to them that they shouldn't have taken my stand-offishness personally. I kept my distance from just about everybody because I knew that any one of them could turn on me at any moment. If there was one lesson that school taught me, and that I have carried through my life, it is "Trust nobody."

My family moved from New Hampshire to Iowa just before I started the first grade. While living in New England, I had been getting my hair cut in a way that my parents thought was cute but which I thought was the most embarrassing thing in the world: *Bangs*, for God's sake. You see bangs on little boys in the East, from time to time (they're less popular in the rest of the U.S., where little boys more usually have their hair clipped short), and I cannot for the life of me understand why parents would inflict such a haircut on a son unless they were trying to traumatize him.

Everyone thought my insistence on always wearing a hat, when I was four and five years old, was an adorable idiosyncracy. I didn't have the nerve to explain to them that I wore a hat to cover up the bangs that made me look like an ugly little girl.

Sure enough, on my first day of first grade, at this new school in the Midwest where all the other boys wore their hair a quarter of an inch long, the first person I encountered was a vicious-faced girl who sneered at me, "You look like a girl! You got bangs!" (And I couldn't cover them, because we had a "no hats in the building" rule, which struck me as senseless and arbitrary.)

That set the tone for my dear old school days. I knew already that I was ugly; I knew already that I looked like a girl; this girl was merely confirming all that, and reminding me that I wasn't going to be getting any breaks at this new school.

As time went by, I learned other useful facts: I was a hopeless athlete, who generally got picked last for games; I was a pussy who couldn't or wouldn't fight back when picked on, but would run home crying to Mommy instead; I was an "underachiever" who'd often be dressed down by the teacher in front of the whole class ("If only you'd *apply* yourself, Joe!"); I had "kooties"; I exuded some sort of foul aura, if not an actual odor.

Then, around the third grade, I started getting fat. By the fifth grade I was downright Cartmanesque, and I stayed that way for several years thereafter – dropping a lot of weight when I hit puberty, but remaining at least moderately chubby till I was about 20.

As if all that weren't enough, as I got older, I started taking an interest in girls. My big problem was that I liked the pretty ones, and it's an odd fact of nature that people usually hook up with boyfriends or girlfriends who are more or less equal to them in terms of physical beauty. Thus, on the rare occasions when I found that a girl was attracted to me, it would be more an occasion for embarrassment than for gratification.

College was no better: Simply, it was four years of doing nothing and learning less, at a cost of tens of thousands of dollars, so that I could tell future prospective employers that I was a college graduate.

So, to sum up, I came out of my schooling with a nearly debilitating paranoia; a conviction that I was a total failure as a human being; an awareness that I was personally repulsive; a terror of achievement; and a blinding hatred of the human race.

How To Get Kicked Out Of School

When I was a student, an English teacher gave the class an assignment that we all enjoyed: to write an essay defending something indefensible (like mugging old ladies), or attacking something sacred (like UNICEF).

I was reminded of this when one of my recent correspondents, who was ending her career as a high school student, told me that one of the requirements of her final examinations would be to write a one-paragraph "essay" on the Holocaust (i.e. the depredations of Adolf Hitler and his henchmen in Eastern Europe in the 1940s). This struck me as preposterous for two reasons.

First, the assignment's too easy. Since when is writing a single paragraph about *anything* a task worthy of a final examination for 17- and 18-year-old students? I suppose the exam that covers mathematics will require them to add four and five, on the grounds that adding five and six involves "carrying," and thus is unfairly tough.

Second, the assignment's too difficult. It requires an experienced and gifted writer, of a professional level, to develop a worthwhile statement about any complex matter in a single paragraph. This assignment encourages the student to consider the Holocaust in ridiculously simplistic terms.

For a person of that age, who wants nothing more, at the moment, than to pass the exam and get out of school, there can be only one way of fulfilling the assignment. Some 99% of the one-paragraph "essays" will read something like this:

"The Holacaust [sic] was the most terrible thing in the history of the world. Millions of Jews were killed by Adolph [sic] Hitler. Every time he conquered a country, Hitler ordered the Jews to be rounded up and killed. This was because of hate and prejudice. We must make sure that nothing like that ever happens again."

As far as I can see, this assignment's purposes are (a) to verify that the student has at least a vague idea of what the Holocaust was, and (b) to oblige him to declare his abhorrence of genocide. Both objectives insult the student's intelligence.

Undoubtedly, one or two Junior Skinheads will write something moronic, along the lines of, "the Holocaust never happened," or "Killing Jews rules." Their diplomas will be withheld, their parents will sue the school system, they'll undergo court-ordered psychotherapy. We all know that routine by now.

A more testing poser might be, "In one paragraph, defend or attack the following proposition. Resolved: The Holocaust was the most reprehensible event in human history."

Could a critic of the Holocaust, in one paragraph, say something more than, "It was really, really, really, really bad"? Alternatively, could a Junior Skinhead defend the Holocaust in a way that came anywhere near to rationality? A high school student who wants nothing more out of life than to make trouble might plagiarize, with my blessing, any of the following three efforts.

I.

"To paraphrase Joseph Fouché, the Holocaust was worse than a crime: It was a blunder! In the midst of a two-front war in which they were vastly outnumbered, the Germans diverted an extraordinary amount of manpower and other resources from the battle lines to the 'killing centers' in Poland. It could be argued that the

Reich needed to round up and concentrate Jews and other 'undesirables' to more efficiently pillage their property, which Germany
needed to finance its military adventures. However, the money
gained from these anti-civilian operations cannot compensate for
the loss of fighting personnel. Those who died in the killing centers could more profitably have been kept alive, providing the la-
bor necessary to the conduct of the war, and – if the Germans
wished it – killed once the war was won. Adolf Hitler blew a win,
in great part, because of his impatience to kill people he could
have slaughtered at leisure once his war aims had been met."

II.

"From the Nazi point of view, considering the circumstances, the
mass killings of Jews, Gypsies, Slavic intelligentsia, and other 'undesirables' was entirely justified. The Nazis felt that Jews and
Gypsies, lacking national loyalties, sucked the lifeblood out of any
nation or community into which they were introduced, without
producing anything of value in return. In the case of the Gypsies,
at least, historical facts support that belief. Ordinarily, the dictates
of common humanity might militate against killing these people.
However, in the midst of a world war, simply expelling them from
the Reich would have been utterly impracticable. Rather than feed
millions of people they considered worse than useless, when all
available resources were required for the war effort, the German
government's decision to put these people to death as efficiently
as possible was, if questionable from a humanitarian viewpoint, at
least well-reasoned."

III.

"That the Holocaust was reprehensible is beyond doubt. Other
crimes, however, dwarf it. What is most remarkable about the

Holocaust is not that millions of people were systematically killed. After all, several other dictators – most prominently Josef Stalin and Mao Tse-Tung – made Adolf Hitler look like a piker in terms of the number of people they caused to be murdered in the name of the State. Several other governments – most notably the United States in the 19th century – made similarly successful efforts to eradicate an entire race of people. What is truly amazing about the Holocaust is the way in which Jewish and Jew-influenced propagandists have revised history so as to create the impression that it was the Jews, and they only, who as a people suffered under Hitler. In the long run, the Holocaust turned out to be an incredible public relations coup, without which the State of Israel would never have been a reality. A bargain, indeed, at the cost of only a few million insignificant people. As the late Ethel Merman might have observed, 'There's no business like Shoah business!'"

Any one of these is guaranteed to provoke severe disciplinary action, a sensation in the news media, and years of litigation.

Surnames

It seems to me that surnames, as we know them, have for some time been obsolete, and serve few purposes other than to reflect negatively on their owners, in one way or another.

This is driven home to me every time a phone salesperson addresses me as "Joseph" (or, worse yet, "Joe"), and is surprised when I inform her that I am Mr. Dobrian to a stranger. Just by insisting on maintaining that level of formality, I identify myself as a tight-assed snob.

I also, by retaining that name, identify myself as someone whose forbears were not here for the Revolution. Many Americans frankly regret that their surnames identify them as being descended from ancestors who didn't speak English. A couple of generations ago, it was common practice, if your name were Shlabotnik or Armaducci or Lupescu, to change it to something a bit more manageable and – let's face it – more socially acceptable. Today, many people still wish they could do that, but social pressure in the other direction – to pretend to take pride in one's antecedents whether or not one actually does – often prevents them.

Many of us know the old joke about the Polish immigrant named Stanislaus Shitski, who resolved to change his name to something a bit less obviously Polish, and less unpleasant to American ears – so he became Bob Shitski. The evolution of my own name is a variant of the same joke: My grandfather, upon arrival in the States, changed it from Dobrjan, thinking that Dobrian would be easier for Americans to pronounce. No such luck. If he'd left it as it was, people who knew no better would have voiced the "j" as a consonant, instead of leaving it as a vowel as it is in Polish – but at least there would have been a uniform mis-pronunciation. As it is, I get do-*bry*-an, do-*bree*-an, Dorbian, Do-brynin, Dobarian, Dobrinian, Doberan, Doberman, Dobbern, and other butcheries too grotesque to mention.

My grandfather also confused the issue of our family's ethnicity. I get begging letters from Armenian charities – un-doubtedly because my name ends with "ian." The Home For The Armenian Aged, in New York City, must have every telephone directory in the United States on its computer, and can generate a mailing list simply by doing a search of any name ending in "ian." (They failed to notice that my name couldn't be Armenian. Arme-nian names rhyme and scan with "Armenian," and Dobrian lacks sufficient syllables.)

It's for this very reason – the fact that they are ethnic iden-tifiers – that surnames do more harm than good. Not only are some people abashed by their obviously Slavic, Hispanic, or Jew-ish names; I've also met a few people with good British names who admitted to wishing they could answer to something more exotic than Brown or Hopkins.

(A few years ago, a fellow named Bob Lee had his name legally changed to Roberto León, so that he could qualify for the various state and federal affirmative action programs that favored Spanish-surnamed people.)

Some of the more common English names tend to raise suspicions these days. For instance, Green and Davis (or David-son), are now almost equally associated with Jews who were origi-nally Gruneberg or Grunewald, Davidov or ben-Dovid.

If there is one common surname that can be called "American," and not of some other country, it's Miller. This sounds like an English name, but Miller is not a very common name in the United Kingdom. Millers, in Great Britain, have always had a reputation as crooks who would steal a good percentage of whatever grain was brought to them to grind into flour. (In Chaucer's *Canterbury Tales*, one of the most memorable characters is the coarse, bagpipe-playing miller, who tells the bawdiest of the tales. The Reeve's Tale – almost as racy – is about a miller who steals grain.) In Germany, however, millers didn't have such a bad reputation; thus the name of Müller has always been common there. The wave of immigrants to the U.S. from Germany in the mid-19th century included a whacking great number of Müllers, most of whom became Miller.

(Many surnames that designate a profession could easily be translated into English if their owners wished to cover their ethnic tracks. For instance, Ferrier, Schmidt, Ferraro, Kovacs, Herrera, and Kuznetsov are all Smiths.)

We also, nowadays, have to deal with the question of who takes whose name upon marriage. A few couples choose to connect their surnames with a hyphen, which could lead to problems a generation or two hence, when some poor kid is saddled with a name like Anne Franklin-Vardebedian-Vrdolyak-Kekkonen-Marcovici-Yamamoto-Veraswami-Gudmundsdottir. On the other end of the spectrum of political correctness is a friend of mine who, born with a Ukrainian jawbreaker of a surname, took her husband's Irish name, and retained it upon her divorce – and when she married Husband Number Two, she still retained her first husband's surname, probably just because it sounded better to her.

That, I think, is the healthiest approach. Obviously, it won't do for people to dispense with surnames entirely, as they are required for identification in a society as large as ours. But perhaps we should accept it as normal that when a person reaches adulthood, he should adopt a surname of his own choosing, and only change it further if extraordinary circumstances demand it.

This surname should serve to particularize that individual, as was the original purpose of surnames like Smith, Underhill, Kennedy (Gaelic for "ugly head") and Rasputin (Russian for "low-life"); thus, we might see modern surnames like Cellist, Freckles, Dogwalker, and so forth. Of course, if we want to pretend that this is a free country, we'll have to cope with grotesqueries like Bigschlong or Moneybags, but at least people who chose such names would make themselves objects of scorn, and thus be less likely to reproduce.

The Importance Of Being Brendan

In one of his early routines, comedian George Carlin remarked that he'd always resented his given name, because, he said, George ranks quite low on the List Of Getting Laid Automatically By The Sound Of Your Name.

He's not the only person to discover that there is, indeed, such a list. I, too, have scanned it, and have found that Joseph is right down there in the same low position as George, just a notch above Elmer, Everett, Irving, Marvin, or Francis. We rank considerably lower than other uninspiring names, such as Murray, Phil, Dennis. Even Tim gets more trim.

This isn't to say that George, or Joseph, or Francis never have girlfriends. We do, now and then. But to make ourselves interesting, we have to overcome a severe handicap – like a one-legged man at an ass-kicking contest.

Names go in and out of fashion, and some of them, I'm convinced, lose popularity because parents are aware that they're low on the getting-laid list. For instance, Elmer Fudd was so christened because the name Elmer was perfect for a fat, ineffectual old guy. Even in the first part of the 20th century, Elmer was an "old man's" name. You don't hear of too many boys being named Humphrey, Roscoe, Ignatius, or Ferdinand these days, either.

Therefore, those of you who are planning to reproduce might do well to discuss what you should call your male children if you don't want them to be angry, lonely, sexually frustrated – and resentful of you for saddling them with a name that made them that way.

If you want your son to be a guaranteed chick-magnet, any Irish name is a good choice: Brendan or its variant, Brandon (dead-certain to get you laid by the hottest babe in the room, wherever you go); Brian; Ian; Sean; Seamus; Declan (another sure winner); Conor, Fergus. Use the original Gaelic spelling for extra effect. It helps, of course, if you have the accent to go with it, but that's just an extra. It's the name that matters. George might have the most musical brogue in Christendom, but he'll still have to work for whatever action he gets. (Call him Seoras – the Gaelic equivalent – and he'll do a lot better.)

Italian names have a reputation for getting you laid, but names like Pino, Tony, Fonz[*], Vito, and so forth are not as universally sexy as the above-mentioned Irish names. They have a cult following, but they don't attract women above a certain income level, or women of Anglo-Saxon or Nordic descent, or people of non-urban background.

Two sleepers – names that you wouldn't think would get you laid, but do – are David and Michael. Davids and Michaels are usually not very sexy, but they always have something about them that allows them to consistently beat out a Gary or even a Rich. I've had to contend with so many guys named Michael – and two of them, in particular, were total slimebags who managed, one after the other, to hold sway for years over a woman for whom I would have walked through 20 miles of napalm – that I instinctively mistrust any stranger of that name, and have to be shown overwhelming evidence of his decency before I'll put aside my prejudice.

---

[*] In the 1970s TV sitcom *Happy Days*, a character was known as Fonzie; it was explained that this was due to his full name being Arthur Fonzarelli. The show's writers were apparently too clueless to know that Fonz, or Fonzie, is the diminutive of Alphonse.

Peter is near the front of the list, too, no doubt because of its phallic connotations. It's especially good if you're trying to attract the dreamy, ethereal types. Oddly, though, another phallic name – Dick – is well back in the pack.

My name is pretty far down the list, no matter what variation I use. Joseph conjures up the image of an uptight, over-cultured, bookish, unexciting, and decidedly not very macho guy. As for Joe, there's a reason why that's the first name of the fictitious Joe Average. Joe is plodding, not too bright, and as scintillating as tapioca pudding. Joey might be okay if I dug women with heavy Bronx accents and big hair, who listen to Barry Manilow and Julio Iglesias. Zeppo? Hmmmmm. That might have worked, once, but it's way too late to change now.

A similar list exists for girls' names. Surprisingly, female Irish names are not particularly sexy. Names like Eileen, Maureen, Kathleen, Noreen, Pegeen, Mavourneen, Drisheen, Crubeen, Strychneen, Gasoleen, Thirteen, and Stringbeen are down around the middle of the list. Other names, like Hepzibah, Euphemia, Edna, Ethel, and even Jane, can put a girl at a horrible disadvantage. Joan, which is just a variant of Jane, is for some reason much higher on the sexiness scale.

On the other hand, plenty of girls' names are clear and consistent winners. For example, I loathe all those trendy yuppie shopping-mall names – all those Megans and Brittanys and Ambers – but you seldom meet an Amber who isn't a babe. Michelle – the female version of Michael – has about the same mojo as Michael. A Michelle may not be particularly pretty, witty, or sexy, but somehow she always makes out pretty good.

A few years ago, in a bitter book called *Jennifer Fever*, author Barbara Gordon looked askance at the tendency of older, financially successful men to dump their aging wives and take up with young bimbos – whom the author called Jennifers. And true enough, a lot of these new-model wives were named Jennifer, and they were hot little numbers, too!

For a stretch, in the mid-1990s, I noticed a huge wave of young women named Tara, all of them in their early 20s, all of them excruciatingly babe-a-licious, all of them very much aware of that fact, and all of them way too good to speak to the likes of me. What is it about that name, that made every Tara really good-looking, and stuck-up besides?

Perhaps one day, we will discover why some names are sexier than others: whether it's the juxtaposition of sounds, or some other factor. In the meantime, parents, if you love your children – and if you want them to give you grandchildren – do please consider how well your child's name will work as a mating tool. I cannot stress this too strongly.

That's 'Your Majesty,' To You!

If you belonged to one of several Plains Indian tribes, in the old days, you'd have a "true name," known only to yourself and your immediate family. If by chance some other people found it out, it would be an extraordinary insult and very bad luck if they were to call you by it. Thus, you'd be known by several different names throughout your lifetime, none of them being your true name.

This is not a bad system. Although it's hard to say exactly why, names have a "mojo" to them, and if you ever want to get someone's dander up, just call him by a name that he considers too intimate, or a name that he answers to, but doesn't like.

My given name is Joseph, not Joe. I was called Joe in my childhood, and a few old friends still call me that, and I don't mind if they do. But to new acquaintances, I introduce myself as "Joseph Dobrian," and if they can't call me "Mr. Dobrian" (which I would prefer) then they at least can refrain from giving me the diminutive form.

A good 75 percent of the time, after I've introduced myself as "Joseph," my interlocutor will automatically call me "Joe." If it's someone I'm likely to see again, I correct him. Unfortunately, too often, the conversation goes like this:

"Hi, I'm Karl Miller."

"Hi. Joseph Dobrian."

"Good to meet you, Joe."

"Joseph."

"Right. Joe, the reason I suggested we meet is that I wanted to give you the news on our operation in Brazil. I think, Joe, that you'll find it interesting..."

"Excuse me, I'm Joseph, if you please."

"Yeah. Anyway, Joe, about this Brazil thing..."

Why? He doesn't yet have any reason to piss me off – especially not if he wants me to take an interest in his damn Brazil operation. I suppose it has something to do with the ridiculous notion that if you give someone a name other than the most informal name possible, you're being stuffy.

The bizarre corollary to this idea is that so many people nowadays actually take offense at being called "Sir" or "Ma'am." I call just about everyone "Sir" or "Ma'am," sometimes. I'll say "yes, sir," or "yes, ma'am," for emphasis, or I'll sometimes use the honorific to stake a position, as Dr. Samuel Johnson used to do, as in, "Sir, I can only describe her singing as execrable." I always was taught that "Sir" and "Ma'am" were titles of respect for people you don't know well. I'm amazed, though, at how many times the following exchange has taken place at the end of a conversation:

Me: "Thank you very much for the information, Sir. It was a big help."

Him (grinning, to pretend he's not offended): "Don't call me 'Sir!'"

A certain person recently disputed something I'd written for publication, and sent me a long, abusive letter (including descriptions of some uncomfortable-sounding sexual variations which he advised me to perform upon myself), and he kept calling me Joe, as in "Joe, I pity you." Somehow, the worst part of the whole letter was that this loathsome filth called me "Joe." If he'd done so in person, I'd have warned him once not to do so, and if he'd persisted, I'd have hurt him.

Perhaps that explains why I tend to use people's given names in *inverse* proportion to how well I know or like them. A business associate with whom I'm not very friendly will be "Bill" or "Joan." One with whom I'm friendly will usually be "Mr. Jones," or just "Jones," or (especially if female) might be given a pet name, like "Steph-O-Rooney" instead of just "Stephanie." Perhaps I use just plain first names for people with whom I'm less friendly because this obviously phony familiarity is a barrier against real intimacy.

(With my closest friends, or with women I'm courting, it varies. For some, I'll use the given name, for others, the surname, and for others, I'll invent a nickname, apparently without regard to how highly I esteem them.)

This may have to do with how boys in my neighborhood addressed each other when I was growing up. I'm not sure how this system evolved, but it went like this:

If Jim Wagner and I were playing just the two of us, we'd call each other "Jim" and "Joe." (I tolerated "Joe" back then.)

If Jim and I were playing in a larger group, we'd call each other "Wagner" and "Dobrian."

If I were referring to Jim in conversation with another kid, I'd call him "Wagner," but if I were talking about Jim to my parents, I'd say "Jim" or "Jim Wagner."

If Jim, in conversation with another kid, had to differentiate between me and my younger brother, he'd call me "Big Dobrian" and my brother "Little Dobrian."

If we were talking about the four Peterson boys down the block, we'd refer to John, the eldest, as simply "Peterson." We'd refer to his younger brothers as "Tom (or Tim or Mark) Peterson." But if Mark Peterson were playing with us without his elder brothers, we'd call him "Peterson."

(I would not have dreamed of addressing Jim Wagner's mother as "Emily.")

I'd be quite pleased if we went back to using two forms of the second-person pronoun: "you" for most people, and "thou" for family and close friends. I daresay, though, that with the labored informality that most Americans feel it necessary to impose on each other, anyone who did not immediately address a stranger as "thou" would be considered the worst kind of stuffed-shirt.

I also wish we would be more conscious of titles. A lawyer, a world-class chess player, an orchestra conductor, have all worked their asses off to get to where they are, and one of the perks of their positions should be that they be addressed as "Doctor," "Grandmaster," or "Maestro."

Perhaps I agree with the Indian taboo against speaking another person's name lightly – and I haven't forgotten the old admonition: "That's my name; don't wear it out!"

Boomers, Fading

Among the several factors that differentiated the "boomer" generation from its forebears, arguably, was the way we were conditioned in childhood. Children of previous generations were often taught their place in society, and seldom thought about breaking out of that place and finding a better one. Many children born post-World War II were taught, from very early on, that we could do just about anything we set our minds to do. I, and most of the kids I grew up with, believed that we could, if we chose to, become a U.S. Senator, a Nobel-winning scientist, a glamourous private detective, or an N.F.L. football star. Note the common thread: the ideal of rising to the pinnacle, or near it.

For the past 200 years, in the United States, it has indeed been possible for people with average gifts and strong will to pursue virtually any calling to which they take a fancy. A child of five could decide to be a politician, a scientist, a detective, an athlete — and as often as not, that child would make it to his or her chosen profession.

But individuals of our generation were not conditioned to pursue a certain calling. Rather, the goal instilled in us, by and large, was to make an extraordinary mark: to excel. The important issue was not what one excelled at: merely that one excelled. This may be why so many of us are now taking rather grim assessments of ourselves. Excellence isn't attained because one wants to excel; it can only be reached if one wants to excel *at something.*

A person might say (Indeed I have said it myself, and quite shamelessly), "I want to be rich and famous, and get laid a lot. How I get there doesn't much matter." There is nothing wrong with that sentiment. Wanting wealth, fame, and sexual desirability gores nobody else's ox. However, if those are your goals, your efforts to obtain them will likely be so scattered that you will not succeed, save perhaps through sheer accident. The lack of a coherent plan, and the lack of even an idea of how to formulate one, will leave you so frustrated that you'll spend time you could have used to further your ambitions, simply daydreaming about what it's going to be like when you are successful. Even these daydreams aren't very satisfactory. Since they don't tell you what your success might consist of, their credibility suffers.

Why did (and do) we boomers find it so hard to excel at *something*? My suspicion – much as I hate to agree with just about everyone else in the world – is that TV did it.

Mind you, I'm not saying that TV is by nature a corrupting influence, or that we were scarred for life by watching hours of sex, violence, inane cartoons, and preposterous commercials. There has been, and will always be, plenty of stuff on TV that isn't exactly edifying, but low-brow entertainment existed for thousands of years before TV, and it's never done much harm.

If TV has crippled our ability to excel, it's not the fault of the sentiments expressed in the programs or the ads. What hurt us, I think, was the relentless exposure to glamourous individuals. We took it as an article of faith that everyone who appeared on TV was highly paid and lived a life of almost unimaginable excitement and luxury. We saw hundreds of examples every day that seemed to bear this out. On TV, we saw almost nothing of the mind-bending drudgery that's almost always a part of a great success story. We knew that superlative performance, and the accompanying rewards, were attainable – but nobody ever suggested that to attain them would be any kind of a strain.

This is not so much a problem for the generations that came after us. Today, many TV shows seem to deliberately make a spectacle of trashy behavior. We pity and scorn, rather than envy, many of today's TV personalities.

Many people of my generation got the idea that if we soldiered on through school and scraped our way through college (and most of us went to college simply because everybody knew you had to go — hardly any of us went there with any specific goal in mind) we would, at 21 or thereabouts, magically be transformed into one of those rich, happy, happening people we saw on the tube every day. It was a mighty rude surprise when that didn't transpire.

Children of previous generations weren't exposed to so many exciting people who had apparently got where they were simply by growing older. Therefore, it never occurred to those children to *not* pick a manageable goal and strive manfully toward it. The result, for many, was a satisfying career.

We've seen some exceptions: boomers who decided on a calling, pursued it with a will, and excelled at it, thereby achieving wealth, fame, wild sex, and so forth. (I started noticing at a very early age that people who had resolved to make music their life's work tended to be especially focused, hard-working, and goal-oriented.) Far more of us, however, just plugged along till we ran out of excuses to stay in college. Then we panicked, grabbed whatever job we could find — and now are stuck in lives we find barely tolerable. We can't just chuck it all and go join a rock band, because that would entail a huge downward adjustment in our standard of living, which none of us would be willing to make even if we could be sure it were temporary.

For many of our children and grandchildren, it's likely to get worse. The idea of learning a craft or a trade is dying. People are catching on to the fact that college is an utter waste of four years and hundreds of thousands of dollars — and yet they continue to go, because they've been told that they have to. In many young people, there's both a lack of hope and a lack of desire – and who can blame them, when we seem to be moving closer to serfdom every day? Nobody seems to *want* anything anymore – except maybe to be left alone, or to be taken care of, depending on the choices they've made.

Is it possible to wreak such changes on our society that young people will once again understand that a trade or profession, well and truly pursued, with clearly stated goals in mind, is the surest route to a satisfactory life? And can we fix it so that they can enter that trade or profession without an unmanageable burden of student debt, such that it's hardly worth having the education required to pursue that vocation?

Most important, can today's young people be convinced that it'll all merit the effort? I suggest that it's motivation that we lack, above all. Motivation most often comes from the possibility of self-realization – certainly not from the prospect of enslavement to a collective, nor from the desire to reach an undefinable, unformed, nebulous goal such as "success."

Love, Romance, And Naughty Stuff

'Bad' Girls Get My Respect

Not long ago, I got into one of those discussions that occasionally just spring up, among a fairly large number of strangers who will probably never see each other again. In this instance, the subject of debate was, "Is there such a thing, for a woman, as going to bed with a man too early in the relationship? If so, is there a specific amount of time you should wait between taking the notion to do it, and actually doing it?"

You'll notice that we all omitted the possibility that a man would, if attracted to a woman, fail to seize the first opportunity to stuff her senseless. As a matter of fact, a man who's interested sometimes will hang back the *first* time he gets an offer of sex, from a woman he's attracted to – if, as frequently happens, he's tired and a bit drunk and worried about "erection issues" – but he will invariably take her up on it, on the next date.

Among the women in the discussion, the range of opinions ran from one woman who dogmatically insisted that a woman must commit to waiting 90 days between the notion and the deed, to a woman who admitted, "I sometimes do sleep with a guy right away, but I know it's not a good idea because he won't respect you if you do that."

Of the men taking part, the two least attractive – fellows who were obviously never going to be in a position to find out – agreed that a woman who sleeps with a man "too soon" is going to be regarded as unworthy of respect. A third gent said he wasn't sure. I alone insisted that the conceit that a man will respect a woman in inverse proportion to how quickly she'll sleep with him is absolute nonsense.

I'll grant that there are plenty of reasons why one should not jump into bed with whomever momentarily strikes one's fancy. But I admire a woman who, if she wants to have sex, has it, and doesn't worry much about whether or not that makes her a slut. To assert that one should allow a decent interval between the time she decides she wants to go to bed with a fellow, and the time she actually does it, just so the fellow won't think she's "easy," is silly and hypocritical.

Am I the only man who believes this? I can't imagine that I am, and yet I have never heard anyone agree with me on this point. Is it possible that we are all so intimidated by a grossly out-dated precept that we still feel that we must continue to pro-nounce it, as though it were a sort of shibboleth, even though we rarely adhere to it in practice? Or am I just full of shit?

Several times, I've danced the mattress hornpipe with a lady on our first date. In one case it was only the second time we'd ever met, and with that lady, I went on to have a fairly intense, if brief, romance. When the romance ended it was she, not I, who broke it off; the fact that we remain close friends, 30 years later, is pretty good evidence that I place her respectability level at "above-average" at the least.

I've had other girlfriends with whom I've made a two-backed beast very early in our acquaintance; in each case, if the relationship didn't last, that was strictly due to personal incom-patibility or factors such as distance. It had zero to do with how soon the lady in question had gone to bed with me.

I know a man who is married to a woman who succumbed to his horrid desires on the very night they met. That was well over 30 years ago, and as nearly as I can tell, their marriage is solid. I can cite other instances, involving other people, where the old in-out-in-out took place on nearly as short an acquaintance, and the relationship turned out to have been helped, rather than hindered, by that circumstance.

My suspicion is that women assume that guys won't respect them if they jump too eagerly into the sack, not because there's much evidence to support that notion, but because they know that *other women* will think they're sluts, and just assume that men will feel the same way. Unattractive men, I rather meanly suspect, back them up on this only because they wish to impress upon these women that they – unlike the more attractive men with whom these women sleep – are interested in an intellectual and emotional experience first, and a sexual one second. Deep down, they're just hoping that saying the "right" thing will get them laid – preferably in less than 90 days! I cannot believe that more than a very, very few men sincerely feel that a certain waiting period should be observed, between the desire and the deed, simply in order to prove one's respectability.

I am convinced, furthermore, that the notion that a woman who is sexually active is somehow "bad" is the main cause of teenage pregnancies. Teenagers get pregnant because they don't use birth control. They don't use birth control because if they did so, that would be proof that they were not simply swept away by passion – half-raped in other words. On the contrary, they'd been *expecting* to have sex! And to have sex with premeditation, according to the myth, is proof positive that you're a ho.

To demonstrate your respectability by getting pregnant, when you could have avoided it, is extremely silly behavior – and yet it happens all the time. It seems to me that it's almost as silly to try to impress a man by showing him how long you can hold out. And I assure you, I'll respect a bad girl before I'll respect a silly one, any day of the week.

How Smart Is Sexy?

One of the most annoying clichés one hears, when one asks a woman what she finds attractive in a man, is, "Intelligence, in a man, is one of the biggest turn-ons I can think of." It's annoying not because it's entirely false – I have had several girlfriends who told me that it was my intelligence that attracted them to me – but because it is insufficiently true.

If every woman meant it, who claims that intelligence is the sexiest attribute a man can have, I'd never have time to put my pants back on. As it is, when I'm in the mood for love, I have to seek out that small cult-like sect that puts its money where its mouth is, and values brains over looks, income, or membership in a band.

(I don't, by the way, mean to boast about my intelligence. It's a plain fact, but whether it does me any good is debatable. After all, Manute Bol was awfully tall, but it didn't make him that great of a basketball player.)

There's no doubt that in a few cases, intelligence truly is sexy, to men as well as to women. I've been attracted to women of modest physical gifts and surly dispositions, because they could match wits with me. I've dumped girlfriends who were kind, gentle, good-looking, sexy, and dumber than a bag of hammers.

In other cases, though, intelligence is a turn-off. I'll never forget a blind date I had once: Having been bid goodnight by the young lady rather earlier than I'd have liked, I got in touch, a few days later, with the mutual friend who'd set us up, to find out what could have gone wrong. She reported to me that my date had complained, "He was so intelligent I didn't know how to talk to him!"

If I knew how to "dumb down" my conversation, I would. But that is much more difficult than pretending to be brighter than you are. It's not all that difficult for a man to fake intelligence. Subtle flattery works very well. Just let the woman do almost all the talking, but listen intently, looking right at her and nodding and "ah-hah"ing and "I see"ing from time to time. Don't ask many questions, or you'll risk exposing your lack of intellect, but when you do speak, speak as you listened: softly yet intently, with lots of earnest eye contact. Your interlocutor will go away thinking you're downright fascinating.

Intelligence is really sexy, though, only if it's combined with humor and wit, and many bright people's humor is humorous only to them. One former girlfriend of mine suggested that because my own humor was so esoteric, everyone who socialized with me should carry around a huge book entitled *The Annotated Joseph*, in which all my obscure references would be explained. (And the main reason she was my girlfriend was that she was witty enough to come up with suggestions like that.)

Intelligence in itself is rarely a turn-off, but immodesty in erudition often is, and many bright people are not shy about showing off how much they know. Once again, this is the voice of experience talking.

Many people believe that the less intelligent a person is, the happier he is likely to be. I don't agree with that notion, but it is true, I think, that intelligent people tend to be much more introspective than unintelligent people, and thus can seem unhappy. Even if they are not unhappy, introspective types tend to talk about themselves a great deal. Women, generally, do not find unhappy men attractive, nor do they often like men whose favorite subject is themselves. Guys who haven't much conversation of their own, but are just intelligent enough to shut up and listen, are thus in a good position.

Men, however, often are attracted to unhappy women. This is partly because they have an instinctive urge to comfort a woman who's vulnerable, but partly also because we suspect that sad women are easy lays. The average guy figures that if he listens to her whining long enough, she'll see him as her knight in shining armor and invite him into her bed. The trouble is, most of us don't care to listen to all that gloom and doom on a permanent basis, and it comes as a nasty shock to the lady when we decide we can't take any more of it.

Also, men tend to be fascinated by women who talk non-stop about themselves. This may be, in most cases, because such women tend to be pleasing to look at. A woman who's attractive physically will often have been taught from an early age that she is interesting, and thus she'll assume that any guy will be happy to hear absolutely everything she can tell him about herself.

That's not the whole story, though. I've seen, many times, a woman with only average looks and average intelligence trans-form herself into a fascinating, sexy person through her ability to speak energetically, articulately, and at great length about herself. In other words, a woman who is trying to fake intelligence should often take a strategy opposite from a man's, and talk *more* than she ordinarily would.

Once again, earnestness, intensity, and eye contact can stand in nicely for intelligence. I've passed over women who might have been quite bright, but who – because they were too retiring to talk about themselves – I concluded were stupid. But the ones who went on and on and on about themselves, in breathy, excited voices, gazing right into my eyes as though to im-ply that I was the first and only person to share all their secrets:

they were the ones who fascinated, even if they had bad complexions or big crooked noses. And believe me, it's a real letdown if you discover, later on, that such a woman is stuffed with rice pudding between the ears.

True enough: intelligence can be sexy. I'd like to be intelligent enough to know how to work it.

A Token Of True Love?

Some of us believe that presenting one's ladylove with a diamond solitaire, to denote an engagement, is an immensely old and unalterable tradition – an unmistakable sign of one's love and devotion. In fact, the tradition is not much more than 100 years old. And, far from being a sign of love, that diamond was originally a compensation for anticipated infidelity.

Back in Victorian times, if you and I were engaged, then I, as the man, committed myself to taking care of you financially for the rest of your life. If you broke off the engagement, you released me from that promise. But if I broke it off, you could sue me. If you could establish that I'd broken off the engagement in a particularly caddish manner, or for a caddish reason – because I'd fallen for another girl, for instance – you could collect monetary damages from me. It did happen.

The rationale was that my breaking off our engagement might have deprived you of your livelihood. It would have been a negative reflection on you that might have prevented your attracting a husband in the future. (In any case, if I'd strung you along for long enough, you'd have been considered too old to be attractive.) And if you were a woman and didn't get married, in those days, you were up a creek: condemned to a life of low-paying jobs or sponging off wealthier relatives. Thus, my breach of promise would have been considered quite a serious matter.

The custom of giving diamond engagement rings evolved as a way to protect oneself from legal action. I would present you with a piece of valuable, convertible, portable property, which would serve, in effect, as a hostage to ensure that I kept to the engagement. If you broke off the engagement, you'd be bound to give it back. If I broke it off, you would be left with an asset that could be easily converted into a large amount of cash – an out-of-court settlement of the breach-of-promise suit.

Today, what with women being perfectly able to fend for themselves financially, the diamond engagement ring is no longer a pledge against bad faith. Its purpose today is to convey the following three messages:

1. I've been bought and paid for.
2. Look what a rich man I got.
3. Look how much he was willing to pay for me.

In other words, this custom has become a potlatch: the wanton destruction of assets, to show that one can afford to do it. The custom as we know it today also implies rather clearly that it's proper for a woman to sell her affection to whomever can afford to pay for it.

The diamond industry feeds this notion with advertising campaigns urging men to "ask your jeweler about the 'two months' salary guideline.'" This is a purely fabricated standard that certain loathsome creatures in the diamond business have foisted upon the general public, to guilt-trip men into spending far more money than they can afford on a useless bauble. According to this "guideline," if you're some poor shlub just starting out in the business world, making $2,500 a month, then you had better shell out at least $5,000 for your girl's diamond ring, or you're a piker, a creep, and not worth marrying.

You might counter my arguments by remarking that an engagement ring is, after all, a proof of my love. A proof of my love? How can I be expected to love anyone who expects me to prove it by running several thousand dollars through a paper-shredder?

Recently, a good many women have abandoned the custom of returning the engagement ring if it were they, not their boyfriends, who broke off the engagement. Advice columnists are repeatedly asked whether this is proper, and despite their insistence that it is not, some women do it. I have heard several rationalizations, to the effect of, "Hey, I like the ring; I'm keeping it," or, "He was such a @#$% to me, he doesn't deserve to have it back."

This is of a piece with a letter I saw in one of the late Ann Landers' columns, a few years ago, in which a correspondent complained about the relatively low prices of the wedding gifts being given by members of her circle, and how this negatively impacted her bottom line.

"I'm spending $100 per person on my wedding and reception," was her approximate argument, "so how am I going to turn a profit if these freeloaders are showing up with $50 and $75 gifts?

(Ann Landers published this letter with the notation, "Now I've heard everything," but I can't believe she'd never heard anything like it before. The letter was signed, "Long Island," by the way, and my fellow Manhattanites and I just grinned. We know Long Islanders, you see.)

Oh, one more thing: As long as they're going to wear their engagement rings and wedding rings on the same finger, couldn't certain women at least observe the convention of wearing the wedding ring on the inside – "nearer to the heart" – instead of wearing it on the outside, as a guard ring? Unless they have no shame about publicly admitting that they hold the convertible asset the more dear.

Why Guys Love To Shop

One of our favorite questions for debate has always been, "Is it easier/pleasanter to be a woman, or a man?" We find some strong arguments on both sides of the question, but I can think of one advantage, anyway, that women have over men: They never have to deal with that constant dentist-drill litany, "Why are men so scared of commitment? Why can't men be trusted to be faithful? Why are men such shits?"

It is true that women tend to be more monogamous than men, but this is only a tendency. Two other tendencies are more to the point: First, men tend to be choosier than women in selecting a mate. Second, men and women look at a sexual involvement in different terms.

It's been said that what a woman wants out of life is one mate; what a man wants is to mate with as many women as possible. This is a facile generalization: too facile. Plenty of men want to settle down with one woman – eventually. But men, by and large, will want to shop around for a mate, much more than women will.

Women are more likely to be satisfied with a bird in the hand, even if the bird's a buzzard. Perhaps one big reason why you hear so many women complaining about husbands who are violent, drink too much, neglect the kids, etc., is that these women had a pretty good idea, before they were married, of what kind of men they were dealing with – but they went ahead with marriage anyway, thinking it a more attractive alternative than starting all over and finding someone else.

Besides, for some reason, women tend to assume that they can change a man. They can't.

Most men, if they have grave reservations about a woman, will not go through with marrying her. Even if settling down with one woman is a man's goal, he won't commit to the first woman who'll have him – unless he knows that he's such a poor specimen that he'd better take whatever is offered, and thank God for it. Most of us ask ourselves, "Is this the best we can do?" If the answer is "probably not," we keep shopping.

Unlike women, men realize that they will not be able to change their mates. We won't be able to get rid of your braying laugh, your mood swings, your preposterous opinions, your ghastly musical tastes, or whatever else about you that we might find annoying. We know this, and we deliberately weigh the defects against the assets.

This is not to mention the number of women who sabotage their relationships almost before they have a chance to become serious, by *acting* serious. I can't tell you the number of times I've heard a woman say something like, "I treat him really well; we have nice times together; he says he's serious about me; and still he wants to go out with these other bimbos! I don't get it!"

To this I reply, "He wants to go out with 'these other bimbos' because you are forcing him to shop around. If you're wanting to stay home and talk about 'the relationship,' if you're after him to 'take it to the next level,' talk about his 'feelings,' if you are in any way pushing him toward a long-term commitment, then you are making him say to himself, 'Gee, she's trying to force me to make up my mind! I'd better find out, *fast*, whether she's the best I can do!'"

So, out he goes, shopping. And he's going to find that "those other bimbos," because they haven't been with him for long, are still going to be more interested in having fun than in heavy conversation. They'll not yet have started giving him a hard time just for being a guy. They'll still laugh at his jokes. They'll be more interested in avoiding arguments than in winning them.

Above all, they won't be trying to change him.

Often, a woman will assume that because a man has slept with her, he has at least some interest in a long-term monogamous relationship. The man may, indeed, be interested in that, but it's a mighty dangerous assumption to make. For a man, sleeping with a woman is just one milestone on the long path of the relationship. First you kiss goodnight at the end of a date; then you kiss a lot at the end of the date; then you go to bed at the end of the date. But you're still just dating. Women are more likely to think of going to bed as the deal-closer – like "drinking on it."

Physical fidelity and commitment are by no means synonymous. Many people – of both sexes – are able to feel a strong attachment to someone, indeed to love them as one ought to love a spouse, yet still bed other people. The rationale, basically, is this: If you are my best buddy, and we play golf together a lot, why should you feel insulted if I play golf with some other guy when you're stuck at the office? It doesn't mean I like your company any less, and it doesn't break your leg or pick your pocket.

You might say, okay, but the issue of sexual infidelity can be complicated by matters like pregnancy and venereal diseases, which can be troublesome indeed in a multiple-partner situation. That is true, but these points are almost never brought up when people discuss the morality of "cheating on your partner." Instead, the objection to physical infidelity is almost always the "just because" argument: "It's just morally wrong."

In many European cultures, it's considered quite normal for husbands and wives – who often love each other sincerely and deeply – each to have their little sideshows. All parties are expected to be discreet about it, that's all. This does not strike me as an unhealthy system. If it were more prevalent in this country, we'd probably see a lot more men walking to the altar, instead of being dragged there, kicking and screaming all the way.

Fasting On A Saint's Day

Valentine's Day is a season of restraint for any guy with the barest tinge of romance in him. The main problem is that in most man-woman relationships, the woman's romantic fire is kindled just as the man's is dying down. When he wants to make with the candy, flowers, and bad poetry, she finds it distasteful. Subsequently, at the point where she has come to desire and expect such tokens, the man will find as much romantic inspiration in her as he might in a dish of oatmeal.

Valentine's Day has got to be the most unpleasant of all the holidays unless you happen to be in the opening stages of an idyllic relationship. Once, I lost a client because of Valentine's Day. The lady in question, who can attract men but not keep them, happened to be between boyfriends (and thus flowerless and candyless) on the day. I should have known enough to avoid her entirely on that day, but I didn't – and sure enough, she went bananas over a trivial matter; we ended up screaming at each other and never again doing business.

I'm not saying I couldn't empathize, but at least if I'm going through a dry spell on Valentine's Day, I'll have the decency to shut myself inside for the day and evening so as to protect the general populace from my psychotic behavior. (Such isolation also spares me the sight of happy couples – which, guaranteed, will consist of a gorgeous woman and some loser guy who obviously couldn't carry my jockstrap. I arrange to have my door locked from the outside, because I know that any such sightings will cause me to go postal.)

Even if you happen to have a boyfriend or a girlfriend on Valentine's Day, you're not going to enjoy the day much unless it's relatively early in the relationship. What's really sad is the second Valentine's Day of the relationship: A year ago, you exchanged extravagant expressions, and now the romance has cooled to the point where you sort of toss the candy and flowers at her as though it were any other unavoidable once-a-year expense.

A few Valentine's Days ago, the comic-strip character "Cathy" – funny for once – talked about not wanting her new semi-boyfriend to come anywhere near her during Valentine's week, because she was aware that this guy wasn't the great love of her life, and she wanted to be totally free and clear of him in case something better came along. This was funny in a not-so-funny way, because I've been the guy in his position more than once, and painfully aware of it, and there's hardly a worse feeling than the knowledge that the lady is waiting for a better deal.

We ought to institute a custom, on Valentine's Day, of sending not just flowers and other gifts to our beloved, but dog poop or decayed fish to people who have scorned us. Are you still brooding about that girl who, when you invited her to a Yanni concert, just curled her lip and said, "I don't think so!"? Why, send her a box of chocolate cordials that have been filled with your personal effluvia!

Or dispatch a singing-telegram artiste to her place of business, bearing a bouquet of thistles and a box of candy-coated cigar butts, so that her entire office will hear a description of her rotten personality and inexcusable behavior – being sung, like an Old Norse saga, by a trained performer.

In this way, nice girls will (with luck) get the recognition they deserve from at least one nice guy. The nasty girls, likely as not, will still get plenty of candy and flowers, from many admirers, because guys love girls who sneer at them, almost as much as girls love guys who treat them like dirt. But those gifts will be counter-balanced, and the nasty girls properly chastised, by the mountain of condemnatory missives, boxes of foul substances, and other expressions of animus.

Probably the biggest challenge occurs when Valentine's Day comes up at a point when you've started keeping company with someone but haven't "done it" yet.

I've discovered through bitter experience that some women consider it bad form for a guy to send them flowers or otherwise indicate romantic intentions until they've solemnized the relationship with sexual intercourse. Having crossed that hurdle, you're authorized to let the woman know that you really, *really* like her; in fact you'll be in trouble if you don't. But if you send her flowers before you've slept with her, she'll think you're an over-eager dork, and probably a stalker besides. At the very least, premature flowers will make a woman think you're sweet, and thus not worth bothering about. No woman wants a man who doesn't present a challenge.

(You have *got* to let the woman think that the relationship is her idea, not yours. It's the same principle as looking for a job: If you don't already have one, you can't get one. Women have a special sensing mechanism, known as "laydar," that tells them whether or not a guy is getting it regularly – and if he ain't, they'll ask themselves, "Why should I have anything to do with a guy who's so unpopular?")

If you want to stir up some discord, if your girlfriend happens to work with a bunch of married women, just send a nice bouquet to her at work, rather than to her home. That evening, each of her co-workers' husbands will get their heads bitten off at the least excuse, and will be quite mystified as to why.

Nothing kills romance as surely as does that little gold ring. I daresay that if I ever do get married, I'll insist on separate addresses, possibly in neighboring towns. At least, under such an arrangement, I'd be more likely to discharge my Valentine's Day obligations with pleasure.

Polite Fiction Keeps Romance Alive

For generations, some of the most popular reading for married women (or women who've been with the same guy for a long time, at any rate) has been books and articles on how to maintain or revive the romance in your relationship.

The sad truth is that part of the reason romance cools, over time, is biological. Once your sense of smell has become used to your partner's pheromones, he or she will be less exciting to you, and while you might remain fond of each other, you won't make each other nearly as hot as you once did, and there's no way you're going to get that back.

However, it is possible to maintain some level of romance – if that's what you want – by maintaining a certain degree of mystery. We hear a great deal about the importance of honesty, about how it's critical to be utterly open and up-front with each other, and never hold anything back. In some areas of the relationship, this is true. However, in one critical area, it is vital that your partner never know anything about you. The area to which I refer is the bathroom.

It was no less eminent a personage than Bertrand Russell who once remarked, "Nothing kills romance more quickly than an acquaintance with your partner's bathroom habits." I have heard a few people – invariably women – take the other end of that argument, claiming that there's a touching sense of intimacy in the act of pooping in front of a lover, and that when a couple reaches that level of comfort, the bond between them is strengthened.

Maybe a few women believe that, but I can guarantee you that hardly any man does. Not all women are aware of this, but it's the truth: Men, in general, believe that women of beauty, wit and refinement do not poop at all. Maybe certain unappealing, vulgar, plain-looking women do, but the kind of women we would marry simply do not manufacture or excrete any solid waste matter.

(I must confess, by the way, that everything I have to say about pooping is merely second-hand knowledge. As a gentleman of exceptional quality, I have never had any more personal experience of that function than has, say, Cindy Crawford.)

If a man is forced to confront the fact that his ladylove does, indeed, poop, he is then forced to re-examine his entire opinion of her. Confidence in her physical perfection is shattered. How could any person of real breeding, of real intelligence, produce such vile substances? It must be, after all, that this woman is not the paragon he had always believed her to be, but is instead one of those very ordinary women who will all too soon become old, fat, and dreary.

And the substance itself is not the worst of it. No indeed: as in many other areas of life, style is far more important. It is difficult if not impossible to take a dump in a manner that's æsthetically pleasing – and consequently most of us would prefer not to see it done.

A lady friend who sees eye-to-eye with me on this subject (and who, it goes without saying, has never pooped in her life) once treated me to a graphic description of one of my predecessors "launching a Democrat" in her presence. Needless to say, their relationship went downhill from there.

It seems to me (speaking from ignorance, of course) that the process of cleaning up afterwards would be just as much a turn-off as the act itself; perhaps even more so, as the aftermath would necessarily be so much more indicative of the pooper's habits. If your partner's efforts at policing the critical orifice strike you as haphazard and inadequate, you'll be revolted, probably on a permanent basis. On the other hand, an exceptionally diligent ablution – commendable if executed in private – would necessarily constitute a tasteless display of earnestness if performed before an audience.

(For example, I can't conceive of any way in which one could ascertain the need for further operations – I believe the process is known as "checking the paper afterwards" – with any great degree of style or grace.)

Any way you wipe it, there's going to be trouble in Paradise. Your partner's method of pooping, the accompanying odors, and the repugnant post-op procedures, will inevitably be filed in a prominent place in your mental folder marked "grievances," right alongside her annoying laugh, her habit of eating cottage cheese with her fingers, and her tendency to flirt excessively with strange men once she's had a couple of drinks.

Neither must there be any suspicion—ever—that you or your partner have any experience with intestinal gas. The comedian Bill Cosby once remarked that fathers are the only family members who are allowed to have gas. That is probably because the father no longer has to keep romance alive, and perhaps he doesn't even want to – and besides, his kids think farts are funny.

However, if you have no children to entertain – or if you choose to amuse them in other ways – and if you're not one of those lucky few who never poop or break wind, you must at least maintain the polite fiction that you don't. You must also – even in the face of overwhelming evidence to the contrary – maintain that fiction with regard to your partner.

When she goes behind that door, you must develop a sense of object impermanence, and convince yourself that she has simply disappeared – actually dematerialized – and might or might not return, but will be as perfect as ever if she does. Shut your ears to any unseemly noises; keep your nose to an open window for a good 15 minutes after she has emerged. If you, yourself, poop occasionally, then shut the door; develop techniques to minimize the noise; flush quickly and frequently; light a match or two; clean up with vigor and perfectionism; and keep those scented candles blazing.

Your romance may never be as strong as it was when first Eros struck you with his dart, but at least it'll keep breathing on its own, without your having to resort to self-help books or articles in *Cosmopolitan.*

Other Annoyances Of Adulthood

A Date With John Barleycorn

Among the many unpleasant by-products of our current obsessive health-consciousness is the rash of simultaneously self-abasing and self-congratulatory books by fairly well-known authors (or by ghost-writers, on behalf of less literate celebrities) on the subject of giving up alcohol. But so far, to my knowledge, nobody has written much about how to make the most of the situation if you choose *not* to become an abstainer.

I never drink to excess (unless sometimes when I'm not paying attention), and I would be shocked – shocked – to hear that any of my readers ever over-indulged. However, it will happen to many of us, at least once or twice in our lives, that we will pass an evening in public with a heavy drinker. In situations like that, most people will instinctively try to keep up with whomever is drinking the fastest, and if you're not used to strong waters, the result can be interesting. Even if you do manage to control yourself, you might find that the person you're with is a different person entirely when in drink – and coping with that strange person can be just as challenging as coping with yourself if you're gassed.

The old saying goes, "A woman who drinks heavily is never a cheap date, but she's usually worth it." That's true only if you can stop her at the point where she's had enough to make her willing, but not enough to make her incapably stinking. Get her too drunk, and you'll go home with her, all right: You'll have to carry her to your car in a fireman's lift; listen to her ramble about all kinds of uninteresting subjects (it's possible that she'll forget that she's with you, and start saying unkind things about you as though she were talking to a third party – or, she'll be perfectly aware that she's with you, and will explain to you at some length that you're a worthless dirtbag); haul her to a bed or couch; wait till she's passed out and you're sure she's not going to puke – and by that time, it'll be way more trouble than it's worth to do anything else besides go to sleep yourself.

No matter how much it pains you to do it, if you're on an official date with a woman who's drunk, you're duty-bound to stay in her vicinity, however obnoxious she gets, however many other guys she flirts with, however badly she abuses you, and be ready to get her home when she finally collapses. The only thing that will absolve you of this duty is if she makes it plain that the date with you has ended and a new one, with another guy, has begun.

If you're with a woman who has reached the point of no return, if she's small enough for you to manage, the best policy sometimes is to let her drink all she wants till you can carry her home unconscious. That's often easier than helping her to walk. If you can get her dancing, this will wear her out and speed the process along.

Never, under *any* circumstances, give a drunk person coffee, and never take it yourself if you're bombed. All coffee gives you is a wide-awake drunk. Coffee also tends to dehydrate you, which is what alcohol does anyway.

Concerning the use of alcohol to prime a woman for sex, I'm inclined to agree with the remark attributed to Casey Stengel: "If it ain't happened by midnight, it ain't gonna happen, and if it does, it ain't gonna be worth it."

Drunkenness, by the way, is a situation in which women and men each have certain advantages. Men, being heavier, usually take longer to get drunk. (That can be good or bad.) Women can get as crazy as they like, when they're drunk, and men will put up with it and even take them home afterwards. A man has to remain somewhat civilized, or his girlfriend will go home with someone else – after that other guy has obliged her by knocking the boyfriend's teeth out.

A woman who's in the passing-out stage will always find some kind fellow to help her get home – although it's a crapshoot as to whether it'll be the type of help she wants. A man, no matter what kind of shape he's in, will usually have to get himself home.

Dealing with a man who's drunk in public is easy. Just walk away from him. He probably won't even notice that you've left. If he tries to restrain you, it's a pretty sure bet that even if you can't knock him down yourself, somebody will do it for you. Or, you can just kick him in the belly and make him puke.

If, after all, it's you who's the afflicted party, I've just two words to say to you: "water" and "aspirin."

The best palliative for drunkenness is water, quarts of it. Drink till your teeth float, then pee, and drink some more. In fact, if you're seriously high-schooled, the best procedure is to sit on the toilet with a gallon jug of water in your hand, and just drink and pee continuously till the room has stopped spinning. Then, when you've peed as much as you can possibly pee, take four aspirins (*not* aspirin substitutes such as Tylenol or Advil) and go to bed. You'll still be hung the next morning, but you'll suffer less than you deserve.

Do not go to bed if you're still feeling dizzy. Anyone who's ever ridden the bucking bed knows that lying down at that stage merely encourages nausea. If you want to throw up, take an emetic and get it over with.

Most likely, your body will react to a bout of drunkenness as a woman's body reacts to childbirth: by forgetting how painful it was, so that you'll do it again.

A Most Romantic Illness

For the past several weeks, I've been tormented by terrible pains in my feet. One joint or another becomes so severely inflamed and swollen that I can't take a step without gasping in agony; the foot becomes so sensitive that I can't bear to have a sheet touching it at night. The other day, I consulted my podiatrist, who told me, "Sounds like you've got gout."

My immediate reaction was, that while I did not particularly want to be afflicted, if I had to have some sort of foot disorder, that is precisely what I would have chosen. To prove to myself just how lucky I was, I reported the doctor's diagnosis to several of my friends. Their nearly unanimous response was, "Whoa! Cool!"

Contracting a glamour illness, which gout certainly is, is a rare thing, and as long as it's not terminal, or permanently crippling, it's nearly a cause for celebration.

Gout is a "rich man's illness," much more common in the 17th and 18th centuries than it is today. It's an acidic imbalance in the blood – a mild form of uremic poisoning – which leads to inflammation of the joints, typically in the big toe or elsewhere on the foot. It's usually caused by bingeing on certain rich foods, and on red wine. My diet's pretty lean, I seldom drink red wine, and I never binge on anything, so it's a mystery to me how I could have been blessed with this disorder.

Okay, those are the hard facts of gout. But the facts are nothing compared to the fancy. The pain is quite a reasonable price to pay for the romance of the thing.

Gout. The word, standing on its own, could be a picture:

In his dimly lit but spacious counting-house, Lord Fiddle-faddle sits at his enormous mahogany desk, poring over ledgers listing the revenues from his slave-ships, his plantations in the New World, and his interests in the British East India Company. He's wearing a beautiful bottle-green velvet coat with gold facings, gold velvet knee-britches, long lace jabot and lace shirt-cuffs, and a long, white, full-bottomed wig. At his elbow is a decanter of madeira; he's seen delicately taking snuff from a silver snuff-box as he scrutinizes his profits through primitive-looking nose-glasses.

One of His Lordship's feet wears an elegant buckled shoe. The other, propped up on a hassock, is swathed in bandages.

Standing solicitously behind him, as if waiting for orders, is a skinny, stoop-shouldered clerk, dressed in a dull brown suit and a cheap wig that could do with a fresh coat of powder. On the floor, two dogs play tug-of-war with an immense bone, while a third looks inquisitively up at the nobleman, as much as to say, "What's the matter with your foot, kind Master?" In the background, an eccentric-looking man in black, with lancets and other surgical instruments bulging out of his pockets, and a book under his arm labeled *Physick*, examines the contents of His Lordship's chamber-pot.

I have only just now composed this painting in my mind, but if it were executed, it could certainly be passed off as *Gout*, a satirical work by an anonymous artist, after William Hogarth, circa 1750.

For glamour and romance, the only thing that whips gout is tuberculosis – which is usually fatal, so most of us wouldn't consider it worth the hassle. But an awful lot of famous people died gloriously coughing themselves to death, including Frédéric Chopin, Vivien Leigh, Doc Holliday, Franz Kafka, and the mother of practically every heroine of every romantic novel of the Victorian era. It was quite the thing, to have TB. You died young and in horrible pain, but in the meantime you were soulful and ethereal, with a bright eye and a flushed cheek, with the intense emotions and the heightened sexual drive to which tuberculars were subject. And when your time finally came, you had a pile of love-letters ten feet high at your bedside, and volumes of bad poetry written by the prettiest girls, or the handsomest young men, from 50 miles around.

Nothing else can quite come up to gout or tuberculosis, although modern times have brought us other mildly glamourous illnesses. From the 1950s to the present, a chronically bad tummy has been strong evidence that you're a player. A bottle of Maalox or Mylanta on your desk can serve as a none-too-subtle status symbol.

Emotional disorders aren't considered nearly as classy as they once were, but it wasn't too long ago – the 1960s and 70s – when psychoanalysis was something you bragged about. First, it was a point in your favor if you could afford this Rolls Royce of psychotherapy. Second, undergoing psychoanalysis suggested that you were plagued by a whole gang of interesting demons. Third, even though you were being treated for a serious disorder, you had evidently risen above it enough to have made a success of your life after all. Fourth (and perhaps most important), revealing that you were undergoing psychoanalysis was a sly way of telling everyone that your mother was a shit.

But a gyppy tummy isn't all that interesting. My creative juices aren't quite up to composing a Hogarthian masterpiece entitled *Dyspepsia*. And while undergoing psychoanalysis might make you superficially and briefly interesting to other people, it's not the sort of trouble that will make anyone write you a poem, in lovely calligraphy on the finest cream laid paper, done up with a bright bit of ribbon.

Sure, given the choice, I'd just as soon not have gout. But I found it a mighty handy excuse to go out and buy a classy walking-stick. Never did a man limp home with more élan.

A True Test For The Actor

Acting is a hobby of mine, rather than a profession, but I have trod the boards of the New York stage several times – even done Off-Broadway (as opposed to Off-Off) here and there, and took a huge loss in bankrolling and producing my own play a few years ago. I've got a short but respectable list of parts I always wanted to play, but am now too old to: Macbeth, naturally; Captain Bluntschli in "Arms and the Man"; Captain Queeg in "The Caine Mutiny Court-Martial"; Mr. Day in "Life With Father," to name a few.

One other role I've always coveted is that of Ebenezer Scrooge, in one or another of the countless adaptations of "A Christmas Carol" that plague the stages, movie theatres and TV screens of the entire English-speaking world through the month of December.

So far, the definitive portrayal of Scrooge was probably given by Alastair Sim, circa 1950, in a non-musical, true-to-the-book, British-made film. My next-favorite interpretation of him was given by – of all people – soap star Susan Lucci in the 1995 TV-movie, "Ebbie," in which she played Elizabeth Scrooge, an iron-hearted department store owner in a present-day American city. If you get the chance to see it (it usually runs on the Lifetime channel at Christmastime), you'll find it's a pretty clever show, likewise faithful to the book aside from its updated setting. (The one objectionable element is a Tiny Tim who is so excruciatingly saccharine that you sit there praying that the little bastard will croak, and look sharp about it.)

Unlike many actors in that role, Sim played Scrooge with a sour sense of humor, which he certainly had in the original version of the story, Charles Dickens' novel. "If I could work my will," Scrooge says in that book, "every idiot who goes about with 'Merry Christmas' on his lips, should be boiled with his own pudding, and buried with a stake of holly through his heart. He should!" Or, to Marley's ghost, "There's more of gravy than of grave about you, whatever you are!"

Susan Lucci took the opposite tack, playing the female Scrooge as a high-strung yuppie bitch who can't understand why everyone else isn't as preoccupied with business as she is. This interpretation was successful because so many of us, today, have worked for at least one woman with that too-driven personality, and we recognize it at once.

It was Dickens' ability to tell a story and his attention to detail that made him a great writer. His characters were seldom very interesting in themselves. They were either caricatures (like Scrooge) or colorless people caught up in colorful events (like, say, Oliver Twist).

Mr. Sim and Miss Lucci gave successful interpretations of Scrooge because they gave the character the complexity that Dickens had withheld. Sim did this by giving Scrooge a rough, awkward sense of humanity, even at his worst; Lucci, by drawing a picture of someone who never got over the notion that life is a never-ending battle, in which there's no room for sentiment.

Another important point is that Sim and Lucci were both young enough for the part. Scrooge is often portrayed as an old man, in his 60s at least; more usually in his 70s, but if you read the book, you'll find that he could not have been very old. He had a nephew who appears to be in his early 20s (at least, Scrooge is angry at him for having got married too young, before he could sup-

port a family), who is the first and only child of Scrooge's younger
sister, who, we can assume, was young when she bore him. As
Dickens portrays him, then – and as Alastair Sim portrayed him –
Scrooge is hardly more than 50. Susan Lucci's Scrooge was in her
mid-40s.

The actor will encounter different challenges to playing
Scrooge, throughout the show: in the early part of the story, when
he's just a mean old cuss; in the middle, as he's gradually converted to nice-guyness; through to the catharsis at the end, when
he gives way utterly to giggling benevolence.

In the first part, the most serious pitfall will be the temptation to play him as an ogre, roaring and snapping at anyone who
gets near him. I'd be more inclined to play him as a quiet sort who
wants nothing more than to be left the hell alone, and whose main
weapon is a sort of Socratic irony, usually delivered with the barest
trace of a smile.

The middle of the play doesn't involve Scrooge much,
since it's mainly flashbacks and fantasy scenes involving other
people, with Scrooge as a spectator. Here, in order to be convincing, the actor has to portray someone who's deeply moved but
trying to maintain a stiff upper lip. This is tough to do on stage,
where facial expressions must be somewhat exaggerated.

The scene in which Alastair Sim gives way to riotous, in-
coherent joy upon awakening from the dream sequence was fun
to watch, but only because it was re-written by the screenwriters
to include more physical gyrations than were described in the
book. Take away the physicality of that scene and it becomes almost impossible to play. Playing a villain is a comparatively easy
job. Playing a reformed villain, in such a way that the audience
doesn't yearn for his former villainy, is a test that only the most
daring actor will face. Which is why I want the part.

Christmas Carols

Doesn't anyone ever stop to think about what he's singing, when the fulsomeness of Christmas cheer impels him to burst into song?

Most of the better-known sacred Christmas carols are inoffensive, if you buy the whole Christian mythology to begin with, and even if you don't, if you merely accept the songs as expressions of a certain belief system, you can enjoy them. Some of the secular carols, though, are frightening expressions of the worst traits of human nature.

Take for example "Rudolf The Red-Nosed Reindeer," in which human behavior is allegorically displayed by hooved creatures. Here we have a reindeer who is apparently a solid citizen in every respect, who just happens to have a physical oddity. At any rate, it's implied in the lyrics that the other reindeer subjected him to verbal harassment and social exclusion solely on the grounds of that deformity. There's no suggestion that they ostracized him because he had poor personal hygeine, molested reindeer children, or cheated at reindeer games.

No, the poor bugger was made an outcast because he was different, as so often happens in the human community, and don't we know it! There probably isn't a one of us who hasn't instinctively turned his face away from a disfigured person, or has, as a child, tormented the classmate with the thick glasses and the perpetually snotty nose. Many of us, at one time or another, have been the fat kid, the oddball, the nerd, or just really, really strange-looking. And we all came out of that experience convinced that most people, at bottom, are wicked, and enjoy hurting other people for the sheer hell of it.

Ah, but the worm turns! Every pig, it's said, has his St. Martin's Day, and our hero's Great Leap Forward occurs when Father Christmas gets the idea of using Rudolf's beaconesque beezer as a headlight for his sleigh full of toys.

"Then," the song relates, "how the reindeer loved him [Rudolf]!" Again, the song illustrates one of humankind's most reprehensible characteristics: we're a bunch of butt-kissers. They *loved* him? I don't think so – except in the sense of the old saying, "Everybody loves a winner." Donner, Blitzen, Comet, Cupid, and the rest of those vicious, backbiting scumbags started sucking up to Rudolf because they were just bright enough to see that he was the fair-haired boy as far as Santa was concerned, and if they gave him any trouble, the Jolly Old Elf would turn them into steaks, glue, and lap-robes, and take their antlers down to the factory to be made into cutlery handles.

(No doubt they already knew what Santa was capable of, having found out the hard way, in their youth, when Mr. and Mrs. Claus whipped out the long knife and harvested themselves a feast of Arctic oysters!)

Someone ought to write a sequel to that song. No doubt it would portray Rudolf, now drunk with power, wreaking a terrible and perpetual vengeance on his mates, lording it over them, eating their food, kicking them on the hocks whenever Santa has his back turned, and running whining to his master whenever one of them retaliates.

Speaking of Santa, that song about his "Coming To Town" is another one that deserves a closer look.

It's all very well to advise people to take a positive attitude and present a cheerful countenance whenever possible; it's quite another to suggest that any display of sadness, discontent or disaffection is socially unacceptable. Let's set aside for a moment the rather ghastly implications of the middle of the song ("He's making a list/He's checking it twice/He's gonna find out/Who's naughty or nice" and, further on, "He sees you when you're sleeping/He knows when you're awake/He knows if you've been bad or good/So be good, for goodness' sake!") and simply consider the portent of the opening lines: that any display of unhappiness constitutes "naughty" behavior, for which Santa will punish you by withholding the merchandise you would otherwise have merited.

Life does not always give us what we want, when we want it, and those of us who never express the least disappointment, in this world that is full of calamity and torment, are not generally regarded as mentally balanced. Would you, or anyone you know, actually want to suppress every impulse to shout, cry or pout, however gross the provocation? Are we to keep a merry smile when someone hits us in the face with an ice-loaded snowball, pours turpentine on our Furby and sets it ablaze, and urinates on our collection of baseball cards? That seems to me an excessive price to pay for a few toys every December 25.

Now, let's consider what this song says about Santa. First of all, is he snooping on folks in an invasive manner – peeping into their windows, etc.? And are we not, in this song, implying that this is acceptable behavior? Do you have any idea what would happen to you if you went around spying on everyone on your Christmas gift list, carefully totting up every time he cussed, told a lie, failed to use a seat-belt, or allowed the crabgrass to go to seed?

Finally, let's examine John Lennon's "Happy Christmas/War Is Over." It begins with the rather sniffish, accusatory, "So, this is Christmas – and what have you done?" Thence, it proceeds to exposition of an emphatically simple idea: Merry Christmas and Happy New Year to everyone in the whole wide world.

As Lennon sings this uncomplicated sentiment, a chorus overlaps with the self-righteous mantra, "War is over, if you want it." As though one could stop all wars by wishing for peace, any more than one could cure illness by wishing for health. As though war by definition were undesirable, no matter how horrible the consequences might be if we failed to fight. As though Mr. Lennon were superciliously demanding of all of us, "I, a gentle and enlightened person, choose peace; what's *your* choice?"

Humbug, I tell you! Humbug!

A Satanist's Christmas

I'm philosophically a Satanist; I'm a clergyman in a Universalist sect; I'm an atheist by conviction; my roster of close friends includes far more Pagans, Buddhists, atheists, and Jews than Christians. For those reasons, I'm occasionally asked how I can morally justify keeping Christmas in any way.

Practically any culture that has roots in a cold climate has a winter festival of some sort, and I'm willing to call mine Christmas for the sake of convenience and because, face it, the Christians have done not too bad a job of perfecting their festival. Carols are nice, even if I don't agree with the sentiments expressed in the religious ones, and Handel's "Messiah" is a fine piece of music. More to the point, the Christian Yule, far more so than that of any other tradition, is given over specifically to the cause of mutual goodwill. (This is not Christmas' official raison d'être in any Christian sect of which I'm aware, but it has, over the centuries, become the de facto explanation for why we keep Christmas.)

I believe we have nothing after this life but the grave, and that it is for that reason – not for the sake of any future reward, but because life sucks and then you're a long time dead – that we should treat each other as decently as possible, and if Christmas gives us a few days' excuse to make a little extra effort to do just that, then I don't care if the stinking Christians invented it.

Possibly, if for a few days we make a serious effort to pretend that other people are not that bad (and it's a stretch, I'll admit, but it can be done if you have a few stiff drinks beforehand), we may eventually get to the point where we can stay on our good behavior for most of the year, instead of just for the season.

The recognition of Christmas by municipal governments has come under fire more and more often in recent years, from people who protest that Chanukkah, Kwanzaa, the Norse/Celtic Pagan Yule, and perhaps a few other winter holidays ought to get equal recognition. Just as strident in their protests are anti-religionists who assert that governmental recognition of Christmas suggests that the Christian tradition has some sort of official endorsement that the other traditions lack, and that erecting a crèche in front of City Hall suggests that if you're not a Christian, you're not a part of the community.

These protests are not entirely without merit. While I don't personally mind such an innocuous – and at any rate utterly corrupted – Christian tradition being observed by my government, I do understand how some people might feel that it violates First Amendment guarantees against the establishment of religion.

However, I feel that these non-Christian protesters are being somewhat disingenuous when they claim that such official displays make them feel that they are somehow less a part of the community than are Christians. Many people do observe the religious aspects of Christmas, but in practice the holiday has become utterly secularized, so that in the minds of many of us it is no more religious than the Fourth of July, and symbols like the star and the crèche are mere advertising icons – like Alfred E. Neuman or the *Playboy* bunny – which serve to remind us, "Oh, yeah, it's time to act nice again!"

By raising a stink about these displays, the protesters are likely to accomplish the reverse of what they claim to want. At best, they make nuisances of themselves; at worst, they actually manage to have the displays removed; in any case, they cause sensible folks to resent them for being killjoys. It is barely possible that these protesters are not protesting simply because they enjoy being offended, confronting other people over fancied slights, and imposing their will on those folks just for the sake of doing so. But it surely does seem that that's what they're about.

Besides, there's nothing in the rules that says a Jew, Hindoo, or Parsee can't put up a Christmas tree and sing carols. I've met plenty who do, and I've never met a Christian who would criticize them for it.

You'd think that in a city as diverse as New York, where Christians are by no means in the overwhelming majority, Christmas wouldn't get as much play as it might in, say, Lake Wobegon, Minnesota, which is 50% Catholic, 50% Lutheran, with nothing else even considered. On the contrary! New Yorkers do it big, we do it well, and nary a squeak of protest do you hear.

Christmas is far and away the best time to be in New York City. Weather-wise, December is almost always the city's most beautiful month: It's sunny and 30 to 40 degrees, most of the time; the sun goes down at about 4:30, so you come home from work in a cheerful kind of darkness; the bitter-cold, icy, slushy part of winter is still a month away.

On or about December 1, the Mayor lights the giant Christmas tree in Rockefeller Center, and The Season begins in earnest. The tourists come sweeping in (but in December nobody minds); we force ourselves to go to the office party even though we all hate doing anything with our co-workers; the theatres are packed; people take to baking cookies and making artsy-craftsy decorations; on weekends, Midtown turns into the world's biggest mosh pit, with everyone getting in everyone else's way and laughing it off instead of getting angry.

In the capital city of the world, where it's been commercialized to the max – fallen into the hands of Satan, some might say – Christmas comes nearer to reaching its romanticized ideal than it could in any Rockwellian village.

Explaining Myself

The Ol' Silver Bullet

A dry martini is like a bed: Even though you might never want to, you might, sooner or later, be called upon to make one. As a public service, therefore, I impart to you the wisdom of the world's leading expert on the production and consumption of dry martinis: me.

Cocktail hour is an appointment I never miss. Putting away a large, ice-cold martini before dinner is as important to me (and probably about as indispensable to my health) as taking a whiz first thing in the morning.

Every martini-drinker has his or her own ideas on how to make a martini. It's a personal matter, and on many points, reasonable people can differ. For instance, loud arguments can be heard as to how much vermouth a proper martini should contain. At one end of the spectrum are those who advocate four parts gin to one part vermouth; at the other are those who say that the word "vermouth" should merely be mentioned loudly enough to make the gin cringe.

Another debate of import concerns the garnish. A green olive is the standard of one camp; that of the other is a twist of lemon peel. A tiny minority prefers a pickled onion, which, if used, makes the drink not a martini, but a Gibson (and I'll tell you why later).

Some say that a martini should be shaken with ice; some say it should be stirred. A few prefer a martini on the rocks; most prefer to strain it into a chilled glass.

Still, trust me on this: My way is the best way.

In a pinch, you may drink a martini out of any kind of glass. But if you can get your hands on a set of real, delicate, long-stemmed, wide-mouthed martini glasses, do so. A martini served in the proper glass tastes immeasurably better than the same liquid served in, say, a wineglass.

Long before you propose to drink a martini, you should have rinsed your martini glass in cold tap water, shaken off the excess, and put the glass into your freezer. I keep at least two martini glasses in the freezer at all times. If you're caught short, you can chill a martini glass by filling it with cracked ice and water and letting it sit for a few minutes.

Pour four ounces of gin and about a tablespoonful of dry vermouth into a cocktail shaker. Take four or five ice cubes, one after the other. Holding each cube in the palm of your hand, bash it a good one with the back of a heavy tablespoon, to crack it into chunks. Drop the ice chunks into the cocktail shaker. (Don't use crushed ice. It'll melt too fast, and make your martini too watery. A martini should contain some melted ice, but not much.)

Put the lid on the shaker and shake it good and hard, with serious back-and-forth action, for at least five seconds (count them!).

If you stir, as opposed to shaking, your martini will simply not be cold enough. There are many ways in which a tyro might fuck up a martini, but none surer than by not serving it just short of frozen. Anyone who tells you that shaking a martini "bruises the gin" is probably also capable of talking about "bending air." They're probably also the sort of person who's capable of describing a wine as "round," and it's even possible that they like to brag about how they never watch TV. Ghastly people; you or I would not care to associate with them.

It's true that shaking the mixture will make it slightly cloudy, but in my opinion it looks better that way.

Take the glass out of the freezer and strain the liquid into it, discarding the ice. With luck, the glass should be filled just short of the rim.

Take a lemon and shave off a two-inch strip of peel, taking *great* care not to cut into the fruit. (The least suggestion of lemon juice will utterly ruin a martini.) Take the piece of lemon peel and twist it over the drink, allowing the lemon oil to congeal in droplets on the surface, then drop it into the glass.

(You can always spot a martini-drinker: He's the guy with a partially-peeled lemon in a ziplock bag in his fridge. I don't use an olive, partly because I don't want anything salty in the drink, and partly because an olive displaces too much gin.)

Some people prefer to take the initial sip while standing in the kitchen; others prefer to carry the glass – carefully – into the living room and sit down before reverentially starting in on it. In either case, the Rite of the Martini is concluded by taking that first sip, and sighing in helpless ecstasy, "Ohhh, *Christ*, is that good!"

Some heretics believe a martini can be made with vodka instead of gin. While it is true that you can follow the above recipe, substituting vodka for gin, and produce a liquid that a few people will drink, it is not a martini, not no way, not no how. A "vodka martini" is fit only for sissies. Period.

I like Bombay gin the best. It's a fragrant, spicy gin with a lot of character. *Don't* use Bombay Sapphire, the so-called premium brand. Its higher alcohol content destroys the subtlety and complexity of the beverage.

Oh, yes: Why does a martini become a Gibson when garnished with a pickled onion? Well, many years ago, there lived an American diplomat named Gibson who was a teetotaller, but who didn't want people to feel uncomfortable about drinking in his presence. (How polite of him, and such a change from today, when some folks feel that it's proper to insult people who indulge their minor vices!) So, at parties, he would drink water in a martini glass, with a pickled onion floating in it. Everyone assumed it was his own exotic variation on a dry martini. And today, it is!

I Don't Know A Thing About Art

My tastes in art are hopelessly vulgar. I'll admire just about any painting, sculpture, or photograph as long as it has naked women in it (except Michelangelo's *Aurora*, who looks like a hung-over Arnold Schwarzenegger with breast implants). If there's no nudity, I'll settle for an oil portrait of an old, rich European, or one of Pieter Breughel's paintings of ugly Flemish peasants, or Joseph Wright's *The Experiment With An Air Pump*. David Hockney is about as revolutionary as I get. In other words, I like art that looks more or less like what it's supposed to represent. In architecture, I go for the Batmanesque monstrosities of Hugh Ferriss, or what one critic called the "federal prison style" of Albert Speer.

Plenty of decent, honorable people enjoy abstract, surrealistic or other types of non-realistic art that are lumped under the umbrella term, "modern." (At least, I'm willing to stipulate that plenty of the people who admire that sort of art are decent and honorable.) As far as I'm concerned, the question of what constitutes good or great art is an entirely personal one, and utterly divorced from either morality or intelligence.

Yet, I just got done characterizing my own tastes in art as vulgar, and if you caught me with a few drinks under my belt, I might characterize your tastes as pretentious if they run to the modern. Then you call me a hick and a philistine; I call you a precious little poseur. Hauling out the heavy artillery, you tell me that the only people who share my tastes are Republicans and Nazis. I reply that your tastes reveal dangerous psychopathic tendencies, or else a nature that is simply evil.

Okay, I exaggerate. But it is true that people sometimes actually take offense at another person's tastes in art, and often feel somewhat threatened by art that they don't like.

People like me, who don't care for non-realistic art, feel threatened by it because it makes us feel stupid. I look at Jackson Pollock's random spatterings, and I say, "For God's sake, this man just stood there in front of his canvas, throwing paint at it till he ran out; then, he managed to convince a bunch of art critics that if they couldn't see the Emperor's wonderful new clothes, it must be because they were unfit for their posts or hopelessly stupid! The oldest trick in the book!" But then my next thought is, "Damn it, is it possible that I *am* hopelessly stupid, and that other folks *can* see merit in this shit?"

My suspicion is that people who don't care for realistic art are afraid of their own emotions. When Andrew Wyeth's "Helga" paintings were published, a few years ago, they were immediately heralded as a great find by the low- and middle-brow art-lovers – the "I don't know a damn thing about art, but I know what I like" crowd – who have generally comprised Wyeth's following. At the same time, those paintings were pilloried by the sniffish, academic-minded "I have no idea what I like, but I know what I'm *supposed* to like" crowd, on the grounds that Wyeth is "merely an illustrator."

The question of how good an artist Wyeth is, is debatable. All I know is that his nude portraits of a plain-looking middle-aged woman are jackoffable-to. Could Pollock have made any such claim?

The same vicious epithet – "illustrator" – is also hung on other painters who painted realistically, such as Edward Hopper and Norman Rockwell. Rockwell is pilloried for being hokey and sentimental, and perhaps he is, but his work is moving because you can look at one of his paintings and say, "Yeah, I've been there, and that is exactly how it felt." Hopper may have been the first painter to put sound on canvas. You can look at *Night Hawks* and hear the scratching sound of the woman idly playing with her matchbook. Look at *Compartment Car*, and you'll hear the chugging and banging of the train. Look at *Office In A Small City*, and you'll hear the deafening silence. This is strong stuff; sometimes a little too strong for someone who prefers the coldness of cubism or the whimsy of surrealism.

Another danger of realistic art is that it can be used to make political propaganda. Painters like Goya, Delacroix, David, Hogarth, Rivera, Kahlo, and Picasso were political as hell. But what sorts of paintings have, historically, been considered politically effective and thus dangerous? Not the modern, less-than-realistic ones. Excepting Picasso's *Guérnica*, what piece of non-realistic art has had serious political impact?

On the other hand, there's a reason why so much of the heavy-handed, painfully realistic work of German artists under the Third Reich has been suppressed till recently. It was feared that these by-the-numbers paintings of sturdy peasants and heroic warriors, these massive statues of rampant horses and big naked guys with muscles, might stir up just a little too much passion.

About 25 years ago, *Spy* magazine ran a feature called, "My Kid Could Do That," in honor of the standard insult applied to abstract art. What they did was to organize a group of a dozen or so children, ranging in age from five to 12, give them each an abstract painting or sculpture to work with, and tell them, "Either copy this piece, as exactly as you can, or do an original piece in the same style as this one." The results were then displayed in a gallery in downtown Manhattan, with no indication that they'd been executed by children.

You know what? Nobody caught on. The kids *could* do that.

How I Dress

I'm one of the best-dressed people I know. No false modesty here. I'm not *the* best-dressed, partly because I can't afford a top-of-the-line tailor, and partly because I inevitably wear a little cat-hair, which some people believe is not in good taste if you're a serious man of business. And some people would assert that I'm not well-dressed at all, because if I were, my clothes would not attract attention.

I would not advise most men to dress as I do. If your profession calls for emphatically plain, ultra-conservative business attire, my look is not for you. If you don't like it when strangers remark on your attire, ditto. Still, a lot of people have told me, over the years, that they wish they could dress as I do (or wished they had the nerve to dress as I do), and quite a few women have told me they wished more men would do so. As a public service, therefore, I'll list just a few choices I make in putting myself together that I consider crucial. Some of these choices break the rules – but it's usually okay to break rules if you know you're doing so, and why.

I consider cowboy boots perfectly acceptable for business. Most men look great in cowboy boots – more macho, more domineering – because of the pointed toe and the slight heel. No laces, so you get a cleaner look. And you never have to worry about the color or the condition of your socks. President George H.W. Bush ("Bush 41") favored cowboy boots with a business suit. He didn't wear a bowler hat, as I sometimes do, but Doc Holliday and Bat Masterson did.

I always wear a hat – and for business, when I lived in New York City, it was almost always a bowler. It's the first thing people notice about me, and it's how they remember me: "The guy with the hat." Many fashion experts say men should not wear hats with business attire, because hats are outdated and look silly. That's nonsense. Certainly most men would feel uncomfortable wearing a bowler to work, but a good-quality fur felt fedora (not cheap wool felt) will lend authority to any man.

Most experts on business dress decree that your suit should be either blue or grey. Period. Maybe a tan suit in summer, but that's it. In general I agree. But I sometimes break that rule and wear black, or white linen in summer. A man can't carry off a black suit unless he's distinguished-looking to begin with. To wear white, on the other hand, you have to have a hint of jocularity about your overall attire. (Think of Mark Twain, or James Abbott McNeill Whistler.)

I dress stylishly, not fashionably, and the key to that policy is to get your suits tailor-made. If you know where to go, you can get custom-tailored suits and shirts for not much more than you'd pay for off-the-rack, and they're more economical in the long run.

Custom-made suits and shirts will last longer. Off-the-rack suits usually have some styling detail that will make them look dated in a couple of years, so that you have to give them to Goodwill and buy new ones. The standard Joseph of Iowa suit consists of a double-breasted jacket with roped shoulders (a profile much influenced by Ermenegildo Zegna), a waistcoat that buttons higher than usual, and trousers with a very long rise. You could never buy such a suit in a store. It's emphatically different from modern standards, but it borrows ideas here and there from the past 100 years or so.

Because I have established this retro look, my clothes will always look current – for me – and thus I have suits I've worn for 20 years.

If you want to look your best, your clothes have to fit. Got one shoulder slightly higher than the other, as I have? Your tailor can take that into account. Got narrow shoulders and a big belly? An oversized butt? Do you walk with a stoop? Want to make your short neck look longer or your long neck shorter? A good tailor can't change your build, but he can camouflage it.

Most critical, perhaps, is the fit of your shirt collar. Mortimer Levitt, the late founder of The Custom Shop chain of haberdasheries, once told me that the average man thinks his proper collar size is a full inch smaller than it actually is – so he buys his shirts accordingly, and strangles himself. That's why men hate to wear ties, and look for any excuse to unbutton the top button of their shirts. If your shirt collar fits, you won't even notice that you're wearing a tie.

Probably next most critical are the length of your jacket sleeves and your trouser legs. Your jacket sleeves should show about a quarter-inch of shirt cuff when you're standing straight with your arms at your sides. Asian men, especially, tend to wear their jacket sleeves half-covering their hands. They'd look more businesslike in a kimono.

To get the right length to your trouser legs – breaking over your shoe-tops but not enveloping them – always, always, wear suspenders. Never a belt. This is elementary, and yet so few men know what a huge difference suspenders make. For one thing, if you wear suspenders, you'll want to buy your trousers bigger in the waist, and with a longer rise, which makes them more comfortable. That is, you'll be wearing them higher – the top of the waistband just under your ribcage – and loose enough that they'd slide off if you didn't have suspenders. Thus, your trousers will hang straight down your legs, and always to the length you want.

(If you wear a belt, your trousers will inch downwards, the bottoms will bunch up and flow over your shoes so you'll tread on them, your gut will hang over your waistband, and you'll look like a slob. Got it?)

I avoid dark shirts. Colored shirts are fine, but they should always be of a light color. Wear a dark shirt with a business suit and you'll look like you haven't quite grown up yet. And never, ever let your shirt be darker than your tie unless you're trying to pass for a low-ranking Mafioso.

Carry two handkerchiefs: one for show and one for blow. Your for-show handkerchief can be plain white linen, folded to form a line across the breast pocket of your jacket, as President Ronald Reagan did, or you may use a colored silk square – usually of a color that relates to your tie – loosely stuffed into your breast pocket. I often choose a pocket square that relates not to the main color of my tie, but to an accent color. For example, if I'm wearing a blue tie with red and yellow stripes, I might choose either a red or a yellow hankie. Never wear a handkerchief that exactly matches your tie.

Finally, don't fear to experiment. Sometimes you'll buy a shirt or tie that doesn't look as good on you as it did in the store. Those are your "fashion failures," and you may give them away with a clear conscience. As you gain experience, you'll have fewer of those – and more compliments, if you're vain enough to care about such things.

My Own Designs

You rarely, these days, see a man in the business world who is well-dressed enough that you'll remark on it. As business attire becomes more and more casual, men seem to be paying less attention to the science of looking good in a suit, and it seems to be far more common now, than it was when I was a kid, to see businessmen in poorly made, ill-fitting, carelessly worn suits.

This is not entirely the consumer's fault. Manufacturers, for years now, have been making suits in lighter-weight fabrics that are less flattering than those used a couple of generations ago, and are constantly making small but significant changes in the design of their suits that cause those suits to look outdated in five years or so. Sure, it's possible to get a good suit off the rack, but it usually requires some hunting, and in any case, in my observation, most men (and their wives and mothers, who often choose their clothes) just don't know how to buy off the rack.

Nor do they know how to wear suits bought off the rack. If I had a dollar for every man I've seen walking down the street with his jacket sleeves dangling over his knuckles because he didn't know enough to get them shortened, I could retire. Not to mention the fact that most of the guys who work the fitting rooms in department stores know as much about altering a suit as I know about neurosurgery.

My own solution, which I discovered many years ago, is to get my suits custom-made by a Hong Kong tailor. Many of these fellows make the circuit of major American cities, passing through each two or three times a year, bringing with them hundreds of fabric swatches and patterns, and setting up shop in a hotel room for a few days. A customer comes to the hotel room, chooses a fabric of which he wants the suit to be made, and discusses patterns and detailings; the tailor then takes all measurements, and a few Polaroids of the customer in his underwear. In about two months, a brand-new custom-made suit arrives from Hong Kong. You can easily get a good suit from a Hong Kong tailor for not much more than you'd pay for a comparable suit off the rack – and for considerably less than you'd pay for a ready-made suit from a top designer.

A medium-priced custom-made suit from a reputable tailor is a huge bargain, when you consider that you can get just what you want. You're not at the mercy of people who are in the business of ensuring that a suit will look out-of-date in a few years. Instead, you can get a suit of timeless styling that you can wear all your life and perhaps even hand down to your son.

For instance, a few years ago, if you wanted a double-breasted suit, if you bought off the rack, you had to settle for that ghastly six-button-one-to-button styling, which made most men look fat. The traditional six-button-two-to-button jacket was very hard to find. Now, those six/one suits are as outmoded as the leisure suits of the '70s, just as I knew they would be. (I'm partial to three-piece double-breasted suits, which have been impossible to buy off the rack since World War II.)

Noël Coward once suggested that a man should gradually widen the lapels of his suits as he ages, ordering them made with lapels one-quarter-inch wider for every decade he is over forty. This is, perhaps, a persnickety detail, but the point is, if you feel like taking his advice, you can do so, if you have your suits custom-made. Buying off the rack, you have to buy jackets with a lapel width dictated by the designer.

My recommendations for buying a custom-made suit:

• Don't just go with the first tailor you meet. Look for a tailor who shares your vision. All tailors have their own ideas of what a man should look like, and yours will try to dress you accordingly. Be sure that he's willing to compromise his vision for the sake of yours – but be willing to listen to his opinions. It's very likely that he knows more than you do.

• Don't get anything "way out." Stick with the basic, conservative designs that have been around for more than a century. A single-breasted jacket should have two buttons, a slightly shaped silhouette, and lapels of three to three-and-a-half inches. A double-breasted jacket should be slightly more shaped, have a "six/two" button pattern, lapels about four inches, and a double vent.

Always get a vest, whether your jacket is single- or double-breasted. It'll make you look that bit more distinguished, and you can always leave it off in warm weather.

• Consider how you like your clothes to feel on you. Do you like close-fitting garments that you're aware of at all times? Or do you like generously cut clothes that fit you more loosely, so that you hardly notice them? Different men have different ideas about this. The fit of your suit will be much like the suspension of your car. Some people really like to feel the road under them, and be aware of every little bump or dip. They usually prefer sports cars. Other folks prefer to barely know that their car is moving. They'll be more likely to go with a Buick or a Cadillac. It's much the same idea, with suits.

• Scyes and rise. Remember the rhyme. And I don't mean "size"; I mean "scyes." The scyes are the armholes of your jacket, where the sleeves are set. Generally speaking, a good suit jacket will have high scyes: the sleeves set close to the armpits. A poorly made jacket will have large, low-set scyes, giving you a more generous armhole. It's easier and cheaper to make a jacket that way, but a jacket with these larger syces will go askew on your body, as you pull and shift about. The higher and narrower the scyes, the more the suit will move along with your body and will thus always look like it fits, whether you're sitting still or dancing the twist.

The rise of the trousers is the distance between the waist-band and the crotch. Ever seen a photo of a guy wearing suit trousers, with his jacket off, from the 1930s or so? Remember how his waistband went up almost to his ribcage? That's a long rise. Nowadays, because men are used to wearing jeans that sit on the hips (and because manufacturers want to save money by using less fabric), most dress trousers have a short rise, and are meant to be worn not much higher than jeans.

Do not allow yourself to buy trousers with a short rise, whether you're designing the suit, or buying it off the rack. You'll look like shit. Take my word for it. You might think you look you're your grandfather, with higher-rise trousers – but you won't, if you're wearing a vest and a jacket over them.

Scyes and rise. Don't forget.

• Consider your shoulders. Do they slope, or are they square? Are they broad or narrow? Depending on your shape, and your tastes, you'll want a natural shoulder, with little or no shaping or padding, or a more padded or shaped shoulder. My own preference is for a very high-set roped shoulder, to emphasize my upper torso. A slender, more athletic man might prefer a less shaped look. I strongly recommend against the totally unshaped, hyper-natural shoulder, which comes into fashion every few years. It makes your jacket look like a shirt, and makes you look like a douche.

• Consider your habits. Are you left-handed? Then have the little pen-pocket on the inside of your jacket placed on the right side instead of the left, so you can reach across your body easily to retrieve your pen. Do you put your hands in your trouser pockets a lot? Get a double-vented jacket so that the jacket will retain its drape when you do so. On the other hand, are you likely to go dancing in that suit? In that case, make the jacket ventless.

• Be honest about your body. Do you have one shoulder higher than the other? Do you walk with a slight stoop? Are you pot-bellied? Your tailor can't cure those imperfections, but he can take them into account when he builds your suit so that they'll be less noticeable when you're wearing that suit.

• Don't suck your gut in when the tailor measures your waist, re-solving to go home and diet until the suit arrives. You're not going to do that. You're going to get bigger, not smaller, so the suit must fit you (just a shade generously) as you are now. Tell the tailor to leave plenty of extra fabric so you can let out the waist of the trousers, and perhaps the back darts of the jacket, when you become a fat old man.

• You can get subtle details, like a buttonhole in each lapel, instead of just the left one – and working buttons on the sleeves, of course. (If you want to reveal that your suit is custom-made, you can leave the last sleeve button unbuttoned. Such a display is a titch vulgar, but the temptation can be overwhelming.) But stay away from silly stuff like Western-style yoke shoulders, or shawl lapels, or pockets with oddly cut flaps.

• On the other hand, don't get the ultra-conservative three-button "Ivy League" suit, which for many years was Brooks Brothers' signature silhouette. That's a ready-made look, designed specifically to *sort of* fit everyone, but not *really* fit anyone. If you like that silhouette – and some men do – buy off the rack and save your disposable income for something else.

• Also, weird colors and loud patterns are *verboten*. The commandment, "Thou shalt wear nothing but blue or grey" really is practically inviolable. Your first suit should almost certainly be dark grey, in worsted or flannel; your next suit should be dark blue. (If you live in a very hot climate and are likely to stay there, I'll allow you to get a linen suit, *after* you've had one made in tropical-weight worsted.) Then you can start buying suits with discreet patterns – pinstripes, glen plaid, nailhead, herringbone – but always blue or grey.

I do occasionally break that rule. I have a chocolate-brown silk suit that makes me look like a prosperous French gangster, and a black pinstripe that makes me look like his American counterpart. But that's the point: I look like a gangster when I wear those suits. I can do this since I'm in a creative profession, but if I were a stockbroker or a corporate lawyer, I'd worry that those suits were bad for my image.

Just the fact that the suit fits you so well will make people perceive you as well-dressed, without your having to resort to ostentation.

Neckties

The traditional Father's Day gift is an ugly tie from the discount bin of Filene's Basement or some other such establishment, and these ties accumulate over the years, to the point where the poor recipient hardly owns a tie that might lend him any respectability.

Most people seem to think that a tie they buy for someone else must be somehow remarkable, if not amusing, to look at. This is a foolish, useless notion. There's a place for "cute," "funny," and "daring" in men's fashion, but that place is in casual wear. Ties are business attire, and one's approach to them should be serious if not downright grim.

True, a tie is purely decorative, but what of that? So are pocket squares. (That is, the one you wear in the outside pocket of your suit jacket is. A properly dressed gentleman should carry two hankies – one for show and one for blow.) So is a woman's silk scarf; so is most jewelry. We don't intentionally buy goofy-looking jewelry, do we?

One can't go far wrong, in choosing ties, if one resolves never to buy a tie that the Prince of Wales wouldn't wear. That means solids, discreet stripes, and small, conservative patterns. That means no florals, no pictures of cunning little animals, no loud patterns of any kind. That's your one big rule. Some others:

• Solid-colored ties are *not* boring. Far, far too many men show up at the office wearing a striped or check suit, striped shirt, and striped or patterned tie. Ideally, the well-dressed man wears *one* patterned garment – suit, shirt, or tie – and two solids. A tasteful dresser can sometimes look good wearing two patterns, but three is almost always disastrous. Any gentleman's wardrobe should include solid-colored ties in navy, maroon, and black, plus whatever other colors are particularly flattering to him. If your husband or father lacks any of these, seize the opportunity to fill the need.

• Avoid *cliché* ties. The classic example of a *cliché* tie is the ubiquitous yuppie tie of the early 1980s: a small grey foulard pattern on a muted yellow background. Originally a stereotypical tie of the senior executive or the high-priced corporate lawyer, it was devalued almost overnight in the '80s, as every over-reaching 23-year-old mouth-breather from Long Island affected it as part of his efforts to make his boss think he was a go-getter. If you have been noticing lots of men wearing a certain distinctive tie for the past few months, do not buy it.

• Mistrust any tie that contains any true white. Classic ties, in which one can't go wrong, include a navy blue or maroon tie with white polka dots, or a navy-and-white stripe, but on the best of these, the white is ever so slightly off: cream, eggshell, or light silver rather than bright white. True white, on a tie, often looks cheap and loud.

• Avoid ties that boast horizontal stripes. On trim young fashion models, they look cool, but on most men, who are not in perfect condition, any stripe that crosses the body horizontally will make them look fatter than they are. Furthermore, these ties have no legs. In a few years, they'll look just as dated as those enormous shawl-like ties that were current in the 1970s.

• When buying a striped tie, take care that it is not a tie that denotes any organization to which the wearer does not belong. (In other words, don't get Dad an Eton tie unless he is an Old Etonian.) The best way to avoid such a *faux pas* is to always buy ties that are striped in the American manner (slanting diagonally toward the right shoulder) rather than the English (slanting toward the left shoulder).

• Never buy a tie that's on sale. They're on sale for a reason – that reason being that they're ugly. If you don't notice that the discounted tie is ugly at the time you buy it, you will notice soon enough. I speak from bitter experience.

Women can spot a cheap tie. So can men, if they develop the eye for it, but women *really* can, and they'll count it against you if you're wearing one. You can sometimes find an acceptable, conservative tie for $25, but if you go below that, you're courting disaster. Cheap ties look and feel cheap: They either have a dull finish or a coarse, metallic sheen, which makes the colors vulgar and garish. The cloth is unsubstantial, and snags slightly when you run your thumb across it. It's far, far better to own five well-made, tasteful ties, than 50 of doubtful pedigree.

To do your father or husband a favor this Father's Day, don't get him a tie at all. Instead, buy him a half-dozen plain white shirts, a full size bigger in the neck than what he normally wears (i.e. if he wears a 15-1/2 neck, get 16-1/2). Some men regard the necktie as the symbol of corporate slavery, and yearn aloud for the day "when I'll never have to put on a tie again." But the tie is not the issue. The reason most men hate to wear ties is that they almost always buy their shirts too small in the neck.

Next year, by which time Dad will presumably be used to wearing shirts that fit, you can get him a *tasteful* tie.

Naked Beneath My Kilt

On special occasions – usually when I'm invited to a black tie event – I go out in public without my trousers. I get many admiring glances, but I haven't been arrested for it yet. There's no law – at least, not since the 1780s – against wearing the kilt.

It's too bad that more men don't wear the kilt. (For some reason, you don't wear *a* kilt; you wear *the* kilt.) It's flattering to most men; it's warmer than trousers; it makes peeing infinitely easier. Besides, no woman has lived until she has danced the tango with a man in a kilt. In this country, though, you see kilts when the New York City cops march in a parade, and that's about it.

Several people have told me they'd like to wear the kilt, but they voice the following objections:

1. I'm not entitled to wear it.
2. I know there are all kinds of rules about wearing the kilt, and I'm afraid I'd break one.
3. I'd be embarrassed to go around without underwear.
4. People would make fun of me.

True, wearing the kilt is not to be taken lightly. It's expensive, for one thing: A good kilt costs $400 and up, and the accessories cost at least as much again. For another, while you will never be laughed at for wearing the kilt (trust me on this), you *could* be laughed at for wearing it incorrectly.

More nonsense has been written about who is entitled to wear the kilt and who isn't, and about who has the right to wear a particular tartan and who hasn't ("tartan" meaning any of the various check patterns – sometimes mistakenly called plaids), than just about any other clothing-related subject. The short and true answers are these:

• It is always appropriate for a man, of any nationality, to wear the kilt, although it is in bad taste to wear certain tartans. Being interested in all things Scottish is a perfectly good reason to wear the kilt, whether your name is Waslewski, Goldberg, Yamashita, or Theotokopoulos.

• A woman wearing the kilt is like a man wearing a dress: It's legal, but it's socially unacceptable unless the woman is wearing it as uniform or is deliberately gender-bending. A woman may wear a pleated tartan skirt, which is a different garment entirely.

• There's no such thing as the right to wear a certain tartan. The Balmoral and the Royal Stewart tartans are reserved by tradition for the British royal family, and it's in poor taste for any non-royal person, aside from soldiers in certain British Army regiments, to wear them, although in practice a great many common people do wear the Royal Stewart – to the point where it's almost regarded as a "general" tartan not associated with any clan, family, or other group. (The Balmoral tartan, by the way, was designed by a German, H.R.H. Prince Albert.) It's also bad form to wear a regimental tartan unless you have an association with that regiment.

The notion that you must be a direct descendant of the historical founder of a clan, on your father's side, in order to wear that clan's tartan, is foolishness. But you mustn't choose a tartan on the grounds that "I like the colors." If you can claim kinship with a certain clan, and wish to wear that tartan, fine. If you can't do that, you may choose a tartan through ties of association or of sentiment – which often means that you'll need to study your Scottish history to determine which clan is of particular interest to you.

(I, for instance, would find it appropriate to wear any of three registered tartans: the Anderson, because I'm a Scandinavian Anderson on my mother's side; the Dress MacLeod, because that was my school's tartan; and the Clerical tartan, since I'm an ordained minister in the Universal Life Church.)

If you're willing to pay to have the cloth custom-woven, you can, of course, devise your own tartan sett – as I have done, twice.

• With the Balmoral or Glengarry bonnet, which most kilt-wearers wear with the kilt, it is in poor taste to wear a clan badge without some particular reason for displaying the arms of the clan represented thereon. To wear eagle feathers in your bonnet, unless you are a clan chief, a chieftain, or a gentleman with your own coat of arms, is damn near a hanging offense.

• You are under no obligation to go commando beneath your kilt. If you feel more comfortable wearing a jockstrap or briefs, by all means do so. Indeed, if you're doing one of the more vigorous Highland dances, or tossing the caber, you'd better! (In olden times, when they wore the *breacan feile*, a full-body version of the kilt, Highlanders generally removed this before going into battle, knotting their shirt-tails between their legs to keep everything in place.)

You may all have one guess as to what is the most frequently asked question I hear when I'm wearing the kilt.

If a woman asks that question, my invariable response is, "I'm a man of few words, ma'am. Give me your hand!" This usually results in a shriek of nervous laughter as the woman clasps her hands firmly behind her back. If a man asks, I reply, "Perhaps a bit of lipstick, nothing more." If he expresses disbelief, I add, "You're welcome to check, if you think you're man enough."

As for the worry that you'll be made fun of, the only person you have to worry about is yourself. If you're too self-conscious to wear the kilt, don't wear it. But do use common sense. You might not be embarrassed to wear the kilt to a job interview, but it would almost certainly make the prospective employer less likely to hire you if you did so – so why cross that thin line between insouciance and stupidity?

Believe me, nobody will ever make fun of you for wearing the kilt. A few people might try, but none will ever succeed!

*

How did I come to devise my own tartan? A rainy day, a flair for design, and a little too much time on my hands.

At the time, the only kilt I owned was in my university's tartan, the Dress MacLeod, which has the advantage of looking especially dashing with evening clothes. Its two disadvantages are that it is too bright a sett to be worn as everyday attire, and that it is my school tartan, not my clan tartan.

Since my Scottish roots are very remote (not to say doubtful), my familial claim to any clan tartan would be tenuous at best. Thus, when I resolved to order a less-dressy kilt (one that I could wear to the pub on Saturday night, if I liked) I decided it would be rather grand to have one made in a tartan sett of my own design. Any reputable kilt-maker will have connections to a weaver who will custom-make any pattern you might devise (although this service doesn't come cheap), and with a little Web-surfing, I made the right connections in a matter of minutes.

I sent my renderings to the kiltmaker, William MacIntosh of Edinburgh, and mentioned to him that I would like to have my tartan registered with Lord Lyon King Of Arms, who is the final arbiter of matters pertaining to Scottish heraldry – such as who is entitled to a certain coat of arms, or which tartan sett belongs to which clan. Mr. MacIntosh informed me, however, that the Lord Lyon will certify a tartan as an official Scottish clan tartan only if it's submitted by the chief of a clan that has been granted arms by the Sovereign.

That let me out, on several counts. First of all, I don't pretend to be a resident or a national of Scotland. Second, no King or Queen of England and/or Scotland has ever granted arms to my family. Third – and crucial in my opinion – is the fact that I claim to be Holy Roman Emperor (as His Imperial Majesty Joseph III), and Sovereign Lord of these United States of America (as His Grace King Joseph). That being the case, it would be ridiculous to pretend that I had been granted arms by another Sovereign, or indeed that the Lord Lyon should have any jurisdiction in my case, *unless* I am claiming that my tartan is a Scottish clan tartan. It isn't. It's not even an American clan tartan. It's the personal tartan of His Grace, and as such, it is not to be worn by anyone else without His Grace's express invitation.

Designing an attractive, original tartan is no easy matter. A good many clan tartans are just about impossible to wear. Anderson, Elliott, Mackenzie, MacMillan, Oglivie, and Clan Chattan, just to name a few, are a bit too loud for most sensible people to be caught dead in. Some others are particularly handsome, but have been so often imitated that they've become rather *cliché* – such as Scott, Wallace, and the "Universal Military" or "Black Watch" (modified versions of which are worn by Gordon, Lamont, Forbes, and other clans). And a few, such as MacIver, MacQueen, and Barclay, are beautiful in their simplicty, but are a bit too simple to be interesting.

I deliberately designed my personal tartan to be tasteful, but distinctly *mine*. It's not one that a lot of people would want to wear. It's extremely somber: entirely black and dark grey, save for a slender red overcheck. It's also a large sett – about eight inches to the repeat – but with considerable variation in the widths of the checks. With luck, it will move well – that is, the intricacy of the pattern and the play of color will be dramatically displayed when the wearer walks or dances. It'll look good on me, because I'm a big, dark man, but it would overwhelm a smaller, fairer person, and the Dobrians in general are a middle-sized, light-haired, green-eyed family.

Since I naturally want to accommodate my family and others who wish to show association with the Dobrian clan, that leaves me with the necessity of designing several other tartans, to satisfy all tastes and needs.

Multi-tartanism is common practice among actual Scottish clans. The largest clans, such as Campbell, MacDonald, and Cameron, have several setts, each denoting a different branch, or dependent family, of the clan. Others, like MacMillan, have old and new setts, which often bear no resemblance to each other.

("Old" and "new," in this context, are distinct from "ancient" and "modern," which refer only to the types of dyes used, and not to the antiquity of the sett. In fact, modern dyes date from Victorian times, while the lighter, softer ancient dyes, intended to mimic the vegetable dyes of the 18th century, are of much more recent invention. Reproduction dyes, which replicate the colors found on kilts made 300 years ago, are the newest of all!)

Some clans also have a dress sett, which is brighter, or a hunting sett, which is more earth-toned, than the basic, everyday sett. The clan Rose, for example, whose tartan is predictably red, has an alternate sett known as Green Rose. Which one you would wear, if you were of that clan, would just be a question of which color suited you better.

Currently in the planning stages are a Dress Dobrian, which will be similar to my own tartan, only on a white ground, with brighter colors, for the ladies to wear in a skirt, sash, or shawl; a Hunting Dobrian, which will allow the wearer to camouflage himself when stalking a deer; and finally, perhaps, a Red Dobrian, for those who insist on something colorful.

Anything, to keep my family from having no other option but the dreaded Burberry.

My Opinion On Fur

I've mentioned that I love animals. I have a houseful of cats, for any one of which I'd take a bullet, anytime. I can't walk past a dog on the street without petting it. If I'm in the country, I can be content all day just hanging out with farm animals.

I also like dead animals. I eat meat, wear leather, and have no problem with the use of animals in scientific experiments. Worst of all, in the eyes of some folks, I think there's not a damn thing wrong with the wearing of fur.

I fail to see any moral difference between eating an animal, and wearing one. We can live without meat; we can live without the skins and pelts of animals; in neither case does the question of *need* arise. And the fact that most people would consider a silver fox more adorable than a trout seems to me to hardly be something we should concern ourselves with, if we are pretending that this is a moral issue.

(You have to love the courage of the animal rights activists, taking on people who wear fur. You'll notice that the percentage of frail old ladies among the fur-wearing population is rather high. I'd have a hell of a lot more respect for the animal-rights crowd if they made a habit of hassling bikers about their leather jackets.)

In general, I don't object to killing farm stock, or feral creatures, if the intention is to eat or to wear. People often consider deer-hunting a greater sin than bird-hunting, and certainly a

greater sin than fishing, because they've seen *Bambi* once too often. The brutal truth, though, is that in many parts of the country,
deer-hunters do both us and the deer a favor by thinning the
population. If it weren't for hunters, deer would overrun the farm-
land, and even at that, many of them would die of starvation.

One method of procuring meat or fur which I do abominate is the leg-hold trap. Some people have proposed banning
such traps outright, and I'm inclined to agree.

Scientific experiments on animals? No doubt some dreadfully cruel experiments have taken place, and no doubt plenty of
them didn't need to happen. But I'm not prepared to say that we
should let a monkey's life stand between us and a cure for AIDS
or multiple sclerosis. Nor can I imagine that any intellectually
honest person would say such a thing. Experimenting on animals
is a horrible necessity, but a necessity nonetheless.

Some animal-rights extremists are hoping for the day
when meat-eating will be entirely prohibited. In fact, they suggest,
if nobody ate meat, there'd be a lot of surplus grain that we could
use to feed starving humans, because we wouldn't be using it to
fatten animals for the slaughter.

But hang on a second. Are these morally pure folks implying that instead of breeding pigs for food, we should eliminate the
species entirely, so that they won't be eating up our corn and pea-
nuts and whatnot? What an interesting suggestion!

Of course, you can't expect these folks to make a lot of
sense. Most animal-rights activists are like anti-smoking extremists. The issue, to them, is far less a motivator than is the pleasur-
able sensation derived by simultaneously displaying their own
righteousness, shaming their moral inferiors, and getting to be the
boss of you.

I often hear, from vocal vegetarians, the argument that
human beings are not naturally carnivorous. That is to say, accord-

ing to them, that it makes as much sense for a human being to eat meat as for a horse or a giraffe to eat meat.

Okay, so what does this mean? If eating meat is, for a human, an unnatural and artificial act, then who taught us to do it? Some demon, who just wanted to do something mean? Why, that's it! That's the whole tree-of-knowledge myth! A talking carnivore – a snake, let's say – said to one of our early ancestors, "Babe, I'm telling you, you don't know what you're missing. Here, try a bite of this burger!" And by golly, that poor human took one little taste, and hooked the whole lot of us. For this, we were kicked out of Paradise.

I wonder, in any case, what the animal-rightsers propose to do about other species that eat meat. I can't believe that they would permit this sort of thing to happen for long. Unless they want to admit they're hypocrites, they'll start passing out literature to grizzly bears, or standing in the way when a lion is trying to run down a zebra, or rescuing a rabbit from the jaws of a wolverine. Hey, I'd bring my video camera along for that!

I have, in fact, heard of people who feed their cats a vegetarian diet. I will be waiting for those people in Hell, and I promise you I'm going to be pissing napalm.

Religion

A Force For Good?

A few years ago, I watched a videotape of a debate held by Intelligence Squared, a London-based debating society, on the resolution, "The Catholic Church is a force for good in the world." Speaking in favor of the motion were the Nigerian Archbishop John Onalyekan and the British politician Ann Widdecombe; speaking against it were the late journalist and social critic Christopher Hitchens and actor/author Stephen Fry. I went into the experience with an opinion, and came out of it with that opinion unchanged, but I nevertheless found the experience extremely interesting and educational.

All four debaters made some noteworthy points, and all four at one time or another engaged in fallacious, circular, or intellectually dishonest argument. The Archbishop, for example, basically argued that the church has been around a long time and has values and guidelines, and that there are a great many Catholics. He suggested that many of them do good works, and it is the spirit that moves them. However, he gave no specific examples, and he did not suggest, let alone prove, that it was the Catholic Church, rather than some other inner belief, that served as the moving spirit. In my opinion, he begged the question.

Mr. Hitchens contended that any merits of the Catholic Church are outweighed by centuries of past crimes, including the Crusades; the Spanish Inquisition; the centuries-long persecution

of Jews (including, he suggested, official tolerance of the Holocaust) and forced conversion of peoples to Catholicism. Of course
he also brought up the many instances of abuses by pedophilic
priests. He objected to the Augustinian concept of Limbo, which
he noted had no scriptural basis and was simply in bad taste. One
serious error that he committed (actually I suspect that it wasn't an
error, but a clumsy attempt at demagogy) was to state that homosexuals can't be Catholics in good standing. In fact they can be,
and many are.

Ms. Widdecombe basically attacked Mr. Hitchens and his
style, and stated falsely that Mr. Hitchens "has to go back to the
Crusades" to argue his point. Not true. He had given examples
right up to modern times. She also asserted that the Catholic
Church does not have the powers of a nation, which Mr. Fry re-
futed by noting that the Vatican is a sovereign state. Mr. Fry also
brought up another non-scripturally-based Catholic concept –
Purgatory – and contended that it was invented to promote the
sale of indulgences, which it almost certainly was. To his discredit,
he went *ad hominem* by asserting that nuns and priests "all share an
attitude toward sex that is utterly unnatural and dysfunctional."

Ms. Widdecombe called him on it, adding that contrary to
Mr. Fry's assertion, the leadership of the Catholic Church is not
obsessed with sex: its critics are. Arguably true, but she dampened
the effect of her rhetoric by remarking that she knew, before it
happened, that her opponents were going to bring up the issue of
the Church's opposition to condom use. Mr. Fry suggested that
that was roughly equivalent to a burglar dismissively saying, "Oh, I
knew you were going to mention that I break into houses."

To my mind, the most enlightening moment of the debate
came when an audience member asked Ms. Widdecombe why she
apparently considered it okay for a woman to serve in the British
Parliament (as she did) but not okay for a woman to be a priest.
She gave the best answer to that question that I've heard yet: that

there's a considerable difference between being an M.P., and being *in persona Christi* at the moment of consecration. "A woman can no more represent Christ," she said, "than a man could represent the Holy Virgin."

On the whole, however, the question-and-answer period was a disappointment. I'm invariably annoyed, at debates, lectures, and other events, by audience members who want to make speeches rather than ask questions. In general, the moderator of this debate controlled those people, but I'd sooner she'd silenced each of them with a well-placed rifle shot. In a situation like this, if you want to make a point, it's almost always easy to state that point as a question. If you do it that way, you're likely to be more on-point, and more likely to advance the discussion, rather than forcing everyone else to sniff your emotional farts.

What I found frustrating about the debate itself was its lack of originality. The affirmative side based its case on the many schools, clinics, pieces of infrastructure, and so on, that the Catholic Church has been responsible for, over centuries, as well as the Church's efforts to spread belief in a moral system. The negative side pointed to the many examples of the Church's violent, aggressive behavior to great numbers of non-Catholics; to its arguably unenlightened views on sex; and to pedophile priests. Nobody bothered to define "good." Nobody broke new ground, raised new arguments. Neither side tried very hard to disprove anything the other side said.

If this debate did anything for me, it reaffirmed my conviction that as entertaining as they might be, debates on such nebulous motions don't serve much of an educational purpose.

This I will say for the Catholic Church: Its adherents are not afraid to debate its merits, or hear them debated. Can you imagine what would have happened if a similar debate had been proposed, let alone held, on the merits of Islam?

Empty Hell, Empty Heaven

A Catholic priest once remarked that because he believed all that the church believed, he believed in Hell — but since he also believed in God's mercy, he believed that it was empty. That's a rather neat way of dealing with the issue. Still, one wonders how many bodies Heaven must contain — since most of the faithful, of any faith that believes in Heaven, believe that anyone not of their faith will not go there.

If there is but one true faith, and all those who do not follow that faith to the letter are damned, yet all of those who are damned are spared the pains of Hell by a merciful God, that leaves an awful lot of us all dressed up with nowhere to go.

I'm not emotionally involved, since I'm an atheist, and I suspect (or rather, I hope) that nothing save oblivion follows this life. But just for my own amusement, I'd like to hear more debate on these questions: What, specifically, makes a Christian a Christian, a Jew a Jew — at least enough of a Christian or Jew to beat the rap when he's finally mugged, numbered, fingerprinted, and haled before the throne of the Almighty? And what, specifically, makes a person an infidel or a heretic despite his profession of Christianity or Judaism?

What, for that matter, makes an atheist an atheist? Some people would say that any atheist worth his salt believes that it can be demonstrated that God does not exist, and that anyone who will not go that far is not an atheist, but merely a wimpy little agnostic. By that standard, I'm not an atheist, because I can't prove that the Judeo/Christian/Muslim God does not exist, any more than I can prove that the ancient Greek Gods don't exist. But I consider myself an atheist because I am convinced beyond a reasonable doubt that no God exists.

But what if I'm right that God doesn't exist, but somehow spiritually impure because I did not believe that God's non-existence could be proven? When I die, will I be punished for not being a hard-core atheist, but merely an agnostic, who lacked the true faith?

In a few religions, you don't have to be doctrinally perfect to achieve salvation. In most, you do. In the Catholic faith, according to canon law, a person who is ignorant of the minutiæ of Catholic dogma may proclaim himself theologically sound simply by saying, "I believe all that the church believes; the church believes all that I believe."

Still, millions of Catholics specifically reject certain teachings of the church, most notably with regard to divorce and birth control. Will these *à la carte* Catholics achieve salvation, or will they be denied the beatific vision?

An acquaintance of mine, an extremely devout "born-again" Christian, once told me a joke about three preachers, which she began thus: "There was a Baptist minister, a Methodist minister, and a Christian minister... ". The clear implication, you observe, was that she did not consider Baptists or Methodists to be Christians. This is common among the more extreme fundamentalist sects. To many of them, the term "Christian" correctly denotes only the holy-roller type. A high-church Anglican is definitely not a Christian by their standards, and Catholics might as well be naked savages, since they worship graven images and perform ritual cannibalism.

Think I'm kidding about graven images? Have you ever seen a crucifix in a Protestant church? You see crosses, right enough, but never one with a body hanging from it. Likewise, you don't see statues of the Holy Virgin, or of the Saints, except in some Anglican ("Catholic Lite") churches.

As for ritual cannibalism, the doctrine of transubstantiation states quite clearly that when the priest intones the proper mumbo-jumbo, the communion bread and wine become the literal body and blood of Christ.

My (admittedly limited) study of the Bible has failed to turn up any specific condemnation of cannibalism. Human flesh is, of course, *treyf*, and blood is not kosher no matter what animal it comes from, but those proscriptions appear only in the Old Testament, and many Christians discount that portion of the Bible as outdated and somewhat embarrassing to them. Therefore, it would appear to me that Protestants would be on solid ground by accusing Catholics of vulgarity, but not of going against the scriptures, by this rather grisly practice.

Then we have the tolerance vs. intolerance debate. Liberal Christians suggest that God will not look kindly on their more conservative brethren, who, in their view, pass judgement on other people when they ought to leave that job to God. Conservative Christians counter that they're merely living their faith by refusing to countenance blasphemy, licence, and other ungodly behavior, and it's liberal so-called Christians who endanger their immortal souls by trying to water down their religion, and not witnessing against heavy metal, *South Park*, and butt-sex.

Jews, similarly, disagree on who's a Jew. The big-tent Jews say, in effect, "If you say you're a Jew, you're a Jew, and if you have a weakness for Shrimp Louie, well, what the hey." The most orthodox insist not only on observation of all the most picayune dietary and sanitary laws, and the performance of the most obscure rituals, but on even the finest points of dress. Thus, you have one ultra-orthodox sect whose menfolk ordinarily wear neckties, and another sect, equally orthodox, that eschews them. Similarly, these sects differ as to style of hat and coat (although these are invariably black or dark blue). So, God's a fashion consultant, now?

It would seem to me that liberal and conservative, ortho-dox, fundamentalist, nonconformist and inclusionist alike, must be tarred with the same brush: guilty, alike, of presuming to know the mind of God. This strikes me as a pretty clear commission of the sin of pride, unequivocally condemned in the holy books of Jews and Christians both. Could it be that all but those who claim to know nothing of God's will and word, must be damned as infi-dels? And what are we to think of those who are so humble that they will not take a stand of any kind on theological issues? We can hardly call them faithful, and thus God's judgement may fall equally heavily on them. Could it be, then, that God sits alone in his Heaven, smoking cigarettes and watching *Captain Kangaroo*?

The Eighth Deadly Sin: Serenity

One of my talents is getting people to talk. I'm a journalist, so I know how to interview people, and I know how to get even the most taciturn interviewee to go into greater detail than "Yes," "No," or "I don't know." I lived for nearly 30 years in a big city, where nobody knows anyone else; where, if you want to meet someone, you have to just start talking and hope he responds. I'm good at that, too: If I want to have a conversation with you, we're going to have one, unless you make it clear that you don't want to be disturbed. You'll find it interesting, too. If you want to talk, I'm good at letting you play your tapes for me while I keep quiet except to ask questions; if you want to listen, I've got plenty of tapes I can play for you. If you want to discuss or debate, I can do that too.

In a way, even the friendliest conversation is a sort of contest, in which the two participants compete with each other in imparting information, sympathy, affection, or well-reasoned opinions. If you accept that description, then I was soundly defeated the other night, by an otherwise perfectly inoffensive person.

This wasn't a date, as that word is generally defined. I took this lady to dinner as a way of returning a favor she'd done me, and since our previous contacts had been purely professional, I had little idea of what kind of a person she was off-duty. I soon found out.

The first bad sign came when I informed her that I was taking her to a German restaurant that had one of the best selections of beer in town. She replied, "That's nice, except I don't drink." In my experience, the only total abstainers I can tolerate are recovering alcoholics – and even that can be difficult. A person who does not drink, and never did drink, is almost never my kind of folks.

Within two minutes of sitting down at the restaurant, I knew we were in bad trouble. Once we'd ordered a martini and a Sprite, I asked her, "What are your interests outside of your work?"

"Church," she replied.

"What denomination?"

"It's a non-denominational Christian church."

"Ah. What are its tenets?"

"Jesus; that's enough."

"Obviously, but I mean, how are your church's tenets different from, say, Lutheran tenets, or Presbyterian tenets?"

"I can't talk about the others; we just concentrate on Jesus."

"So, you haven't made much study of different religions and sects?"

"No."

(Long pause.)

"Which of Jesus' teachings are particularly attractive to you?"

"Love, humility, submission, obedience..."

So there we were. Me, a Satanist, yet a *polite* Satanist, and therefore not inclined to explain to this woman why she was full of crap, yet still trying to get an actual conversation going, rather than just this question-and-answer session.

"How interesting." (Another long pause as I scramble for a foothold from which to lauch a discussion.) "You know, it always did strike me that humility were rather overrated as a virtue. It seems to me that a healthy sense of pride, and a certain reliance on personal power, are much more useful."

"Well, whatever works for you."

By the time the food arrived, I'd been throwing jabs, hooks, crosses, uppercuts, and had hit nothing but air. This lady was winning each round without throwing a single punch in return.

"I have to confess I'm stumped," I finally told her. "You and I apparently live in two entirely different worlds."

She just looked back at me with the same placid half-smile as before. Another long silence.

"So," I tried once more, "has anything particularly interesting happened to you lately?"

"Yes," she replied, "I'm going to a whole new spiritual level now."

"Indeed? What does that consist of?"

"Finding a deeper sense of humility; giving myself more to others; placing myself more below others."

"Ah."

You can't even get off any sarcasm at the expense of a person like that, unless you are making a gross and conscientious effort to insult her, which in this case I didn't want to do. Hence the pauses: It was all I could do to say anything that wouldn't sound like I was poking fun at her.

Only once in the evening was I able to land solidly: During one of the many lags in our conversation, we overheard a fellow nearby complaining rather loudly to his friends about his complicated and unsatisfactory sexual entanglements; we both eavesdropped for a few seconds, and I muttered, "Interesting life that fellow has."

She replied, "When I see someone like that, I just say, 'Thank God I'm a Christian!'"

I cocked an eyebrow in languid mock-astonishment and remarked, "It's odd that someone who's so interested in the teachings of Jesus has forgotten the parable of the Pharisee and the publican. You might want to read it again when you get home tonight." It was impossible to tell from her expression whether she had caught the reference or not: Another long silence followed, but whether that was because I'd succeeded in shaming her, or just because we had to hunt for another topic, I couldn't say.

All through the evening, the dominant thought in my mind was, "Good Lord, how it must suck to be you!" And yet, it obviously didn't suck to be her. Utterly serene, devoid of inner demons, she sat with never-changing expression, answering my questions in one or two words with no elaborations, never asking a question of her own, replying to each of my declarative sentences with slight variations on "whatever." Without question, she went to bed that night completely at peace with herself, and thinking of me (if she thought of me at all) with nothing but pity.

Okay, I guess it is unfair and hyperbolic to call this lady's serenity a sin. This exemplary Christian did me no harm. She was just insufferable.

New Age Maintains Old Foolishness

Since I'm interested in the use of magick in everyday life, I have quite a few friends who are into alternative religions, symbolic or psychedelic rituals, divinations, and other practices that are certain to send them straight to Hell. I also enjoy spending time in on-line chat rooms where magick and witchcraft are the subjects.

(I differentiate between magick – the use of controlled thought and ritual to produce a result – and stage magic.)

In these rooms, you're likely to encounter a good deal of argument among the Pagans (sometimes quite acrimonious) on matters of religious doctrine, history, ethics, magickal technique – in short, exactly the kind of debates you might hear in a room full of Christian clergy. About half the time, this is interesting. Just as often, though, it points up the disturbing fact that bigotry and stupidity know no religion.

Occasionally, these chat rooms are visited by angry Christians looking to threaten us with damnation, or by pitying Christians urging us to read the Bible and come to Jesus. In both cases, their arguments boil down to, "The Bible says it's so, therefore it's so." A lot of the Pagans in these chat rooms (most are Wiccan, but you'll encounter just about any other new-agey tradition as well) are every bit as dogmatic, self-righteous and patronizing – not to mention intellectually dishonest.

(For instance, at least once an evening, some tyro will enter the chat room to ask for a love-spell. Immediately, half the population of the room will be up in her face, telling her that it's "against the rede" to cast spells that manipulate other people. Point one: Any time we dress seductively, engage in witty banter, or otherwise make a conscious effort to attract someone, we are trying to manipulate that person. Point two: If love-spells worked, none of us would be wasting our time in a damn chat room – rede or no rede!)

A great many Wiccans or related Pagans praise their religion on the grounds that it's older than any other (or at least older than Christianity) – as though the age of an idea were proof positive of its validity. In fact, Wicca as we know it today is a new religion – about 60 years old – and its rituals and tenets are based on an extremely sketchy and historically doubtful reconstruction of various pre-Christian Northern European beliefs and traditions. For the most part, these beliefs are as bizarre as those of Christianity. To take them seriously requires faith, rather than reason.

Some Pagans (particularly those of Irish or Scots descent) pretend to a certain social superiority on the grounds that they were born into the religion: The farther back you can trace your family's observation of the "old ways," the cooler you are.

This is an interesting contrast to monotheistic religions, where converts often claim a special cachet over those who were born into the faith. Born-again Christians can't shut up about their new selves; Muslim converts often don robes and burnooses; a convert to Judaism will tend to let drop the remark that she's "just a nice Jewish girl," every 10 minutes.

But at least we can assume that these people converted to their religions as the result of considerable thought. They're not just doing something because their parents did it. Pagans who boast of their family's background in their religion are engaging in snobbism indistinguishable from that which fuels the Daughters of the American Revolution.

In any case, Pagans are rarely able to renounce Christianity, or Jesus in particular. I could buy a lot of gin if I had a dollar for every time I've heard (from someone who claims not to be a Christian): "I believe Jesus was a great man/great teacher"; "I agree with the teachings of Christ"; "If Jesus saw what people were doing in his name, he'd be really pissed off." In general, such comments translate to, "Listen, I don't want to call myself a Christian, because that's so low-class – but I'm going to say nice things about Jesus just so I won't get hit with a lightning bolt."

According to the Bible, Jesus was often unreasonable, irascible, and vicious. Some of his actions are inexplicable unless you want to admit that he was a sado-masochistic sociopath. If I had to choose some other person on whom to model myself, Jesus of Nazareth would not even be on my long list. If there's a modern person who most reminds me of Jesus, it's Charles Manson. And yet, nearly everyone will automatically declare that Jesus was one of the best and wisest of men, because to do otherwise would doubtless invite all kinds of fearsome consequences.

Another frequently-asked question from newcomers to a Pagan chat-room is, "Is a male witch called a warlock?"

Invariably, some five or six people in the chat room will jump on the questioner, explaining that real witches never use the word "warlock," that it's a very naughty word (having been invented by Christian bigots). Male witches, they add, are just called witches (although there are usually a couple of female chauvinists in the room who will only grudgingly admit that there's any such thing as a male witch).

I always tell these newbies that a warlock is an obscure wrestling hold that will, properly applied, cause your opponent to bite his own balls.

Actually, there is another name for a male witch: sensitive new-age guy trying to get laid.

The Awful English Language

How To Speak English

Oscar Wilde was right: The English and the Americans are divided by a common language. While English and American are about 99% mutually intelligible, it's not easy for an Englishman to speak American convincingly, much less vice versa.

But oh, how dearly most Americans would love to be able to speak English like the English – well enough to pass if we wanted to! It can be done, with long effort, and indeed being able to speak English (as opposed to speaking American) might improve one's drab, wretched life. For one thing, it's guaranteed to get you on first base in the dating department.

To overcome the principal difference between American and English, just speak in your normal American accent, but pitch your voice an octave higher. You'll immediately sound more like John Cleese.

Next, learn the standard Middlesex accent. By this I do *not* mean the "received pronunciation" used by the Queen or by BBC broadcasters; instead, I mean the accent known as "Estuary," which has become the standard accent in southern England for anyone born post-World War II. The Duchess of York is perhaps the best-known speaker of Estuary, which is basically received pronunciation with slight Cockney overtones: You have to learn to make the glottal stop on words like "glottal" (pronouncing it, more or less, as "*glock*-ul"), completely relax your lips when prounouncing any vowel, and swallow your "L"s, so that "pint of milk" becomes "pawnk a miwk." If you speak Estuary, Americans will assume that you're fun to party with – because you sound like Fergie, and we all know what she's like!

Having mastered Estuary, learn to speak "Fraffly," which is the standard accent of the upper-upper classes, those just below royalty. The late Princess Diana spoke Fraffly. (Fraffly comes from the phrase, "Weah seu fraffly gled yorkered calm," which is the Fraffly for "We're so frightfully glad you could come.") If you speak Fraffly, you are guaranteed a job as a receptionist in any fancy office in the American city of your choice.

But the accents are only half the battle. You still won't pass unless you pick up on the various differences in grammar, vocabulary, and class-based usage. Here are a few of them:

More so than American, English distinguishes between "U" and "Non-U" (upper-class and non-upper-class) vocabulary. Oddly, the most outstanding characteristic of this distinction is that the upper socio-economic groups tend to use more direct terms, while the lower tend to use euphemistic, circumlocutory, or foreign (invariably mispronounced) terms. For example, the U would say "cake," "napkin," and "toilet," while the non-U would say "gâteau," "serviette" and "lavatory."

Always mispronounce foreign words. The English consider it a grotesque effeminacy to pronounce any foreign word correctly – plus, they want to show those foreigners who's boss. (Thus you'd pronounce "gâteau" as "*gack*-eau," "pasta" as "pastor," and so on.)

"Lemonade" in the U.K. means 7-Up or Sprite or any similar citrus-flavored soft drink, and lemonade is what you should call those beverages. The stuff we make out of fresh lemons is not commonly known over there.

Resist the urge to correct the London *Times* when it says "The Royal Family are at Sandringham," or "Parliament have decided..." English uses plural verb forms with collective nouns, and there are nothing we can do about it.

Never use the American "Mm-hm" noise, the one that means, "Yes, okay, I see." The English don't use it, because it sounds a lot like their "Mm?" which means, "Please repeat." The English are more likely to say "Ah-hah" when they mean, "message received and understood."

Quite a few terms have almost exactly opposite meanings in the U.S. and England A "bomb" is a disaster here, but a smashing success there. "Nervy" means unflappable here, high-strung there. To "table" a motion or bill in legislative debate is to kill it in America; in England it means to bring it up for discussion. "Knickers" are what Bobby Jones wore on the golf course in the States; the Limeys use the term to describe ladies' panties, invariably with a leer and a giggle. (And if you remark to an Englishman that you've torn your pants, he's likely to inquire how you could have torn your pants without tearing your trousers.)

The word "fag" has two principal meanings in the U.K. Most commonly, it's slang for cigarette, but "fagging" also describes the custom, once common to most English public schools, by which younger boys acted as servants for the older boys in exchange for tutoring and physical protection. Author and TV personality Alistair Cooke told the story of the American who asked an English acquaintance, "Do you know Lord So-and-so, by any chance?" The Englishman replied, "Yes, of course, known him all my life. He was my fag at school." "Well!" the American replied, "I'll say this: you English certainly are frank!"

You'll probably want to learn rhyming slang. This is a form of Cockney slang that has to some extent spread throughout England, Scotland, and Wales. (And to the U.S., for that matter. The slang term for money – "bread" – comes from rhyming slang:

"Bread and honey" rhymes with "money.") An illustrative, if highly unlikely, example of rhyming slang might be a Cockney doctor examining a patient who's complaining of a headache: "Feeling ginger, China? I'll have a butcher's at your loaf, then you can scarper home to your trouble." Translations of the key terms: ginger beer=queer; China plate=mate; butcher's hook=look; loaf of bread=head; Scapa Flow=go; trouble and strife=wife.

If you can master a broad Cockney accent, by all means do so. If you then adopt the right hair and clothes, you can get with a band that gets on MTV – and that, my friend, means sexual intercourse with anyone you want to have it with. Just don't let it get too broad, or nobody will understand a word you're saying – whether they're English or American.

*

British accents have long been used (very effectively in many cases) to sell products and services on American TV. A "received pronunciation" upper-middle-class accent, in particular, has long been believed to lend tone to whatever's being advertised. If someone with a plummy accent endorses the product, the reasoning goes, it must be good. More important, you'll reveal yourself as a person of sense, sophistication, and taste – in short, the sort of person who would associate with people who had that accent – if you buy it.

That particular accent was the standard, when American advertisers employed British actors and voice-overs, from the 1950s into the 1980s. Since, then, however, other British accents have been growing in popularity. Over the past generation or so, we've become more used to hearing Scottish, Cockney, and other regional British accents from time to time. (Irish accents are another matter entirely, and not part of this essay: The use of badly faked Irish accents in American advertising practically constitutes an ongoing crime against humanity, and in any case not many Irish people will thank you for calling them British.)

Advertising isn't my racket, so I can't be sure of this, but I wouldn't be surprised to hear that in the past 20 years or so, focus groups have frequently been used to determine just which British accent might be most effective in a particular ad. Consider for starters the red-hatted garden gnome who stars in the Travelocity ads. I don't know any Brit who sounds like he does, and no wonder: His accent is a parody, and a blatant one at that. He sounds rather like Noël Coward would sound if he were doing a bad Noël Coward imitation for laughs. (It's hard to do a clever or funny imitation of yourself, but I daresay Coward could have done it if anyone could.)

How did the creative department come up with that accent? How did they know it would be effective? That has got to be an expensive campaign – and it must be effective, too, because it's been running for years. I would love to find out how many different accents they tried before settling on that one. Did they try other British accents? Scandinavian? German? Baltic?

The Travelocity gnome's accent has remained the same for all the time he's been in business. But consider another imaginary Brit: the GEICO gecko. This cute little iridescent lizard has been pitching GEICO ("Fifteen minutes could save you 15% or more on car insurance!") for more than a decade – also, we must assume, with great success. But while his presence on our TV screens has been constant, his accent hasn't been. When he made his début as GEICO's corporate spokesman, a few years ago, he had not quite the standard pronunciation of a BBC newscaster, but it was definitely a higher-end Home Counties accent, the sort you'd expect to hear from any carefully educated person from South Central England. The public seemed to react well to the accent, which suited the gecko's manner: shy, self-effacing, polite, and slightly nervous.

Then, maybe five or six years ago, the gecko's accent was moved down-market – but in a northerly direction. Somehow, he acquired a Mancunian accent, yeah? He became a little more brash in his manner, a little more working-class. But apparently that accent still wasn't quite right, because in a year or two the lizard became definitely Cockney. Most recently, he has come to sound more Aussie than English.

Why, and how, was it determined that the gecko's original educated accent wasn't quite right for attracting the American *Lumpen*? I can understand why the creative department settled on Cockney. To most Americans, Cockney is a funny, comfortable accent that makes them think of Bert in *Mary Poppins*. The gecko's original accent might have appealed to a viewer with more spending power, and thus would have been ideal if he'd been pitching a luxury product – but he was selling a mundane product and emphasizing its low price at that. Thus, I suppose, a down-market accent was indicated.

But why, in the transition from a middle- to a working-class accent, did the advertisers briefly give the gecko a regional accent with which most Americans aren't familiar? First his address is Westminster, then it's Manchester, then it's Stepney. That doesn't compute. Again, there must have been a focus group, somewhere, that chose the Mancunian pronunciation – but perhaps, after the new accent was introduced, GEICO started losing market share, and the higher-ups decided the gecko's accent was to blame. So, they did another focus group, and this one came up with a different result. Or perhaps, once sales started slipping, one of GEICO's top dogs told his advertising agency, "Look, screw the focus group: You've got to change his accent again. Make him Cockney. This whatchamacallit accent is confusing people. They can't place it. Everybody knows Cockney. Everybody trusts Cockney. Make him Cockney, dammit!" So, the customer always being right, the change was made.

I suppose they could have tried a Liverpudlian accent instead – but would they have used Ringo's Scouse drawl, or Paul's nearly-Irish version? And would either have been effective? These days, those of us who remember the Beatles are getting too old to drive, and younger folks would still wonder, "What kind of an accent is that?"

Cute Accent Beats Big Pecs

A recent ad on TV, for an Italian wine, shows a young man picking up a young woman in the street by charming her with his delightful Italian accent. They go to a quaint little bistro, where they share a bottle of the wine being advertised; she points to the name of the wine, on the label, and asks him, "What does this mean?" The young man sputters for a moment, then drops the phony accent and admits, "No clue." The lady bursts out laughing – and the subsequent journey back to his place, and the squeaking bedsprings, are left to the viewer's imagination.

I can't say that the ad was *effective*, since in my case it did not fulfill its mission. I can't remember, now, the name of the wine – Primavera something, I think – and in any event I know better than to ever buy a wine that's advertised on TV. But it certainly was a *funny* ad, because it was so painfully believable.

An accent frequently gets you into the ballpark, whether you're a man or a woman. Many's the woman I wouldn't ordinarily have looked twice at, who got that second look because English was obviously not her first language. And many's the time I've bemoaned my inability to pose convincingly as a foreigner.

I'd say it's pretty easy to figure out why accents exert such a sexual pull. Most of it is just plain curiosity. On a non-sexual level, most of us are interested in meeting people who come from far away. This interest is translated into a romantic attraction – particularly if it's the man who has the distinctive accent – because of the vague idea that a romance with this exotic foreign person will somehow broaden the woman's horizons and pull her out of the drab wretchedness that is her life. Men, for their part, are attracted to accents because they know other men are, too – so an accented girlfriend is a sort of status symbol.

However, people of either sex are also intrigued by accents for a much more naughty reason, which all of us know and few of us will admit: we hear an accent, and we wonder, "What do her 'oohs' and 'aahs' in bed sound like? What's it like to hear a Russian, Indian, or Irish girl talking nasty while you're schtupping her?" (In bed, so I've been told, some accents are better than others. I have a friend whose girlfriend is an accomplished mimic, and he tells me that they experiment with various accents whilst indulging in the swinish pleasures. My own favorite accent in bed is Afrikaans.)

The effect of a foreign accent on a woman tends to be more pronounced than on a man. Often, her curiosity about the moans and groans is eked out by a secret fascination – shared by many American women – with the prospect of confronting an uncircumcised penis. This particular treat, a foreign accent frequently promises, since that hideous custom of genital mutilation is commonplace in the U.S.A. but not in Europe.

Mayhap a certain accent will lend you a certain persona in the mind of your interlocutor, and it may be a persona quite different from your own. For instance, if you have one of those modern Cockney "Shall we shag now, or shall we shag later?" accents, it's going to make a girl think you've got something going on in your life, like maybe you're in a band, and maybe you're a bit wild. You don't have to *be* wild, just so long as you smile craftily and curl your lip like Mick Jagger. By the time the poor girl discovers that you're only a desk clerk in a hotel, and circumcised at that, it'll be too late.

Some accents are sure winners with just about anyone: any English, Irish, Scottish, or Welsh accent; French; Italian; light U.S. southern; Australian; Scandinavian.

Others are just as sure losers: any really strong U.S. regional accent; Caribbean Spanish; Asian; East Indian; Yiddish (although the Israeli "Sabra" accent has a cult following).

The problem with strong regional U.S. accents, and with Caribbean Spanish accents, is that they're down-market. You hear that accent, and you assume that its owner carries poverty, ignorance, illegitimate children, and a prison record.

Most Asian accents are just not pleasing to American ears. American men, I suspect, are attracted to Asian women despite an accent, rather than because of one, and American women are rarely into Asian men. The Yiddish accent...well, how can anyone be sexy while wearing a beanie?

American Negro inflections can also be very attractive. (The politically correct would have us believe that there's no such thing as a "black voice," but in fact you can almost always identify an American Negro as such by his speech, when you hear it on the phone or radio, regardless of that person's educational level, region of origin, or other variables.) The soft, low-pitched, Barry White-like voice, which many Negro men have, can make women of any color melt into their shoes. I am especially charmed by the careful, over-enunciated accent that many American Negro women assume when talking to a Cauc: One can't help speculating on whether there might not be something wild under that polished exterior.

My own accent is an occasional source of frustration to me. I am sometimes accused of being English or Irish (my accent is "U" New York, with tell-tale remnants of the Midwest), but I'm never quite courageous enough to try to pass myself of as foreign. I do tend to enunciate carefully, and choose my words and structure my sentences meticulously, and a few women have told me they find this sexy. Others, to my horror, have told me, "it makes you sound gay," even though my voice is a light baritone, devoid of any lisp. I guess it's a wash. Either way, my voice – much to my chagrin – evidently does not imply a foreskin.

Yall Read This, Hear?

The question of whether Southerners use "yall," as opposed to "you," only as a second-person-plural formation, or as a second-person pronoun regardless of number, is fraught with controversy. Southerners with whom I've discussed this matter insist – sometimes with great indignation at the idea that anyone could suppose otherwise – that "you" refers to one person, while "yall" refers exclusively to two or more people. Yet I've heard Northerners insist, with comparable ferocity, that they have, themselves, been called "yall," when there was no possibility that more than one person was being addressed.

(On this point, we are as disputatious as on the question of whether grits *are* good, or grits *is* good, and whether there is such a thing as "a grit.")

As nearly as I can figure it, if a Southerner wants to know whether you, as an individual, are coming to his party that night, he'll ask, "Are you coming over tonight?" If he's addressing several people, he'll ask, "Are yall coming over?" If he wants to ascertain that every single member of the group is of the same mind, he'll ask, "Are all yall coming over?" But – and this is the important distinction – if he's speaking to you alone, and wants to know whether you *and your sister* are coming to his party, he'll ask, "Are yall coming over?" It's easy to see how an inexperienced person might take "yall" to be a singular pronoun if, for instance, someone says, "You [the person immediately addressed] are left-handed. I don't see how yall [left-handed people in general] can do innathang that way."

The clearest example that I've found, of the difference between the use of "you" and "yall" when a single person is being addressed, came in Vance Bourjaily's novel *Now Playing At Canterbury*, in which a Southern man admonishes a Northern man whom he's caught dallying with his wife:

"Jane Lee is going to act crazy and want yall to touch her, because she is a crazy woman. But you not going to touch her, because you not a crazy man."

In other words, Jane Lee is in the habit of coming on to men other than her husband, and has apparently done it several times to the husband's knowledge – but the husband is warning this particular man to stay away from her.

The use of "yall" is generally considered a purely Southern idiosyncrasy – as clear an indicator of a person's geographic origins as the use of "*in*surance" instead of "in*sur*ance" – and I can only wonder why it has not become a universally employed device. Partly, I suppose, because of anti-Southern prejudice. According to popular stereotype, Southerners are less intelligent, or at any rate less learned, than Northerners, and certainly far less refined. Many of us Yanks, when we hear a Southern accent, assume that the speaker breakfasts on turnip greens, clay, and Negro babies; dines on moonshine whiskey; and is his own father.

However, even if we are unable to overcome that prejudice, it's about time we admitted that "yall" is useful, and ought to be generally adopted. I was reminded of this not long ago, while chatting with two women. At one point, I had to put a question to both of them. If I had asked, "Are you doing such-and-such?" under the circumstances, they might not have known whether I was asking one of them (and if so, which one?) or both. But since it doesn't come naturally to me to use "yall," I was left with the phrase "you guys," which just didn't sound right when, as in this case, I was addressing two beautiful, willowy fashion models. "You two," "you ladies," and "you folks" are likewise unappealing to both the lips and the ear, and "you people" is what we call phone solicitors when we're scolding them for interrupting our dinner. Thus, I thenceforth resolved to use "yall" in conversation – and just bear it like a man, if I'm consequently accused of having Southern origins.

Another viable alternative is the New York/Irish equivalent of "yall": "yous." This non-standard second-person-plural pronoun has been around, in this country, for at least 150 years, but it has never had anywhere near the success of "yall." While "yall" has gained currency in a huge area, roughly circumscribed by Maryland, Florida, Texas, and Missouri (with pockets of support outside that quadrangle), "yous" is heard today only in a few working-class neighborhoods in the outer boroughs of New York City, plus Nassau and Westchester Counties. One also hears it used by some Irish immigrants, which makes one suppose that the Irish influx of the 1840s was what brought "yous" to these shores.

One wonders why. Conceivably, this was a "backformation" invented by Gaelic-speaking Irish people when they were adopting English. Perhaps they reasoned that since English plurals are usually formed by adding an "s," "you" should get that treatment. But that is not, to me, a satisfactory explanation, mainly because the Gaelic language hasn't any greater distinction between second-person-singular and second-person-plural than has English, so there would have been no reason for the Irish to invent one. Besides, Gaelic plurals are *never* formed by adding an "s."

However it got here, "yous" has no hope of catching on, once again because of its associations with a people stereotyped as stupid and uncultured. (An unfair generalization about the Irish, I'll admit, but not without merit when applied to New York City's bridge-and-tunnel crowd.)

In a few parts of the U.S., one hears the word "yins," which is evidently a contraction of "you ones," as "yall" is a contraction of "you all." "Yins," however, is so little used that one can't regard it as more than a curio.

We could, of course, solve the problem of distinguishing between singular and plural by reserving "you" as the plural form only, and reverting to "thou" when addressing one person. Traditionally, "thou" was reserved for close friends, family, inferiors and animals. It would have been discourteous to call a stranger, or your boss, "thou." But in today's over-egalitarian society, where you're considered stuffy if you don't address strangers by the diminutive forms of their given names, it would seem inevitable that if we revived the use of "thou," then "you" in the singular would quickly become outdated – even though if of my subjects were addressing *ma majesté*, the King-Emperor.

This would seem as acceptable a practice, on the whole, as the use of "yall." The only problem with it is, nobody will bell the cat. Whichever of us is the first to use "thou" in everyday speech will be laughed at, and asked "Art not thou supposed to be wearing one of those funny hats and endorsing oatmeal?" till he gets tired of it and goes back to "you."

If, on the other hand, a Northerner can learn to use "yall" as naturally as a Southerner uses it, he can explain it away by saying, "I picked it up in the Navy," or, "My mother's from Tennessee." Meanwhile, its use will spread, to the point where, in a generation or so, nobody will think twice about it, and we can, at last, draw a distinction for which most English-speakers currently lack the wherewithal.

Euphemisms

How do we determine what is a socially acceptable term for various bodily parts or functions, and what is not? In other words, why is it okay to talk about "sleeping with" someone (when in fact you probably didn't sleep a wink), but other terms for the same act are considered unprintable, and in some cases a basis for legal sanctions? How did "vagina" get to be a correct clinical term, while the Middle English "queynte" evolved into a word that many people consider the most obscene in our lexicon? Why couldn't it have been the other way around?

(And I don't want anyone writing me back with sorry explanations like, "because the F-word and the C-word are just ugly words!" You're going to have to do better than that.)

In some cases, it's easy to see why one term is more socially acceptable than another. For instance, "pee" is considered fairly genteel, since it's an abbreviation of a naughtier word. But how did that naughty term come to be regarded as vulgar in the first place? In Elizabethan times, everyone used it. (If you wanted to be excruciatingly proper, you "made water.") Nobody bothered to say "urinate."

One thing that most "bad" words have in common is that they are of Anglo-Saxon origin, while the "proper" or clinical terms usually come from Latin or Greek, or less frequently from another language.

Some of the slang terms that are considered reasonably genteel are also of foreign origin. "Ca-ca" has its roots in Hebrew, and "poop" is just the English spelling of the Dutch *poep* (in Dutch, "oe" is pronounced like the oe in "shoe"), which means dung. ("Poppycock" comes from the Dutch *paapekaak*, which also derives from the Hebrew, and means soft dung, as opposed to the dried stuff, I guess.)

This is similar to what went on in ancient Rome: Only the lower classes spoke Latin; the educated classes spoke Greek, although it was not the native language. Julius Cæsar never said *"Et tu, Brute?"* He said something equivalent, in Greek. Even at the point of death, he had too much dignity to speak the language of *hoi polloi*.

What I think is hilarious is that euphemisms for animal dung often sound like food. Have you never put a cow pattie on a bun, or made a pie of horse apples, or enjoyed a few buffalo chips with salsa?

I've recently been reading the diaries of the British politician Alan Clark, who refers to a bowel movement as a "thompson," as in, "I had to fly to Geneva first thing this morning, which precluded the possibility of a thompson after breakfast."

Mr. Clark also uses the yeccch-inducing term "greywater" as a synonym for diarrhœa. It's been said that the Eskimos have some dozens of words for snow, and the Bedouins have at least as many terms for camel, but we seem to have at least as many words for diarrhœa as we have for all other types of fæces put together!

Often, dance-related metaphors are used to describe this disorder of the bowels. The "Green-Apple Quickstep," is perhaps the most picturesque synonymous phrase; travelers in Mexico sometimes find themselves doing the "Mazatlán Mazurka." Even "the trots" implies a dance of some sort.

(I've heard someone refer to a large, solid stool, expelled with unusual force, as a "flying axe-handle," which I consider a true sockdolager in the pantheon of euphemism.)

Mr. Clark is the only person I know who uses a surname to describe a bodily function. But both surnames and given names are used as synonyms for the penis, the most popular being "johnson," "dick," "peter," "willie," and "john thomas." Worst of all, I've heard several fellows refer to their male members as "Mr. Happy." Who wants to date a guy who has a smiley button between his legs?

Every family has its own special euphemisms, which in some cases get passed along to other families, through marriage or close friendship. Thus, if I were to return to Earth 500 years from now, I might meet someone only remotely connected to the Dobrian family, who nonetheless refers to the male genitals as "credentials," and who, instead of urinating, "does a screecher."

Even using terms that are generally accepted as *the* most proper and clinical can get you in trouble with some folks. An America Online member recently had her privileges suspended for using the word "breast" in a chat room where the subject of discussion was breast cancer. The company that pays Howard Stern's salary was fined $1.7 million by the Federal Communications Commission because Stern used the word "penis" in a broadcast.

When I was in high school, three of my classmates formed a fairly good jug band, and often performed in the lunchroom or at school assemblies. Their signature piece was a ribald song called "Charlotte the Harlot." They once performed this song at a school assembly and were subsequently given a good talking-to by the principal. He didn't mind the song's risqué subject matter so much; what he objected to in the lyrics was the word "vagina."

It would seem to me that if everyone stopped being shocked or offended by certain words, they'd lose their attraction in a huge hurry. When Big Bird says "shit" on *Sesame Street*, we will have taken a great step away from the idea that mere nouns and verbs have some sort of evil mojo, whereas other words that describe the same things are somehow less powerful.

The unfortunate trade-off, though, is that there might, then, be no need for some of our more picturesque expressions. Somehow, it's more fun to excuse yourself to shake the hand of the unemployed, or to launch a Democrat.

Which reminds me: It's been far too long since I've made a two-backed beast. I generally have to content myself with whipping the lizard.

A Nimrod In Search Of Daffisms

We owe a great debt to Daffy Duck, for the almost incredible change he single-handedly wrought upon the English language.

Our language is perhaps more fluid than any other. New words and expressions work their way into the language, and old ones disappear, at a fantastic rate. Other old words stick around, but their meanings slowly evolve – or sometimes metamorphose with remarkable suddenness – into something utterly different from what they once were. Yet others (and these are by far the most maddening to a pedantic know-it-all such as myself) change their meanings, or are debased to the point of meaninglessness, due to the shocking ignorance of the general public.

Take the phrase "eke out." The standard definition of "eke out" is "supplement," as in, "I eked out my salary by winning at the racetrack," or "The Thanksgiving turkey was eked out by stuffing, candied yams, cranberry sauce, and other goodies." This phrase came to be because "eke" is the old-fashioned word for "extra." "Nickname" is a modern version of "eke-name," meaning "extra name."

Still, simply because "eke" rhymes with "squeak," most people believe that to eke something out is to barely achieve it, as in "The horse eked out a narrow victory." My teeth hurt every time I hear someone use the phrase in this way, but short of draconian legislation, there's no way to make people stop it.

Another one that gives me douche-chills is "The proof is in the pudding." What is this phrase supposed to mean? And how do you find the proof in the pudding? By biting down on it unexpectedly? This grotesque piece of nonsense is actually a butchering of the sensible maxim, "The proof of the pudding is in the eating" – in other words, "Performance is the only valid test."

Now, about Daffy Duck: Sometime in the 1950s (I don't know exactly when the cartoon was made), he managed to convince a great number of English-speakers that a certain word means something entirely different from what standard dictionaries say it means. Here's what happened:

The plot of this particular cartoon has an irascible caveman (with his good-natured but stupid pet dinosaur) ineptly trying to kill and eat the infamously malicious little black duck. The caveman comes a cropper time and again, meeting the dreadful injuries and humiliations that inevitably befall anyone who menaces a Warner Brothers anti-hero.

At one point, gloating over his adversary's failures, Daffy sneers, "Well, well, my little Nimrod..."

Here, the duck was using the term "Nimrod" strictly in accordance with the definition supplied by Webster's New World Dictionary (Second Collegiate Edition): "...the son of Cush, referred to as a mighty hunter: Gen. 10: 8-9...a hunter." In other words, he was saying (sarcastically), "Well, you're quite the mighty hunter, aren't you?"

Given the context, however, just about everyone who saw that cartoon took the word "Nimrod" to mean "loser," or "clownish nincompoop." Since the word was so pleasing to the ear, a thitherto obscure term quickly gained wide usage with an entirely new meaning, and it has been used thus ever since.

As one who hates to see English corrupted by ignorance, I naturally deplore this amazing shift. However, I can't help but marvel at it. If a foul-tempered (and fictitious) celluloid animal –

not even a mammal! – can accomplish so much, just think how many other times something of this sort must have happened in the 1500-year history of our language!

I would beg all my readers to send me similar examples that they've encountered (with as thorough documentation as they can supply, of course). I don't pretend that I'll ever be able to stop anyone else from committing these vulgar errors, but it may be that I am currently misusing certain words and phrases as innocently as anyone who has ever used "Nimrod" as an insult.

In the meantime, I grudgingly raise my hat to the little black duck. In homage, I have just invented a new word, to describe any word or phrase that is commonly misused through ignorance: Daffism.

Such misuses are, of course, deththth-*picable!*

Pedantic Corrections

We observe an alarming trend, not only among business writers (who can almost be forgiven, since most business writers know nothing about business), but among high-ranking business executives, who ought to know better, to use the term "stakeholder" to mean "anyone who has a 'stake' in the enterprise under discussion – be it an investor, an executive, a lower-ranking employee, or a dependent business."

In fact, "stakeholder" has exactly the opposite meaning. A stakeholder is a person (or a company) who is *disinterested* in the matter at hand, and so is entrusted with the property under contention. For instance, if the ownership of a famous painting were in dispute, the painting might be kept in a bank vault while the question of ownership was being settled; in that case, the bank would be the stakeholder. If you and I bet each other on the outcome of the Super Bowl, we'd give our money to a third person – the stakeholder – to give to the winner when the game was over.

The solecism is due to two factors: the confusion of "to have" and "to hold" and the confusion of "a stake" and "the stakes." I *have* a stake in the outcome of the game (that is, the money I've bet). However, a disinterested third party is *holding* that stake. My stake is joined by your stake (or, in a business enterprise, the investor's stake is joined by that of other investors, employees, outside suppliers, etc.) to form *the stakes*.

Thus, "stakesholder" might be less confusing than "stakeholder," but a person who *has* a stake in the matter under discussion is neither. "Interested party" has more syllables, but does not lack accuracy.

*

There is no such rule as, "You can't end a sentence with a preposition." The 18th-century scholar, Bishop Robert Lowth, is generally cited as the authority who handed down that rule – but he never did! Here is what he wrote: "[Ending a sentence or clause with a preposition] is an Idiom which our language is strongly inclined to [sic!]; it prevails in common conversation, and suits very well with the familiar style in writing; but the placing of the Preposition before the Relative is more graceful, as well as more perspicuous; and agrees much better with the solemn and elevated Style."

*

To "beg the question" does not mean to invite or raise a question. I'm almost willing to impose the death penalty (or at any rate severe corporal punishment) on the next person I hear saying something like, "She said she couldn't go out with me this weekend, which begs the question, 'Who else is she spending time with?'" (Note that the imaginary speaker of this imaginary statement is also too ignorant to use "whom.")

Begging the question is a rhetorical fallacy, one that you'll encounter frequently, in which the desired conclusion is assumed in the premises. A primitive example would be, "He didn't rob the bank, because I know him, and I know he would never do that." One that is slightly more subtle, since it doesn't explicitly use the conclusion as a premise, is, "I know Jesus was the son of God, because it says so in the Bible, and the Bible is the revealed word of God."

In the latter example, the speaker is also using the "argument from authority," another rhetorical fallacy that you'll see again and again. You'll often see the two fallacies working hand in hand, as in, "I know prostitution is wrong, because the law says so." There, also, you have the substitution of one concept for another: "wrong" and "illegal" do not have a one-assumes-the-other relationship.

*

Probably most of us, at least when we were children, have dragged one of our feet up to our mouths to bite off a jagged toenail. However, excepting people who (a) are exceptionally limber and (b) have mouths the size of basketball hoops, none of us would be able to get more than one of our own toes into our mouths, even if, for whatever reason, we might want to.

I mention this because of an expression commonly used, that has no business existing: one that should make anyone who hears it want to shake the offending speaker by the shoulders and scream, "Don't you *ever* use that expression again, you goddamn idiot, or I will personally rip you in half lengthwise and eat cornflakes out of your hollow skull!"

The expression, "to put one's foot in one's mouth," has gained wide acceptance as a synonym for "to feel embarrassment at having said something stupid, inappropriate, tactless, or excessively revealing." This expression has been around since at least my early childhood, and for all I know it could have been coined generations ago. Despite its age and currency, though, this usage is based on a gross misunderstanding of the expression whence it evolved.

The original expression, which is centuries old, is in the form of criticism: "Every time you open your mouth, you put your foot in it." "To put your foot in it," is a venerable slang term for "to blunder" – "it" being a euphemistic term for that foul-smelling brown stuff that you're likely to step in if you're not watching where you're going. In other words, "Every time you open your mouth [to speak], you embarrass yourself."

Thus, when you see an old friend for the first time in years, and blurt out, "Jesus, you've put on weight!" you have "put your foot in it," or stepped in doo-doo. Having done that, *do not* put your foot in your mouth without washing it first.

Neither Basic Nor Newspeak, But Prime

In this essay, I employ a form of the English language which, according to those who promote it, leads to clearer expression and more exact usage. I invite the reader to perceive anything peculiar about the English I employ throughout this piece. (Anything more peculiar than usual, I mean.)

Fairly recently, along with "racism," "sexism," "fattism," and the many other politically incorrect isms, I've heard the term "lookism," which I gather means treating people more or less well depending on their degree of handsomeness. I sometimes hear lookism condemned in connection with everyday social intercourse; in other words, one might act more politely to a pretty bank teller than to an ugly one, and according to those who condemn lookism, one should not behave thus. In this context, I admit that the situation exists and that in an ideal world it ought not to.

Some extremely P.C. people – the least handsome of the bunch, naturally – complain bitterly about people's tendency to prefer good-looking people as dates and/or mates. They condemn such behavior as shallow, unfair, elitist, and just plain naughty. Right; like any of us will feel inspired by a spirit of egalitarianism to go out and ask someone for a date just because we know nobody else will, or to marry a hideous person because we see it as our duty to an enlightened society to do so.

One can hardly blame this more extreme group for holding these views. For much the same reason – envy – poor people often become Communists or Socialists. Understanding their feelings, however, doesn't inspire rational people to concur with them. Most of us, male or female, do consider looks when we choose a boyfriend or girlfriend: men, primarily because we'd rather have sex with someone we enjoy looking at; women, primarily because they want a good-looking man to father their children; both men and women, because we like appearing in public with a handsome escort.

I attribute the fact that men treat handsome women better than plain ones, even if we have no intention of dating them, mainly to the fact that most men have sex on their minds literally all the time. Sure, we might get distracted by our work, or by breaking news on CNN, but even at that, a sexual undercurrent will prevail. I mean, if I see a commentator on TV, I'll assess what she says *second*. First, I'll determine to what degree I would like to have sex with her. If I meet a new female client, even if I know that no way will anything ever happen between us, I'll make the same determination, even before she has told me what kind of work she wants me to do. Most men act thus, consciously or not. The one snap judgement that men make, in the moment that they first clap eyes on any woman, boils down to, "Hot, or not?"

Of course, I assess a man's looks too, but only incidentally will I remark that Larry King looks like someone's grandmother, or that Jay Leno probably has to walk on his heels to keep from toppling over on his face from the weight of his jawbone. My general opinion of a man's looks, in any case, depends less on his structure than on his dress and grooming.

Men and women both have the same question in mind when looking at a strange man: "Threat, or no threat?" We have not lost our animal instincts, after all; we know that any other person could attack and eat us. (In the case of a man looking at a woman, though, the "Hot or not?" question takes priority over "Threat or no threat?")

Women also make snap "Hot or not?" judgements of men, but I suspect that they don't do so immediately or instinctively. Of course, many women find a man hot if they feel slightly frightened of him, but that attraction comes later. First, they must answer the more critical question, "Do I need to run away/defend myself?"

I do believe in physiognomy. I believe that I – and most people with good intelligence and perceptions – can generally tell "nice person" or "nasty person" by the general characteristics of the person's aspect. This has nothing to do with "handsome" or "ugly." Abraham Lincoln, one of the wisest of men, looked like a baboon. Cute little Marlo Thomas has a widely known reputation as a shrew. John F. Kennedy, indisputably a handsome man, had the most cold-blooded eyes I've ever seen. Your best friend, the person you most trust in the world, could not have such eyes.

(Among professional politicians, you frequently find utterly bland faces: handsome enough perhaps, but with no trace of good or bad evident in them. I explain this by suggesting that many politicians long ago stopped thinking in terms of good and bad, and thus their faces, too, have lost contact with those concepts.)

Asked to perform a physiognomic self-appraisal, I would profess myself stumped. Others, no doubt, can tell me about my face. I can say nothing about the character it conveys, except to report the reactions that I observe. I recently went drinking with a co-worker, who informed me, once we'd downed a few, that certain folks at the office have nicknamed me Satan. I get that kind of thing a lot; on the other hand, I get far more smiles from pretty women on the street than a man my age has any right to expect. (I admit to getting a few nervous shudders, too.) Strange dogs, often, will strain at their leashes to greet me, but whether they can instinctively spot an animal-lover, or merely recognize me as Lord of the Flies, I can't say.

*

Have you caught the stylistic affectation yet? Can you identify the characteristic that makes the above essay, and the continued writing below this paragraph, a different form of English?

I regard with great suspicion any sort of contrived jiggery-pokery with our language that purports to make it simpler, easier to use, less ambiguous, less open to grammatical solecism, or more politically correct. Somebody (or bodies) tried, back in the 1970s, to introduce neuter pronouns, like tey, ter, tem, so that one could say, "Give each child a lollipop after tey has recited," instead of offending females by using "he" to refer to "each child," or offending both male and female sensibilities by resorting to the hideous "he or she" (or worse yet, the wimpy s/he) every time one refers to a person of variable gender. This strikes me as a reasonable proposition, and I'd gladly use neuter pronouns if I knew of some way to popularize them to the extent that everyone would understand what they meant. But we can't force artificial neuter pronouns on the general populace, most of whom already have enough trouble making sense when they write or speak.

(To anyone who thinks we can enforce a new way of speaking, I remind you that the U.S. Government considers the metric system our "official" system of weights and measures. They have, however, singularly failed to persuade the American public to use that system on an everyday basis. Do you know how many kilometers you walk to and from work, or your weight in kilograms, or how many milliliters of coffee you drank today?)

Charles Kay Ogden, the inventor of Basic English – possibly the most ambitious effort to simplify our language – claimed that by using Basic, one could reduce the language to only a few hundred words and still express any idea. (Estimates vary as to how many different words comprise English, but many scholars conclude that it has the largest vocabulary of any known language.) However, Basic comes a cropper pretty quickly when it tries to describe any idea in two words or fewer.

For instance, since Basic eliminates words like "urine," you must use the term "body water" – but how does one distinguish among perspiration, urine, tears, and spit, all of which count as body water? One could, I suppose, use circumlocutions such as "body water that comes from the bladder" or "body water that comes from the pores," except that neither "bladder" nor "pores" exist as words in Basic, either! That leaves us, I fear, with the necessity of composing a good-sized explanatory paragraph to accompany each use of "body water," to indicate to the reader or listener the precise sort of effluence under discussion. If we all had to talk that way, not much would get said, as we'd die of old age whilst thinking up those long (yet Basic, let's not forget!) euphemisms.

Why, I wonder, would anyone want to simplify our language, anyway? I say, the more words we have, the more shades of meaning, the more ways to tweak a sentence one way or another, the better. After all, if someone offered you a box of 16 crayons, or a box of 64, which would you take?

One major purpose of Newspeak, which George Orwell invented as a futuristic form of English in his novel *Nineteen Eighty-Four*, was to make it impossible to utter a politically incorrect idea. In the course of that book, one of the scholars working on a Newspeak dictionary boasts happily that Newspeak contains fewer and fewer words all the time, and that as words left the language, so would ideas. Eventually, he said, Newspeak would eliminate the expression of any but the simplest, most politically pure thoughts.

(This adds to my argument for a large, lexicographically abundant language, rather than a streamlined, watered-down pidgin. If we wish to avoid an utterly oppressive, utterly stultifying society, we must welcome the expression of any ideas, however outrageous – and for that, we need as many words as we can cram into our heads.)

I noticed a small example of the reasoning behind Newspeak the other day, when I read a report of certain busybodies demanding that the word "nigger" not appear in the new edition of the Merriam-Webster Dictionary, on pain of protests and boycotts. These people have the idea, apparently, that to pretend that a word doesn't exist will somehow end its existence. I suggest that they all shut their eyes and plug their ears; that way, no naughty ideas of any kind will exist, and I can go ahead and look up "nigger" in the dictionary to my evil, racist little heart's content!

The renowned logician, mathematician, and philosopher Bertrand Russell, in his essay, "The Metaphysician's Nightmare," suggested – in jest – that we might profit by the complete elimination of any negative construction. In other words, we should *not* use *not*. (Thus, instead of saying, "I cannot find that book," one might say, "I have only found books other than the one I need.")

The stylistic device I've employed so far in this essay depends on the elimination of a certain word, phrase, or construction. I find it an interesting device, and it certainly does stretch one's grey cells. However, I do not advocate the widespread use of it, or of any other language reform. Language reform tends to attract the most annoying type of Socialist, animal-rights activist, nudist, feminist, anti-glutenite, pacifist, and World Federalist: exactly the sort of people who, I suspect, secretly harbor the same goals as Orwell's fictitious student of Newspeak.

*

The trick revealed:

Up to this point, in this essay, I have **refrained from** using any form of the verb "to be." As I've just demonstrated, one can easily express any idea without that verb. To omit it **forces you to** think carefully about structure and usage with every sentence you write. But enough. I've learnt my lesson, which is that by reducing my use of "to be," I can improve my style. Having absorbed that, I can go back to using, in moderation, the dread verb of existence.

The fact that it **forces you to think before you speak or** write appears to be the main advantage of "E-Prime," as linguistics experts call this "be-less" variant form of English. Nothing about the verb "to be" automatically **makes a sentence in which it** appears less literate, less grammatical, less stylish. However, use of it does lead to two stylistic tendencies to which many of us are prone, and which many teachers, editors and other authority figures condemn: overuse of the passive voice, and of "it is," "there is," or "there are" constructions.

Eschewing "to be" makes it well-nigh impossible to employ the passive voice – i.e., "The window was closed by Jane," rather than "Jane closed the window." Therefore, those readers who guessed that my trick was to avoid the passive voice were partly right, but only incidentally.

(I've been told that certain military schools, most notably The Citadel, absolutely forbid the use of the passive voice – ah, but once those cadets become officers, they discover the passive voice with gusto, as anyone who has ever spent much time reading official military communications will attest.)

Many people find "it is/there is/there are" constructions objectionable because they tend to conceal who did it, how it happened, and other relevant information; thus, many experts reject "There are gold deposits in my back yard" in favor of "I discovered gold deposits in my back yard."

The above prejudices at least make more sense to me than does the notion put forth by many people that we should, as much as possible, avoid using foreign words or phrases if an English equivalent exists. I mentioned, in a recent column, that I was particularly fond of the German term *Schadenfreude*, but that, indeed, is a word that has no one- or two-word English equivalent. I like to use and hear foreign terms even when an English equivalent might exist, because I find a big difference between "equivalent" and "satisfactory equivalent."

If I'm drinking with someone in a bar, I don't mind his raising his glass and saying, "*prosit*," "*na zdrowie*," or "*slàinte mhath*." A foreign toast lends a bit of extra comradeship to what would otherwise be a vulgar rite of self-intoxication. I also would have no objection to someone saying "*mea culpa*" instead of the currently popular "my bad."

When I use a foreign term, I choose it because it is in some way a better usage than the English equivalent. For instance, I'm fond of the phrase, "*pour épater la canaille*," as in, "Mussolini's corpse was strung up in the streets of Milan, *pour épater la canaille*." The phrase translates as, "in order to thrill the rabble," which would be just as good except that *canaille* is a far more satisfying word. It's impossible to pronounce without twisting your mouth into a contemptuous sneer ("cah-*naiiiiiii*-yeh!") that tells your interlocutor exactly how you feel about the people you're describing.

Yiddish terms are particularly satisfying, and they provide shades of meaning that can't easily be found in English, such as the difference between a *Schlemiel* and a *Schlimazel*. Both are unfortunate fellows, but the former is a bumbling loser, while the latter is merely luckless. In other words, the *Schlemiel* is the guy who knocks the flower-pot off the windowsill, just as the *Schlimazel* happens to be passing underneath.

Another precise (and thus useful) Yiddish word is *Mensch*. Literally, the word simply means "man," but it connotes a degree of moral uprightness and indomitability of spirit such as no English term will. (Our nearest equivalent might be "prince," but *Mensch* implies more mental – and perhaps physical – toughness.)

French has a good many terms that are useful to English-speakers: *bête noire* and *enfant terrible* come immediately to mind. Literally, they mean "black beast" and "terrible child," but the definition of the former is "one who serves as a constant annoyance or harbinger of bad luck, usually in relation to a specific person or group." Thus, Kenneth Starr was President Clinton's *bête noire*, and Don King is professional boxing's. An *enfant terrible* is "a young and/or innovative person whose behavior is conspicuously unconventional or controversial; one who rocks the boat." Madonna, at the start of her career, might have been called an *enfant terrible*; so might Marlon Brando have been, or Jerry Brown, or Muhammad Ali.

It is, however, important to pronounce foreign terms correctly if you're going to use them. One of my favorite hair-pullers is when I hear someone pronouncing *coup de grâce* ("blow of mercy") as "coo day grah." First of all, an unaccented final "e" in French is pronounced as a schwa, not fully voiced as in Spanish or Italian. Second, the word *grâce* is pronounced "grahss." If you say "grah," you're saying "blow of fat," which might have some private meaning but is not a widely used expression.

As bad is the current mispronunciation of *lingerie* as "lawn-jur-ay." The correct pronunciation is "lanj-ree" (rhymes with "man free"), and I am apparently the only American who knows this.

Next best thing to using foreign words creatively and correctly, I suppose, is to invent a few imaginary words, in imaginary languages, attach definitions to them, and see if they catch on. After all, look how much money the Häagen Däzs people have made so far.

B Words And C Words

In a recent garden-variety celebrity-sniping-at-celebrity incident, a certain film actress referred to a certain woman of letters as a "fucking bitch." Informed of this, the woman of letters remarked, "What struck me as most offensive about this is not that she'd call me a 'fucking bitch' so much as that she'd call *anyone* a 'fucking bitch.' What an ugly, misogynistic term. ... One step away from the c word, if you ask me."

She is by no means the first person, nor will she be the last, to raise the double standard when it comes to gender-specific epithets. For some reason, of the many finely nuanced terms for "disagreeable person," those most commonly used refer to gender-specific parts of the anatomy, or to persons, animals, or things of a certain sex. A man might be a dick, a prick, a sonofabitch, or a fuck-stick. A woman might be a bitch or a cunt or a cow. Less frequently is a person granted a genderless epithet, such as pig, jerk, rat, or slimebag – and in any case such terms are generally felt to lack strength.

This is the way of our language and culture – and always has been. To cry misogyny, at this late date, over a term of common abuse, strikes me as misguided at best, sanctimonious at worst. I cannot accept the notion that "bitch" and "cunt" are misogynistic terms – that is, terms that connote a dislike of women in general. Nobody, after all, would seriously suggest that to call an individual man a dick or a prick is to express a dislike of all males. (Men, rarely, are called bitches or cunts, and when they are, it means much the same as when one of those names is applied to a woman.) Nor would anyone suggest that to call someone a fucking bitch implies a general distaste for the act of fucking.

"Dick" and "prick" are, of course, extremely common terms of abuse, as well as slang terms for the penis. They are considered pretty equally naughty in the anatomical context, but, as epithets, those two words have different meanings.

A dick, usually, is someone who is aggressively stupid, or obnoxiously ridiculous, or generally dislikable – but not knowingly vicious or cruel. It's a more general, more loosely defined term than "prick." "Dick," also, usually connotes a mild to middling dislike, rather than hatred.

A prick, on the other hand, is a person who's vicious and cruel in a sneaky, dirty, underhanded way – yet in a way that's small-time, rather than monstrous. A prick is someone whose behavior is not actually criminal or seriously injurious, and yet so mean-spirited as to make him despicable.

To give specific examples, Larry King was a dick when, in his biography, he fabricated friendships with people he never knew: obnoxiously ridiculous. Burt Reynolds was a prick when he made that guy spill his drink all over himself on the *Tonight* show: a cheap-shot artist.

In my observation, the meanings of "bitch" and "cunt" differ considerably one from the other, yet those meanings are less distinct than those of "dick" and "prick." "Cunt," oddly enough, is most usually used as the female equivalent of "dick." It usually connotes a woman who is oafishly dislikable, although it can connote one who is truly detestable, depending on the user and the context. "Bitch" is commonly used to connote an aggressively ill-tempered woman – a scold, a nag, a harridan – *and/or* a back-shooter. It's roughly equivalent to "prick."

Why is "cunt" generally regarded as perhaps the most obscene, least printable word in our lexicon – even more horrible, according to many folks, than "fuck" or "nigger"? This, to me, is a mystery. Nobody, not once, has ever offered me a well-thought-out – nor even a vaguely reasoned – explanation for this. The only explanation I have ever received is, "It's just an ugly word." In other words, "Ick." In other words, "Because."

(This abhorrence of the word "cunt" is not universal. For one example, an ex-domestic partner of mine, who is as annoyingly female-chauvinistic and politically correct as anyone I'd care to meet, routinely refers to that part of her anatomy as her cunt, and even refers to her gynæcologist as her cunt-doctor. I once asked her why she, of all people, was not offended by that particular word, and she very sensibly replied, "Why should I be?" In France, the word is *con*, and it's considered a rather mild epithet: about as strong as "loser" in English, and equally applicable to a man or a woman.)

Whether or not one chooses, oneself, to use terms like "bitch" or "cunt" or other gender-based words of commination, it's hard to escape the conclusion that each of these words has meaning other than to disparage the gender as a whole. Whether or not the actress alluded to above was justified in calling the authoress a fucking bitch, it must be assumed that she chose the compound epithet as a metaphor for "exceedingly contemptible woman," rather than, "exceedingly contemptible, like women in general." If, indeed, she had used the phrase, "exceedingly contemptible woman," would that phrase be deemed misogynistic because it specified the gender of the person being vilified?

Testifying About Hysteria

On several occasions, from several women, I've heard objections to the use of the word "hysterical" to describe certain excessive, uncontrolled expressions of anger (and, occasionally, sorrow, fear or other emotions). The contentions are several:

• Putting aside the question of whether the "hysterical" behavior was in fact excessive, uncontrolled, or at all obnoxious, it's inaccurate, rude, and sexist to ascribe it to the woman's uterus or the workings thereof. (The etymological antecendent of "hysterics" is the ancient Greek *husterikos*, from *hustera*, or womb.)

• When men lose their tempers, the behavior is seldom or never called hysterical, nor is it commonly attributed to a male sexual part.

• By dismissing certain behavior as hysterical – which most people use to mean "temporarily irrational and over-emotional" – we deny the validity of what might have been a very reasonable anger.

• It's politically incorrect to impart, simultaneously, a pejorative and a feminine characterization to anything. (That, after all, is why we stopped giving hurricanes girls' names only.)

I won't call these women's objections to "hysterical" an hysterical reaction, of course, since their arguments are not entirely without merit, and at least appear to be well-reasoned. However, they don't hold up, when you consider that "hysterical" is just one example – and an understandable one, at that – of attributing certain behavior to a person's being a man or a woman.

Throwing a tantrum, lashing out at someone with vehemence that suggests insanity, hurling the best china across the room: that is, in fact, behavior more typical of a woman than of a man. When a man does it, we consider him un-manly, and we use the feminine-sounding term "hissy fit" (which might stem, etymologically, from the verb "to hiss," or might be related to "hysterical," in which case we might want to spell it "hyssy fit") to describe the episode.

I've heard women contend that however one might describe the behavior, it's incorrect to ascribe it to one's having a womb. In general, however, that is the very thing to which one must ascribe it! People with wombs are more likely to display a certain identifiable sort of rage, than people without – just as people with balls are more likely than people without to drive aggressively, keep an untidy apartment, and crush beer cans on their foreheads.

Women have excused themselves to me, more times than I can count, for their capricious rages or other unpleasant behavior, on the grounds that "I'm PMSing." That, it would seem to me, is admitting that one's behavior does indeed have something to do with one's womb.

Men have their peculiar ways of displaying anger, and some of those ways are disagreeable, but men are more likely to express anger quickly and in few words. And they do express it. They don't snap, "nothing!" when someone asks them what's wrong.

Women might properly object to "hysterical" if typically male behavior were never attributed to male genitals. But we have countless examples of such expressions. If I'm in a car with a reckless driver, I might admonish him to "stop driving with your dick." He in turn might say to me, if I'm making a fool of myself over a woman, "Don't let the little head think for the big one." No man takes offense at this, because we are aware that our behavior is, occasionally, prompted by our testosterone, and we would never deny it. Why can't women face the analogous truth about themselves?

Could we accuse a woman of a certain age, who contracts an unsuitable marriage because she feels time running out, of "thinking with her womb"? Beyond question, we could, and it would be sheer hypocrisy to call it an unfair accusation.

Aside from the question of whether or not certain behavior should be implicitly classified as masculine or feminine, we should note that a great many English words evolved from other words that had to do with the reproductive equipment. "Pen" and "penis" are etymologically related. "Testify" and "testimony" are etymologically related to "testicles," because when you testify, you stake your balls on the truth of your statement. (Many of us are familiar with the expression, "Put your balls on the table," as a variant of "Put up or shut up.") Thus, one very politically correct person suggested that women ought to "ovarify" when giving evidence in court.

It is true, I'll admit, that when a woman is upset and lets people know about it in strong terms – while remaining controlled and rational – that behavior is sometimes called hysterical, quite unfairly. There is that double standard by which a man can be admired for asserting himself, and a woman denigrated. That is unfortunate, but we are not going to eliminate the problem by pretending that each display of anger is as meritorious as any other, or by pretending that some behavior is not typically feminine, or masculine.

We live in a time when boys and men are more and more often hearing their gender disparaged; when popular movies and TV shows continually portray women as smart, loving and capable while men are foolish, weak and bungling; when every self-help book in the world might as well be titled *Woman Good, Man Bad*; when our increasingly feminized educational system is trying to turn little boys into little girls; when pop psychologists and other self-appointed busybodies demand that men "get in touch with their feminine sides." (Anyone who suggested that women "get in touch with their masculine sides" would undoubtedly be laughed out of court.) Under those prevailing conditions, it would seem, unpleasant behavior that's common to men must be bred or conditioned out of them, while unpleasant behavior that's common to women must not even be remarked upon.

If what we are striving for is legal and social equality between the sexes, then such a course is sheer folly. We must, I think, let men act like men, and women, like women – and if the gender-inspired behavior of either becomes excessive, call their attention to it.

Matters Poetic

Battle Of The Sexes Extends To Verse

There is, in my observation, such a thing as "guys' poetry" and such a thing as "girls' poetry." Many of us noticed this early in life, in school, when the teacher would require us to read a favorite poem to the class. Given an anthology of all the poems read by a class of, say, 30 kids, you'd probably have little trouble guessing which were chosen by boys, and which by girls. This gender-based difference in taste continues into adulthood. Men enjoy Robert Burns' poems and songs, while women often think they're silly and crude; women prefer the work of Emily Dickinson, which most men find facile and anæmic.

This is good in a way: If everyone liked the same thing, after all, there'd never be any experimentation, and poetry – and our language with it – would decay like a dead fish, with analogously pleasant results. The negative effect of this difference, though, is that it's difficult for a man and a woman to have an intelligent discussion of poetry, and harder yet for a man to write a poem for a woman, or vice versa, that will have the desired effect.

I like to read poetry aloud – my own or somebody else's – and I often participate in readings, as a featured reader or as part of the open pool. I've heard a lot of poetry, both good and bad, but to judge its quality, I invariably finding myself judging a poem not merely as a poem, but as "guys' poetry" or "girls' poetry."

I think I noticed this difference even before I could read. My parents often read poetry to me; two of our standard volumes were A.A. Milne's *When We Were Very Young* and *Now We Are Six*, and I still have a lot of those poems by heart. Looking back, I can recall that my father would usually select poems that told a story, were funny, and had a distinctive meter and rhyming pattern: "Disobedience," "The Dormouse And The Doctor," "The Knight Whose Armour Didn't Squeak," "The Old Sailor." My mother preferred poems that were indistinct as to image, but would conjure up a sort of emotional identification in the reader's mind: "Happiness," "Binker," "Halfway Down," "Come Out With Me."

This may be why, in my observation, men are more likely than women to write formal poetry. Women want a poem to create a feeling; men want a poem to systematize a complicated idea.

That is not to say that a man can't be profoundly moved by a poem – but he'll be moved most often by the specific, rather than the general. Thus, for example, Ezra Pound's "The River-Merchant's Wife – A Letter" will literally make me weep, while Stevie Smith's "Not Waving But Drowning" will cause no emotional reaction at all – even though I clearly understand what she's trying to say, and can see that it is a very well-written poem of its kind. "The River-Merchant's Wife" deals with emotions that are peculiar to its narrator, and what makes it a well-written poem is that it makes the reader feel the narrator's emotions vicariously. "Not Waving But Drowning," being more general, enables the reader to relate its emotions to those that are peculiar to herself – and that is its strength, to a woman, and its weakness, to a man.

Perhaps that, too, is why men prefer narrative poetry, while women prefer rhapsodies on a theme. I have yet, for instance, to meet a woman who reads Rudyard Kipling's poetry for choice; just as unlikely would it be to meet a man whose favorite poet is Sylvia Plath. Kipling's "Danny Deever" tells, in linear form, the story of some men being forced to watch an execution:

While most of us have never been there and done that, Kipling takes us there and shows it to us, and we feel the horror that the men in the poem felt. Plath's "Daddy" starts with a near-universal theme (a woman's confused and conflicting feelings about her father) and expands on them, verse by verse, moving in a sort of spiral, painting no picture, but – I must assume this, since the poem is so universally acclaimed – reminding the individual reader of her own feelings for her own father.

Men also enjoy, more than women do, poems that do not touch the emotions, but which make a social comment, or are satirical or ribald. Thomas Hardy's "The Ruined Maid" makes a point, humorously. A man will fall apart laughing on reading it, while a woman might only smile and admit that the poem was clever.

I've also never heard a woman praise a poem for its rhythm. Louis MacNeice's "Bagpipe Music" is a guys' poem not only because of its content, but because, when it's read aloud, it sounds like a lively bagpipe air.

I don't mean to imply, by the way, that men always write guys' poetry, and women always write girls' poetry. Several of Robert Frost's poems – I think immediately of "The Road Not Taken" – are much more appealing to women than to men. Gwendolyn Brooks' "We Real Cool" is as hard and macho a poem as anyone would want to read. But this kind of crossover is rare. In general, the constant and never-ending misunderstanding between the sexes is nowhere better illustrated than in our respective tastes in poetry.

The Moon In Poetry

By now, no doubt, all of us have received as many emailed chain-letters and forwards as we ever want to see in this or the next world. One came my way just the other day, under the heading, "This is the sweetest forward." It contained a brief poem, and a promise that love would come my way if I e-mailed copies of it to seven people.

I enjoy writing and criticizing poems, so I figured I'd take a close look at this one before I forwarded it. It turned out to be fascinating: more conducive to deconstruction, explication, and discussion than many poems generally regarded as "classics."

I suspect it's by Arthur Anonymous, the enigmatic poet known for the timelessness of his work. (Arthur was probably named after the ancient Indian mystic, Sid Arthur.)

A Lover's Dream

As I sit and stare at the shimmering moon,
I also sit here and hope to see you soon.
Then I realized I won't be able to see you tomorrow,
so I would sit here and cry in sorrow.
Now I only uphold a dream which I hope come true
and that one dream is to be with you.

STUDY QUESTIONS

1. Discuss the poet's use of the moon as a symbol of romantic love. Does he break new artistic ground here? Specify and explain.

2. Discuss the importance of universality to "great" poetry. Is there a line between "universal" and "banal"? Does this poem cross it? Defend your position.

3. Diagram the scansion of the poem, line by line. Did the author have a specific scheme of accented and unaccented syllables? Discuss the lack of uniformity in number of syllables per line. Was this the author's intention? If so, what was his purpose?

4. Observe the scansion of line three: - - / - - - - - /- - - - - / -. (There; I've given you part of the answer to question three!) Can a pattern be discerned? Compare and contrast it with other unusual scansions in the poetry of any age.

DECONSTRUCTION

As I sit and stare at the shimmering moon,

Does anyone actually stare at the moon out of wistfulness, or only for the fun of finding shapes in it? Also, does the moon shimmer? ("Shimmer," I believe, is made up of "shine" and "glimmer," and implies an unstable liquid or metallic effect. A reflection of the moon, in a pond or on the blade of a sword, might shimmer, but the moon looked at directly has a dull and steady glow.)

I also sit here and hope to see you soon.

We already know the speaker is sitting, so "also sit here and" is superfluous. And in what sense is "see" used here? "Catch sight of"? "Spend time with"? Or is it used in the more modern sense, as a euphemism for "have regular sexual intercourse with"? (As in "I'm not seeing anyone right now.")

Then I realized I won't be able to see you tomorrow,

This fact only just dawned on the poet? Remarkable! And what's this "I won't be able to"? Which of them is unavailable, the poet or the beloved? If the former, the credibility of the poem is destroyed: If you want to see someone badly enough, you'll find the time somehow. The excuse, "Oh, gosh darn, I just remembered I have that meeting tomorrow afternoon, and there just won't be the time to see you otherwise," isn't going to cut it. If the latter, he must have known, *before* he sat down to stare at the shimmering moon, that he wouldn't have a date the next day. It's mysteries like this that make poetry so fascinating: If the author isn't on hand to explain, scholars can debate these fine points till kingdom come.

so I would sit here and cry in sorrow.

"I would," in this context, can only mean, "I wish to." It can't mean, "It is my habit to," and it doesn't mean, "I shall," or "I am fixing to." But why is it necessary for the poet to specify that he is crying "in sorrow"? We wouldn't assume that he's crying for joy – unless, of course, he's joyful at having just thought of an excuse for avoiding his ladylove on the morrow. We can only regret the paucity of biographical material on Arthur Anonymous. Was he often ambivalent in affairs of the heart? Alas, his trail grows colder every day.

Now I only uphold a dream which I hope come true

"Uphold" is an interesting word choice. "Dream" is an acceptable synonym for "objective" or "wish," but "uphold" implies a degree of effort, or of striving against an opposing force – and if the objective be sincerely desired, or the wish keenly felt, little effort should be required to keep it in one's bosom. Again, we see the poet's ambivalence and inner conflict.

As for "which I hope come true," it's hard to determine whether the author merely mis-conjugated "to come" – in other words, meant to write "comes" – or whether the intention was to use the verb in the rather pretty but largely obsolete subjunctive mood, as in "if he come."

and that one dream is to be with you.

The word "one" seems to have no place here except to change the meter of the line from an anapest-anapest-iamb pattern to iamb-iamb-anapest-iamb. In other words, it serves approximately the same function as a "titty bum." Poets of modest talent sometimes introduce nonsense syllables into a line in order to make it scan to their satisfaction, but here the poet has used such a complex and original scansion throughout that it's hard to see how any but the most exacting reader would miss that syllable.

A poet of Arthur Anonymous' stature could hardly be accused of carelessly inserting a superfluous syllable into a poem – into the climactic line, at that. An explanation must exist – as must exist the scholar who will one day unearth it.

The Immortal Memory[*]

I think I was about six years old when I first was exposed to Robert Burns. I clearly remember I was looking at a small book of poetry, probably the best-selling anthology in the United States, entitled "101 Famous Poems." In it were 98 poems written in English, and three in Scots: two by Robert Burns and one by a later poet, Alexander Anderson. Bear in mind that I was only six, and although I could read pretty well for my age, I could not come anywhere near reading those three poems.

I showed the three offending poems to my mother, and I asked her, "What is the meaning of this? Are these two poets just trying to be clever, or cute, or something, using this... this... *slang*, this *accent*, this..."

At this point, my youth got the better of me. I knew what I wanted to know, you see; I just lacked the vocabulary to put the question properly. What I was trying to ask, in my ignorance, was, "Why can't these guys write their poems in good plain English, instead of using this debased vernacular?"

My mother explained – not quite accurately – that these poems were examples of what we call "dialect," like, for another example, the tales of Uncle Remus, or the comic strip *Pogo*, both of which used American Southern dialects, and both of which I

---

[*] This is a speech, delivered by Joseph Dobrian on January 22, 2000, at the New York Caledonian Club's annual Burns Supper.

was also learning to appreciate at that age. She went on to explain – again, not quite accurately – that poems like these, or tales like the Uncle Remus stories, were ways of recording for posterity the everyday speech of people who lived in marginalized cultures in another age.

It wasn't until many years later that I learned that what Rabbie Burns was after was not the cryopreservation, if you will, of a dying patois. Rather, his purpose was to prop up and revive a true national language, that had been slowly dying for centuries.

He did not succeed entirely. As a spoken language, Scots is still bedridden, and it's coughing up blood, and there's no improvement in sight. But at least – and largely because of Rabbie Burns' efforts to keep it alive – Scots is today recognized as a language in its own right.

The popular misunderstanding had long been that Scots was merely a bastard offspring of English. Rabbie Burns, and others who wrote in Scots, have forced scholars to study the family a little more closely and concede that English and Scots are *brother* tongues, equally legitimate offspring of the language spoken by the Angles. One brother settled in the South, married the Saxon language, and took the name English. The other brother settled in the north, married the Gaelic language (and took as his mistresses the Scandinavian, Flemish, and French languages besides) and called himself Scots.

The trouble was that English – from the beginning – was the bigger, wealthier, and more powerful brother of the two. And just as an individual human being might ape the mannerisms of the richer, more refined folks next door, it was natural for the Scottish people to incline away from their own Scots language, and speak English instead.

Some 450 years ago, the religious reformer John Knox was criticized for being too English in his speech.

More than two hundred years after Knox, the Scottish philosopher David Hume became one of the leading advocates of English, as the proper language for Scotland. When he died, someone suggested that he died confessing not his sins, but his Scotticisms.

When Dr. Samuel Johnson visited the Scottish Lowlands, in Rabbie Burns' own time, he commented as follows:

"The conversation of the Scots grows every day less unpleasing to the English; their peculiarities wear fast away; their dialect is likely to become in half a century provincial and rustick, even to themselves. The great, the learnéd, the ambitious and the vain, all cultivate the English phrase, and the English pronunciation."

On visiting the Highlands, he added:

"By subsequent opportunities of observation, I found that my host's diction had nothing peculiar. Those Highlanders that can speak English, commonly speak it well, with few of the words, and little of the tone by which a Scotchman is distinguished. Their language seems to have been learned in the army or navy, or by some communication with those who could give them good examples of accent and pronunciation."

In this context, it's no surprise that Rabbie Burns did not write in Scots in his everyday correspondence, nor did he speak it as his everyday language. He spoke English, and a self-conscious English, at that. An old friend of his, Professor Dugald Stewart, wrote as follows about Burns' speech:

"Nothing, perhaps, was more remarkable among his various attainments, than the fluency and precision, and originality of his language, when he spoke in company; more particularly as he aimed at purity in his turn of expression, and avoided more successfully than most Scotchmen, the peculiarities of Scottish phraseology."

A true Scottish nationalist might, in hindsight, condemn Burns for being so douce in his approach to the language of Scotland's oppressors – but others might point out that by adopting English, he may have merely been trying to conquer his conquerors, as certain individual Scotsmen have succeeded in doing, over the past four centuries. If you doubt that it's ever been done, just consider such typical "Englishmen" as Harold MacMillan, David Niven, Alec Douglas-Home, and Charles II.

But as a poet, Rabbie Burns used the Scots language – and in so doing, he achieved a level of excellence that the English language could never have given him.

Rabbie Burns did write many poems in English, and most of his English poems share two common characteristics. First, they're not very good. Second, to call them "gloomy" would be the understatement of the millennium. They are veritable invitations to suicide. Perhaps the most famous of his English poems is "Man Was Made To Mourn," but as it's rather a long one, it might actually result in a few deaths if I were to recite it here and now. So, to give you an example of Burns' English style, I'll read you a short one, entitled, "To Ruin":

All hail! Inexorable lord
At whose destruction-breathing word
The mightiest empires fall!
Thy cruel woe-delighted train
The ministers of grief and pain
A sullen welcome, all!
With stern-resolv'd despairing eye
I see each aimèd dart
For one has cut my dearest tie
And quivers in my heart.
Then low'ring, and pouring,
The storm no more I dread,
Tho' thick'ning and black'ning
Round my devoted head.

And thou grim pow'r, by life abhorr'd,
While life a pleasure can afford,
O, hear a wretch's pray'r!
No more I shrink, appall'd, afraid
I court, I beg thy friendly aid,
To close this scene of care!
When shall my soul, in silent peace,
Resign life's joyless day?
My weary heart its throbbings cease,
Cold-mould'ring in the clay?
No fear more, no tear more,
To stain my lifeless face,
Enclaspèd, and graspèd
Within thy cold embrace!

Burns, here, has written two rather long stanzas, and all they say is, "I feel like crap and I wish I were dead."

Now, though, let's turn to another poem that addresses the same notion – sudden and utter ruin. To my mind it's a superior poem for three reasons. First, it does what every high-school English teacher tells his students is the key to great poetry: it uses the specific to make a universal statement. Second, it is outward-directed: not a commentary on the author's inner torment, but on the common condition of all creatures. Third, the author has written it not in English, but in broad Scots. The poem, of course, is "To A Mouse, On Turning Her Up In Her Nest With The Plough, November, 1785."

Wee, sleeket, cowrin, tim'rous beastie,
Oh, what a panic's in thy breastie!
Thou need na start awa sae hasty
Wi' bickerin brattle!
I wad be laith to rin an' chase thee
Wi' murd'ring pattle!

I'm truly sorry man's dominion
Has broken Nature's social union,

An' justifies that ill opinion
Which makes thee startle
At me, thy poor earth-born companion,
An' fellow-mortal!

I doubt na, whyles, but thou may thieve:
What then? poor beastie, thou maun live!
A daimen icker in a thrave
'S a sma' request;
I'll get a blessin wi' the lave,
An' never miss 't!

Thy wee bit housie, too, in ruin!
Its silly wa's the win's are strewin!
An' naething, now, to big a new ane,
O' foggage green!
An' bleak December's winds ensuin
Baith snell an' keen!

Thou saw the fields laid bare an' wast,
An' weary winter comin fast,
An' cozie here beneath the blast
Thou thought to dwell,
Till crash! the cruel coulter past
Out thro' thy cell.

That wee bit heap o' leaves an' stibble
Has cost thee monie a weary nibble!
Now thou's turn'd out for a' thy trouble,
But house or hald,
To thole the winter's sleety dribble
An' cranreuch cauld!

But, Mousie, thou art no thy lane
In proving foresight may be vain:
The best laid schemes o' mice an' men
Gang aft agley,
An' lea'e us nought but grief an' pain
For promis'd joy.

Still thou art blest, compar'd wi' me!
The present ainlie toucheth thee:
But, och! I backward cast my e'e
On prospects drear!
An' forward, tho' I canna see,
I guess an' fear!

Rabbie Burns was a man who frankly admitted that life was in many ways a source of frustration to him. He was, without question, a man given at times to deep gloom – and yet, the poems that he wrote in the Scots language, by and large, almost always had an element of fun, or of humor, or at any rate of empathy, no matter how serious the subject matter.

Far be it from me to suggest that Scots is inherently a happier language than English, or a more literarily effective language – but in the hands of Rabbie Burns, it certainly was.

There is, I think, something about the Scots language that invites ribaldry and irreverence, and this comes out in Burns songs, more so than in his poetry. As many of us know, Rabbie Burns was not only a preserver of Scots as a literary language; he was also a collector of that language's traditional naughty songs – and believe me, with the possible exception of French, probably no language has a greater collection! He also wrote a number of such songs. It wouldn't be much of an exaggeration to say that for every song that Burns produced for general consumption, there was another that he wrote strictly for the amusement of bachelors and other wicked people.

We're all familiar with Burns the composer of tender, touching love-songs. "A Red, Red Rose" is probably the best known of these; "John Anderson" is another. But what not everyone knows is that Burns' love songs, and his less presentable ones, were sometimes just two sides of the same coin. My own favorite of Rabbie Burns' love songs, the one that never fails to get me choked up when I hear it, is one that's somewhat lesser known, called, "Sae Flaxen Were Her Ringlets." To me, the beauty of this song lies equally in Burns' lyrics, and in the tune. I'll only sing you one stanza because I'm painfully aware that I'm no singer:

Sae flaxen were her ringlets,
Her eyebrows of a darker hue,
Bewitchingly o'erarching
Twa laughing een o' bonnie blue.
Her smiling, sae wyling
Wad mak a wretch forget his woe;
What pleasure, what treasure,
Untae these rosy lips tae grow
Such was ma Chloris' bonnie face
When first her bonnie face I saw,
And aye ma Chloris' dearest charm,
She says she lo'es me best of aa.

Well, as I was researching tonight's presentation, I discovered a letter that Burns wrote to a friend about this very song, in which he reveals that the tune was not his own composition – few if any of his tunes were – and that his lyrics were a replacement for some much older verses, of unknown origin. In the letter, he writes:

"Do you know, my dear Sir, a blackguard Irish song called, 'Oonagh's Waterfall' or 'The Lock That Scattered Oonagh's Piss'? Our friend Cunningham sings it delightfully.... You may be pleased to have verses to it that you may sing it before ladies."

In other words, all my life I've been getting all misty-eyed over a tune – and a blackguard Irish tune at that! – the original verses to which deal with a rather naughty sport that's known to its practitioners as "golden showers."

In its way, this is as illustrative a story as can be told, to explain Rabbie Burns' legacy. Rabbie Burns is a hero to people of Scottish ancestry or Scottish affinities because of the prestige he brought to the language and culture of Scotland. In the world at large, though, his fame has only partly to do with the charm of his language. He's also beloved because he's perceived as a great poet who is nonetheless emphatically human. There is nothing mystical or God-like about Rabbie Burns. He was not, for instance, a Robert Frost, whom we revere as an almost supernatural perceptor of human thought. He was not a Lord Byron, who apparently saw himself as a direct descendant of ancient Olympus. Burns was, in many ways, an ordinary man with ordinary limitations, a man cursed with endless questions but blessed with few answers, a man keenly aware of the utter fecklessness of the human race.

To conclude then, I'm forced to admit that my initial violent reaction against his poetry, based on his use of this outlandish language, was perhaps a bit hasty. However, it was also providential. In the many years since, I've enriched my own life beyond measure, through my study of the language, history, and culture of Scotland – a study I might never have pursued had I not been so offended by my first encounter with Rabbie Burns that I took the trouble to get to know him a little better.

And over my years of acquaintance with him, I've come to agree with a recent biographer of his, who pointed out that Rabbie Burns does not, all that often, make us think. He doesn't. But he makes us laugh, and he makes us cry, and the laughter and the tears that he brings to each of us, intensify our awareness of both our common humanity, and of our individual existence. It's with deep gratitude for that laughter, and those tears, that I now propose the immortal memory of Robert Burns.

Food

Food As A Study Aid

"I'm not a glutton," the old boxing champ Archie Moore once asserted. "I'm an explorer of food." A fine sentiment, I say. By treating gastronomy as a discipline to be studied, you're likely to learn considerably more about the human condition than you would through more conventional studies of history, philosophy, and anthropology.

For instance, many of us know that the Potato Famine in 1840s Ireland caused considerable immigration to the United States, but without knowing the history of the potato in Ireland, it's hard to understand why the failure of one crop would have brought such catastrophe, or why the Irish still blame the English for what happened. Most of us don't know how the potato came to be a staple food of the Irish, or that it was unknown there a few centuries ago.

People who are fond of those extra-salty, mummified Southern hams that have to be cooked for days before they're fit to eat might be interested to know that the ancient Romans ate similar hams, which they cured by burying them at the seashore and letting them absorb salt water for a few months.

Connoisseurs of fine old wines might be surprised to find that their hobby is a relatively new one, and dependent on the discovery that excellent bottle-stoppers could be made from cork trees. The use of corks as bottle-stoppers was not widespread till about 1700. Prior to that time, most wine was stored and shipped in barrels, and not decanted into bottles till served at table. Thus, wine didn't keep well, and had to be drunk rather young. It was the use of cork stoppers that allowed wine to be stored in nearly air-tight bottles, and kept to mature for years.

If you want to know what wine tasted like in the time of the ancient Greeks, buy a bottle of retsina, a cheap Greek wine with a strong flavor of pine tar. Back about 3,000 years ago, the Greeks lined their wine-barrels with pitch to make them water-tight. They found that this made the wine taste nasty, but in time they got used to it, and even when better storage techniques were invented, many Greeks still preferred resinated wine.

I'm on this subject because of a dinner party I gave the other night, at which I served dishes from *Pepys At Table*, a book of recipes for the many foods mentioned by Samuel Pepys in his famous diaries.

Samuel Pepys – pronounced "peeps" – was a high-ranking civil servant in England in the time of King Charles II, and his diaries provide an amazing lot of information about what middle-class private life was like in 1660s London.

From his diaries, we know that Parmesan cheese was such a prized item in Pepys' time that when the Great Fire swept through London in 1666, he "did dig a pit in the garden [for] all the papers of my office that I could not otherwise dispose of. And in the evening Sir W. Penn and I did dig another and put our wine in it, and I my parmazan cheese as well..."

Pepys was lucky to be alive at a time when fashions in food and drink were going through an adventurous stage. Foods, and people's attitudes toward food, go in and out of fashion just as surely as do styles of clothing, and in the late 17th century a veritable gastronomic revolution was taking place. Europeans were settling the Americas, and sending back exotic fruits, vegeta-bles, and native recipes – and that strange Mexican substance for which they'd just about sell their children: "chocolatte." In England, the common folk generally had to get by on bread, cheese, salt fish, and beer, but the middle and upper classes were enjoying their first exposure to continental cuisine. (Charles II had just returned from exile in France, and many French chefs, sensing a friendly business climate, had come to England. Thus we see how the end of the English Civil War raised the standard of eating for at least some Englishmen.)

It's fascinating to read about all this, and I intend to learn the history of other countries and eras by sampling their cuisines, as well, but one thing saddens me a bit: the likelihood that we may have by now discovered everything that is edible on our planet.

Moreover, many foods that were once considered delicacies are now completely out of fashion, and thus virtually unavailable. When, for instance, has any of you seen mutton for sale at a butcher shop – not lamb, but mature mutton? King Charles II used to keep a cow on the grounds of his palace so that he could have "syllabub" – a punch made by taking a bowl half-full of white wine and filling it the rest of the way by milking a cow directly into it. Unless you have similar facilities, where can you get raw milk today?

Other prized foods of centuries past – passenger pigeon, aurochs, sea cow – have been hunted to extinction, and will never be tasted again.

If it's new gastronomic thrills we want, I have an idea. I hear we taste a lot like pork – and I daresay we've got more flavor than those dried-out extra-lean pigs that today's farmers are breeding in response to the never-ending demand for low-fat everything. Jonathan Swift suggested eating Irish babies as a way of lowering their numbers, but almost any other group of undesirables would do just about as well, I should think.

Imagine how Pepys would have reported the experiment.

"Up early this morning with my wife, to make pyes of the serving wensh we had lately caught a-thieving. Later out and about, delivering the pyes to various of our friends as presents, then to church. At night we eat a legg of the wensh, stoffado, along with some cheese-cakes and mull'd claret, then out walking with my wife till very late. And so to bed."

Outdated Food

Foods go in and out of fashion just as do styles of clothing, but it seems that till recently, food fashions have changed with an almost glacial slowness. It's only been in the past 60 years or so that we've seen real revolutions in how and what we eat.

We foodies – people who make a study of cooking and eating – each have our own special interests. Some of us will latch onto a particular type of ethnic cooking, Chinese for instance, and learn everything we can possibly learn about it. Others will indulge a personal dietary requirement, such as keeping kosher or being a vegetarian, and see how well we can cook within that self-imposed limitation.

My own obsession is with the cuisine of particular historic periods. When I throw a dinner party, I might provide a Restoration feast, with food such as might have been served in England around 1660, or an Ancient Egyptian banquet featuring 4,000-year-old recipes.

If we're talking historic food, one of my favorite types and eras would have to be "gourmet" American cuisine of the 1960s.

When I say the 1960s, I'm not talking the tacky late 60s, the time of love beads, Laugh-In, and the White Album. I'm talking about the worldly, classy early 60s, the pre-Beatles 60s, the 60s of Jack and Jackie Kennedy, James Bond, *Butterfield 8*, the Mercury flights, and those cool narrow neckties.

In the 60s, it was important to show off your sophistication, and people used food to do this, just as, nowadays, they use
food to show off how virtuous and health-conscious they are.
Those snooty, self-righteous health freaks who take an almost
decadent pleasure in telling you the exact nutritive components of
a rice cake, probably have parents who, 50 years ago, also used
food as a boasting tool – but at least they encouraged other people
to take some pleasure in it. I'm talking about people who served
their guests beef stroganoff – that's red meat and sour cream,
folks, serious cholesterol – with baked Alaska for dessert. None of
your low fat this and heart-smart that. A meal was a celebration,
not a medical exercise.

Probably it was World War II that started the gastronomic
revolution in this country. Our soldiers came back from Europe
and Asia having been exposed to foods other than overcooked
meat and boiled vegetables. Subsequently, overseas travel became
easier and cheaper. By the late 1950s, Americans were discovering
garlic (previously thought fit only for illiterate Italian immigrants),
wine (ditto), and rare meat (once considered a foppish French affectation, but by this time accepted as a sign of great sophistication).

Nowadays, people take garlic in pill form: deodorized garlic, to benefit the heart. This is typical of our sterile, joyless approach to dosing our bodies with the proper chemical com-
pounds. In the 50s and 60s, people ate garlic because it was *sooooo*
nasty. It had an exotic horrible/delicious flavor and it made you
stink like nobody's business – and that was the fun of it!

Greek food is *very* 60s. Anything Greek was big then. The
films *Never On Sunday* and *Zorba The Greek* taught us that the
Greeks were a rough, joyous, life-affirming bunch who danced,
laughed, never worried, and could teach us stuffy, timorous
Americans a few things about how to have a good time. A prolif-
eration of popularly-priced package tours brought thousands of

middle-class Americans to Greece to see for themselves. Greek food lent itself to parties. It was either bite-size *hors d'œuvres*, for cocktail parties (dolmades, cubes of feta, pita that you dipped in hummus), or dishes that were easy to make for a big crowd, like moussaka. If you had the nerve to attempt them, your Greek cookbook contained a few flaming dishes that would allow you to wow your guests by creating a low-yield nuclear explosion right on your buffet table.

A good 60s dinner party just about has to feature moussaka, or beef stroganoff, or paella, a Spanish dish of rice, chicken, and shellfish. If you're serving cooked vegetables, let them be smothered in plenty of creamy sauce. Garlic bread, made with tons of butter, is a must. No "healthy" salad dressings, remember! Green Goddess dressing, which is mayonnaise-based, is probably the quintessential salad dressing of that period – and if you use homemade mayonnaise, it'll involve raw egg, which is *really* spitting in the eye of the health police.

For dessert, if you haven't the time to whip up baked Alaska, how about chocolate-covered ants? I don't even know if they're available nowadays, but they were quite the thing, back then.

Naturally, you need to have a well-stocked bar on hand, and learn how to make a martini, Manhattan, Rob Roy, pink lady, and other such concoctions. If you're serving beer, it mustn't be anything good, because in the 60s we Americans didn't know anything about beer, aside from the watery domestic swill like Schlitz, Falstaff and the like. (Heineken was considered quite exotic back then.) You'll have to have red wine on hand to satisfy your heart-smart friends, of course, but don't forget the delightfully mediocre white and rosé wines of that era: Lancer's, Mateus – and retsina for the adventurous.

The music has to be right, too. Keep your dateline in mind: We didn't listen to rock, or soul, or R&B, back then, unless we were beatniks, in which case we would not have had a party like this one. Lay in some Herb Alpert, Hugh Montenegro, Percy Faith, The Shadows, and the *Never On Sunday* soundtrack, and you're golden.

(If you're radical-chic, you can listen to Pete Seeger and Peter, Paul and Mary; in that case, your cuisine should be less Western, more Chinese, Russian, or Arabic.)

Oh, and before your guests arrive, scatter ashtrays all over the apartment, and never be without a lit cigarette. If you don't smoke, you'll just have to make an exception, this once. It's the 60s, and thank God for it!

Iowa Cuisine

Oftener than not, if I'm asked where I live, and I say "Iowa," my interlocutor will reply, "Oh, yeah, potato country, right?"

"No, that's Idaho. Iowa is corn and pigs."

This exchange is so standard that it rolls off my tongue as easily as I pronounce my name. Few people know much about Iowa except that it's west of New York, and full of hillbillies.

"No, we have hicks and hayseeds, not hillbillies."

So, when I gave one of my famous dinner parties in my Manhattan apartment not long ago, I decided to introduce my guests to the cuisine of Iowa.

I hear some wiseguy in the back of the room remarking that the cuisine of Iowa is based on one central ingredient: Jell-O. It is true that Iowa contains probably the world's greatest trove of Jell-O salad recipes. Most Iowans eat these concoctions – which might contain marshmallows, canned fruit, fake whipped cream, and even more horrifying ingredients – as a prelude to the main course, although any civilized person who was daring enough to try them would probably take them as dessert.

Indeed, I served a couple of such Jell-O salads at my little party the other night – one of them a sort of Frankenstein green, the other a day-glo magenta. Only a couple of my guests could be induced to touch them.

Like any other regional American cuisine, that of Iowa has certain ethnic influences. German, Scandinavian, and Czech – and, surprisingly, Mexican – are the main ones.

For such a meat-eating people, Iowans come up with a remarkable variety of salads – such as taco salad, another item on my party menu. This is a huge conglomeration of ground beef, red beans, lettuce (iceberg, of course!), tomato, onion, avocado, and crushed Doritos, in a spicy cumin-based dressing. This is an example of the many half-Mexican, half-Midwestern dishes that Iowans have adopted from the Mexican migrant workers who work in our melon and soybean fields.

Pea salad – a mixture of peas, cubes of processed cheese, hard-boiled eggs, sweet pickle juice, and Miracle Whip – is almost never seen outside of Iowa. This and the pickled ham (a legacy from the Amish communities of east-central Iowa) were the dishes my guests found most interesting.

One typical Iowa dish that I did *not* serve was hamburger meat, minimally seasoned, broken up into little pebbles as it cooks, which you scoop up with an ice-cream scoop and serve on a bun with ketchup. The sandwich filling is called "loosemeats" (a plural noun, like grits), but the sandwich is called a Maid-Rite, after the restaurant chain that popularized them. These are occasionally inflicted on children in school cafeterias in other parts of the country, but only in Iowa do people eat them by choice.

But my party was not complete, because you can't have a proper Iowa feast without serving fresh, native foods that you can't get anywhere else, at least not of the same quality. These include various types of melon, tomatoes, sweet corn, and Iowa-raised meats.

Many people outside of Iowa have heard of Iowa corn, but you will not experience the real thing unless you're right near the source. The window of opportunity for really good sweet corn is tiny – approximately from August 15 to September 5 – and what you eat must have been picked within the past 12 hours or so. (Leave it too long, and its sugars turn to starch, leaving a bland flavor and a disagreeable texture). Iowa tomatoes are just like tomatoes anywhere else, but bigger, redder, smoother – and if you bring them straight from the back yard to the kitchen, two minutes before dinnertime, and slice and serve them immediately, they'll still be hot from the sun when they get to your plate, and won't need anything on them but salt and pepper. Cantaloupe (mainly grown near the town of Muscatine), with a scoop of vanilla ice cream on top, is the quintessential Iowa summer dessert.

No matter where you live in the U.S., the last pork chop you ate probably came from Iowa. But in Iowa you can get pork freshly killed and minimally processed. There's no more typically Iowa party than a Saturday-night pig roast in July or August, and nothing easier: All you need is a whole young pig (killed and cleaned), bread and ketchup for sandwiches (substitute homemade barbecue sauce if you want to get fancy), plenty of baked beans (and fresh-picked corn if it's late enough in the year), a tanker-truck full of beer, some reefer, and a local garage band that plays mostly early Doobie Brothers and absolutely no Grateful Dead.

(Speaking of reefer, Iowa produces some surprisingly good strains of weed: Iojuana, we called it in my day.)

Where Iowa surpasses itself, though, is in its beef. I'm a steak man (very rare, please), and I've eaten steak all over, but never had better than what you used to get at The Lark Supper Club, in Tiffin, Iowa (pop. 460), a quiet, dimly-lit, windowless place with dark walls, old-fashioned muzak and overstuffed banquettes, where everyone talked in whispers: real 1950s swank, set down in the middle of a tiny Iowa prairie town.

This, too, is something New York City could never duplicate. New York restaurants might serve Iowa beef, but never with the understated élan you'll encounter at a fancy restaurant that stands only a few hundred yards away from a grain elevator.

You're Going To Die Anyway

If bread be the staff of life, then surely cheese is an indispensable grace note thereupon. To my mind, few of life's pleasures are equal to a little Gorgonzola with a glass of port, or a Limburger so strong it fizzes in the mouth, or a Parmesan so ancient that you could put a piece of it in a sock and beat someone to death with it. Few sandwiches are as satisfying as those made with sharp Cheddar – either with mango chutney, or with tomatoes, cucumbers, sprouts, and hot English mustard, and on hard crusty bread in either case. And what's the point of pizza, if you don't specify "triple cheese"?

And yet some people would gainsay me. Not because they don't like cheese, but because of our current passion for self-denial. I mean, look at us, these days! We don't drink (except for one glass of red wine a day, taken as medicine). We don't smoke – hell, we *can't* smoke. We don't eat beef or pork or eggs. We don't smoke weed. We aren't supposed to have sex without full armor. We have a President who finishes his blowjobs into the sink, smoked pot but didn't inhale, and chews cigars because Hillary won't let him smoke them. And even at that, by comparison with some of us, he's just a wild and crazy guy.

I happened to overhear a conversation between two rather stereotypical women at my gym the other day: the type of women who spend half of their waking hours working out, and the other half measuring exactly regulated portions of tofu, egg whites, rice cakes and soy milk. One of them was a stringy, sexless woman of about my own age; the other a dancer of about 25, so grotesquely hard-bodied that I was tempted to check her for knotholes. Stringy was telling Hardbody about this great Mexican restaurant she knew, where they serve fat-free this, fat-free that, fat-free the other, no animal products except for cheese...

"Oh, but I don't eat cheese!" Hardbody replies, a tad self-righteously.

What the hell is that all about? Obviously, her reason for abstinence from cheese was so that she might be able to pee in front and crap behind a little bit longer than the rest of us – but why would anyone want to extend a life lived without cheese?

"I don't eat cheese," to me, is as outrageous a statement as, "I don't watch TV," or "I don't go out in the evenings," or "I don't masturbate": an artificial limitation imposed on oneself to give oneself a false sense of purity.

Lately, dairy products have become flavor-of-the-month with the Health Nazis. "Lactose intolerance" is a currently fashionable disorder. Practically any dairy product contains some animal fat, and we all know that animal fat is naughty, naughty, naughty. Drink the occasional glass of milk, eat the occasional piece of cheese, and you might as well buy your coffin, some folks would have us believe.

I know of a fellow who is six feet tall and weighs 130 lbs., who eats two meals a day – a bowl of oatmeal, and a serving of kale and cherry tomatoes, and that's all – because he figures that by keeping to this meager diet, he'll live to the age of 125 or 130 or thereabouts.

So, what if he does? Meanwhile, he doesn't exercise, or work, or party, because he hasn't the energy to do anything except stay home and live – I was going to say "from meal to meal," but perhaps "from dosing to dosing" would be more to the point. Why does he want to do that for 130 years?

How dreadfully he must fear death! Death, itself, is most likely not so horrible, but the journey toward it, it seems to me, must be tedious slow if you're doing nothing but pressing on the brake.

It's okay to be amused by people who take such attitudes, but bear in mind that their kind of thinking will lead – and soon – to warning labels on Hostess Twinkies, and perhaps, one day, to "cholesterol taxes" on bacon, and FDA regulation of candy.

An excellent example of what the Food Fascists have already done to us – an example that's especially vexing, less than a week from Thanksgiving – is that largely due to their propaganda, turkey is no longer the delightful festive treat that it was a generation ago. It has been bred, over the years – at the insistence of the many health nuts who eat it as their staple meat – to contain less and less fat, so that it's almost impossible to cook a turkey without drying it out. Even prepared with the best will in the world, with all the love and skill that Grandma can muster, it's likely to come out tough, insipid, and as interesting as pressed sawdust.

We eat so much of it, anyway. There's turkey pastrami, turkey bacon, ground turkey for turkey burgers – all of this to supposedly provide a more healthful alternative to real pastrami, bacon, and hamburger. Walk into any deli with a salad bar in New York City, and you'll find whole roast turkeys hacked into thick slabs, which you'll eat because turkey is low-fat, it's cheap, and you remember that way back, when it was still something special, you liked turkey.

I usually serve goose on Thanksgiving – a far more tasty and interesting bird, which, during the roasting, yields up a quart or more of rendered fat, which is the best stuff in the world for frying eggs or sautéeing a steak. This year, by way of a change, I'll be serving roast rack of venison – a meat that was more likely than turkey to have been served at the first Thanksgiving feast. I shall do my best to forget the fact that venison is low-fat.

Presidential Tastes

Since as far back as we've had Presidents, the American public has been interested in their eating habits. President Clinton's peckishness was a standing joke, prior to his conversion to veganism. The patrician George H. W. Bush's handlers invented the story that he had a fondness for pork rinds, in order to make him appear more folksy. We've had Ronald Reagan's jellybeans; Richard Nixon's cottage cheese with ketchup; Lyndon Johnson's constant losing battle with the scales; and so on, back to George Washington's appetite for madeira and his wife's fruitcake.

Why has this always been such a compelling subject? Probably because of the old expression, "You are what you eat." It's impossible to know much about anyone without learning their habits at table and bottle.

It's no surprise that Jefferson was our most sophisticated eater, and wrote extensively about food, wine and cooking. But who would have thought that Ulysses Grant, a professional soldier, couldn't bear to eat meat that had any blood in it, or that he was squeamish about chicken because he didn't want to eat anything that went on two legs? Or that Franklin Roosevelt, who showed such decisiveness in his economic policies, couldn't bring himself to fire a housekeeper who deliberately fed him dishes she knew he hated?

The White House has seen some huge eaters: Theodore Roosevelt, William Howard Taft, Chester Arthur, Grover Cleveland, and the aforementioned Slick Willie. Of Lyndon Johnson, it was said that "he would eat anything that wouldn't bite him first."

Abraham Lincoln, on the other hand, was notoriously indifferent to food; he often had to be reminded to eat. Once, when he was having breakfast at his desk, a visitor remarked, "I see you drink milk for breakfast, rather than coffee." Lincoln, who'd been eating rather mechanically as he concentrated on his work, looked at his tray for the first time and said with some surprise, "As a matter of fact I do prefer coffee, but they don't seem to have sent me in any."

Richard Nixon's plebeian tastes in food were well known. When they were dining alone, the Nixons would enjoy economical middle-class dishes such as meat loaf, enchiladas, or tamale pie. Nixon's critics used even this against him, claiming it as proof that he was a hick as well as a hack.

Harry Truman, in his diary, described a typical meal at the White House when his wife and daughter were home in Missouri:

"A butler came in very formally and said, 'Mr. President, dinner is served.' I walk into the dining room... . Barnett in tails and white tie pulls out my chair, pushes me up to the table. John in tails and white tie brings me a plate, Barnett brings me a tenderloin, John brings me asparagus, Barnett brings me carrots and beets. I have to eat alone and in silence in the candle-lit room. I ring. Barnett takes the plate and butter plates. John comes in with a napkin and silver crumb tray – there are no crumbs but John has to brush them off the table anyway. Barnett brings me a plate with a finger bowl and doily and John puts a glass saucer and a little bowl on the plate. Barnett brings me some chocolate custard. John brings me a demitasse...and my dinner is over. I take a hand bath in the finger bowl and go back to work. What a life!"

At least, by then, Truman was rid of the tyrannical Henrietta Nesbitt, the housekeeper he'd inherited from the Roosevelts. Mrs. Nesbitt, it seemed, had served Franklin Roosevelt oatmeal for breakfast, every single day, ignoring the clipped-out newspaper coupons for other breakfast cereals he pointedly sent her. He disliked broccoli, but Mrs. Nesbitt insisted on serving it to him. ("It's good for him; he *should* like it," she would explain.) "My stomach positively rebels," Roosevelt complained in a note to his wife, "and this does not help my relations with foreign powers. I bit two of them today." But Mrs. Nesbitt stayed on; even the Trumans put up with this behavior for some time before giving her the axe.

Alcohol, as well as food, has been an issue for Presidential historians and trivialists. Franklin Pierce, probably our worst President, was called by critics "the hero of many a well-fought bottle." Three other Presidents held in low esteem by Posterity – James Buchanan, Ulysses Grant, and Warren Harding – were also heavy drinkers. Truman drank rather a lot, too, but spaced his drinking throughout the day, so it did him more good than harm.

Grant, though not a big eater, set one of the best Presidential tables on formal occasions. One invariable item on his menus was Roman punch, which was made chiefly of lemon sherbet mixed with rum, served in a scooped-out orange skin. But Grant's successor as President, Rutherford Hayes, decreed that no alcohol would be served at the White House during his administration. (New York's elegant Senator Roscoe Conkling sneered, after a dinner at the Hayes White House, "It was a splendid occasion; the water flowed like champagne!") The staff, taking pity on the imbibers, continued to serve Roman punch between courses – but, according to Hayes' memoirs, "the joke...was not on us but on the drinking people. My orders were to flavor [the oranges] strongly with the same flavor that is found in Jamaica rum. ...There was not a drop of spirits in them!"

One White House staffer noted that such, indeed, had been President Hayes' instructions – but the only people who'd been served the non-alcoholic oranges were the Hayeses; everyone else at the table got the genuine article!

This story is of a piece with what most of us remember about Hayes: that he was a decent, incorruptible man who entered the White House via a stolen election, engineered by his underlings while he remained blissfully unaware. Analogous parallels, I don't doubt, can be drawn on the eating and drinking habits of our other 43 Chief Executives.

Fancy A Cuppa Cha?

You just can't get a decent cup of tea, in this country, outside of a private home. Even hotel lobbies and tea shops that pride themselves on providing a charming afternoon tea will almost invariably serve you with a pot of fairly hot water and a selection of tea bags – which have never yet produced drinkable tea. The craft of making tea has been utterly lost to Americans (except for a few aging hippies, who are likely, in any case, to use some flavorless, fragrance-free variety of green tea). Most of us don't even know that there's a difference between tea made with tea bags (with most people trying to wring two cups out of one pathetic bag of pulverized leaves) and tea made with whole, loose leaves, in a pot.

We're a coffee-drinking nation; we have been since the Boston Tea Party, and I would agree that coffee's the superior beverage in the morning, at least, when we need a good wake-up jolt. Still, we're missing out on a lot by maintaining our ignorance of tea. It provides, I think, a pleasanter sort of high in the afternoon and evening than does coffee; furthermore, a love of tea will introduce you to a great deal more poetry, lore, and minutiæ than will a love of coffee.

The definitive essay on how to make tea properly has already been written: "A Nice Cup Of Tea," by George Orwell, appeared in England's *Evening Standard* on January 12, 1946, and can still be found in anthologies of Orwell's essays and journalism (which by the way are better writing than most of his fiction). I won't go over ground that Orwell has covered except to express my agreement with him on a couple of points.

First, use loose leaves, and put them directly into the pot (or use a muslin infuser if you must) as opposed to imprisoning them in a ball or a basket – and use a lot of them. As one of the characters in James Joyce's *Ulysses* remarked, "When I makes tea I makes tea, and when I makes water I makes water; God send I never make them in the same pot!"

Don't use this wimpy green jasmine slop that you get in Chinese restaurants. You want your end product to be as black and thick as molasses. Bring the pot to the kettle, when you're putting in the hot water, so that it'll be still boiling when it hits the leaves, and give the pot a good shake before you pour.

Orwell is also quite right when he advises against using sugar. Tea, he contends, is supposed to be bitter, just as beer is supposed to be bitter. If you must sweeten your tea, the way to do it is to eat cake or cookies with it; never put sugar (or honey) directly into tea.

This issue – that of putting sugar in tea – gives you an idea of how tea has been used over the centuries to make a political, social or æsthetic point. One of the funniest political cartoons I've ever seen was published in 1792, when King George III, during a nationwide austerity program, announced that the Royal Family would be giving up sugar in their tea. The cartoon, by James Gillray, shows the King, the Queen, and five of their daughters at tea. The King, sipping contentedly, is crying "O delicious! Delicious!" while the hideously grinning Queen Charlotte encourages her sulky Princesses: "Oh, my dear Creatures, do but Taste it! You can't think how nice it is without Sugar, and then consider how much Work you'll save the poor Blackamoors by leaving off the use of it! And above all, remember how much expense it will save your poor Papa! O it's charming cooling Drink!"

The use of milk in tea is also supposed to be fraught with import, and in fact it is. Some people put milk into the cup first, and then add tea, and some do it the other way round – and for some reason the higher your social standing, the more likely you are to put the tea in first, and then add milk! I believe it was Evelyn Waugh who wrote, "All nannies, and many governesses, put the milk in first." This strange tendency has developed into a synonym for "tacky," widely used in the United Kingdom: "My dear, she *is* rather milk-in-first, isn't she?"

The difference between afternoon tea and "high tea" is also one of social class – but the difference is exactly the opposite of what you might think. Afternoon tea is what the middle and upper classes take as a light snack at four or five in the afternoon: tea, bread and butter, cucumber sandwiches, cakes, scones, and perhaps a glass of sherry afterwards. High tea is taken by the working class, slightly later in the day – say, 6:30 – and it constitutes their evening meal, being usually more substantial than afternoon tea. (One story, probably apocryphal, has it that the term comes from "high T," an abbreviated form of "high time we had something to eat.")

One might be tempted to believe that only ignorant American lummoxes make the mistake of referring to the more upper-class of these two repasts as high tea, but I've heard Brits and South Africans (who can be more English than the English) make the same mistake. What sets my teeth on edge is when a supposedly sophisticated travel writer tells her readers about the charming oh-so-veddy-British hotel in Boston or Vancouver where you can get "high tea" on silver service in the delightful Victorian lobby every afternoon. In that context, the misusage is *really* "milk-in-first"!

Politics And The Law

Social Justice

A capitalist and a socialist are standing side-by-side on a street corner, watching a man drive past in a big expensive car. The capitalist thinks, "One day, I'll be able to afford a car every bit as nice as that one." The socialist thinks, "One day, I'll have that son of a bitch out of that car."

When I'm explaining Libertarianism – especially when I'm explaining it to children and teenagers – I'm often accused of not caring about social justice. When I ask what the questioner means by social justice, I'm usually told in vague terms that it means some sort of redistribution of wealth. In other words, taking from the rich and giving to the poor. I have to disappoint people by replying that that isn't my idea of social justice.

I'll invariably get a shocked laugh from a classroomful of kids when I give them the example of Robin Hood. "When I read the story of Robin Hood, when I was smaller than any of yall," I'll say, "when he died at the end, I jumped up and cheered! He was nothing but a common mugger who should have been hanged in the public square!" Apparently none of the kids had heard that opinion before.

Most libertarians believe in the principle of nonaggression. That is, we believe that you should not be allowed to initiate force or fraud against another person. If someone starts with you, you may retaliate – but you mustn't start with anyone. And when I look back on my schooling, I reflect that for generations, children have been taught from an early age to glorify and romanticize the initiation of force, to admire people who start with others.

Consider Robin Hood. We've always been taught that he was a good guy because "he stole from the rich to give to the poor." Really, does that make him a good guy? He waylaid people on lonely highways and threatened them with death if they didn't hand over their money. To me – and to any decent person, I should think – there would be the end of it. You don't do that. If you do it, you're deserving of punishment and universal odium.

But apparently not, in the case of Bob Hood. He gets a pass because, after all, he stole money to give to those who pre-sumably needed it more than the person from whom he took it.

Would you buy that argument, if someone stopped you in a dark alley, put a knife to your throat, went through your pockets, and explained that he was thinking only of the downtrodden and the underfed? Would you walk away from that experience think-ing, "Gosh, what a good guy! And I sure deserved that treatment, for presuming to carry money on my person!"? Would you root for the mugger, and root against the cops who were trying to ar-rest him?

But, you might argue, Robin Hood only mugged rich peo-ple! Okay, then: Are you saying it's fine to waylay and rob people whom you think have too much money? How much is too much, and who gets to decide? Is it okay to kill these rich people if they resist? How about if someone decides that you're rich enough to get that treatment?

(In any case, according to the legend, Robin Hood didn't just rob extremely rich people. He mostly just robbed whomever looked like he might have money on him, such as a farmer coming home from market with the cash he'd just made for his produce.)

We encounter many Robin Hood types in American cul-ture. Perhaps our best-known example is Jesse James. I well remember learning in school, at the age of 12, several poems and songs about the heroic Jesse James who stole from the rich to give to the poor. Laying aside the question of whether the motive justified the act, the plain truth is that Jesse James did nothing of the kind. In real life he was a guerrilla fighter during the Civil War (on the Confederate side), and took to robbing banks and stagecoaches afterwards. His robberies benefited only himself and his gang – and never amounted to a huge pile of money at that. During several of those robberies, the James Gang killed one or more innocent parties.

I recall the classroom discussion of those poems. Several of the boys, who knew a little about the Wild West, pointed out that in fact the James Gang did not rob the rich to help the poor. But never once did we debate the issue of whether or not his robberies should have been excused if indeed he'd had altruistic motives. Why didn't we?

Probably the most egregious recent example of a Robin Hood type is Che Guevara: a terrorist and murderer, responsible for the deaths of some hundreds of Cubans, but all forgiven because (according to legend) he was acting on behalf of "the people." You'll see his image on t-shirts in college towns all over the U.S., particularly at left-wing demonstrations. Of course as a Libertarian I will defend anyone's right to wear such a t-shirt, but I'm sometimes tempted to ask a wearer, courteously, what he finds admirable about Che. I resist that temptation, though, because I'm afraid of hearing a response that would cause my head to explode.

One can understand a reflexive, unthinking admiration for a rebel, a trickster, particularly if he can in some way be made to look like a champion of the underdog. But to admire a common thief and murderer – or to deny that that was what he was, or to somehow rationalize his behavior – seems to me to require a despicable attitude.

An Insane Legal Concept

Since the early 1980s, the plea or verdict of "guilty but mentally ill" has gained popularity in American courts. I believe it's an evil, unjust verdict, and should be abolished.

"Guilty but mentally ill" is a new, and very American, jurisprudential concept. Its inception was the result of a well-known Federal criminal trial, *U.S. v. Hinckley,* in which the defendant, John Hinckley, Jr., was on trial for attempting to assassinate then-President Ronald Reagan. Mr. Hinckley was found "not guilty by reason of insanity," and currently remains confined to a hospital, with little prospect of ever being released except on occasional weekend visits to his family.

That verdict didn't go down well with the Wad. The most loudly reported opinion from the man in the street was that it was a miscarriage of justice; that Mr. Hinckley was a malingerer; that if he could be found not guilty by reason of insanity, any criminal could escape punishment by offering the same defense. A cry went up to abolish the insanity defense entirely, or (as finally was done in some states) to institute a verdict of guilty but mentally ill.

By use of the latter, a defendant who is determined to have been mentally incapacitated at the time he committed his crime will, while serving his sentence, receive psychiatric treatment till brought to a level of mental health at which he can understand that he's being punished for something. At that point, he'll be allowed to serve the rest of his sentence as a regular prisoner, just as if he'd been fully responsible for his criminal act.

This practice, apparently, was instituted to satisfy the great many people who feel that punishment, rather than justice, is the main purpose of the criminal justice system, and that therefore even someone who commits his crime as the result of a devastating mental illness – perhaps not even knowing that he committed a crime at all – must take the consequences just the same as if he'd committed his crime in full possession of his faculties.

This strikes me as some of the most blatant evidence that the average American is wicked, stupid and sadistic. What we're saying, in effect, is this: "Okay, you had a heart attack and started staggering around, clawing at the air. In the course of your flounderings, you hit this woman in the eye. That's assault and battery, and as soon as you've recovered from your heart attack, you're gonna do 90 days in the county jail."

*

The M'Naghten Rule, which most states use to define insanity, is pretty clear. It states that a defendant is not guilty, by reason of insanity, if he is so impaired as to not have known what he was doing, or, if he did know what he was doing, didn't know that it was wrong. This rule may or may not have been applied correctly in the Hinckley case; it's debatable. What's indisputable is the fact that Hinckley's acquittal on the grounds of insanity was an extremely rare instance. Any criminal lawyer or judge will tell you that the frequency of successful insanity pleas is, and has always been, infinitesimal.

I can think, off-hand, of only three other instances where that defense was used successfully, and in two of those cases, the defendant's insanity was only nominally the main point of the case for the defense:

• In the case of *Virginia v. Bobbitt*, in which Lorena Gallo Bobbitt was tried for mutilating her husband, Ms. Gallo's clear subtextual defense was "The son-of-a-bitch had it coming to him." The jury apparently agreed, and on that basis, they acquitted her. Ms. Gallo was subsequently released after a few days' evaluation in a mental hospital.

• In the 1946 case of *U.S. v. Pound*, the poet Ezra Pound claimed that insanity drove him to make anti-U.S., pro-Fascist propaganda broadcasts during World War II. He was subsequently confined, in relative luxury, to a mental hospital for 12 years. Nobody really thought Pound was crazy. The subtextual defense was, "This is one of the world's most eminent living poets; we can't hang *him* for treason!"

• In the third instance, the defense was used to secure a *harsher* sentence. When the first assassination attempt on a U.S. President took place (on Andrew Jackson, in 1835), there was no crime on the books for which the would-be assassin, the obviously delusional Richard Lawrence, could be charged – other than simple assault, for which he could get only a few days in jail! Therefore his lawyer, Francis Scott Key (otherwise famous), pled him not guilty by reason of insanity to ensure that society would be permanently protected from him.

*

A criminal defendant is either insane or not. If insane, he cannot be held responsible for his actions, nor punished for them, beyond the confinement necessary to prevent further criminal behavior and/or to effect a cure. This must necessarily be somewhat unpleasant for him, but – since there can be nothing punitive about it – it's society's duty to make it pleasanter than prison. If he was *not* insane, at the time of the crime, then he is responsible for his actions, and by God let's ship him off to the big house. Certainly we can, and should, provide him with psychotherapy or whatever else, within reason, that he might require to improve his mental health, but that should be available to any prisoner, regardless of whether he's claiming serious mental impairment.

The purpose of prison must be to rehabilitate the prisoner, or to protect society from him: not to punish. Else, we might as well revive the lash, or the stocks, or bodily mutilation, and thus save the taxpayers a fortune.

Victim's Rights = Pernicious Hysteria

Advocacy for "victim's rights" seems to be a popular adjunct to our current mania for dealing out ever-harsher punishments to criminals. Along with calls for longer sentences, the abolition of parole, more prisons, and more executions, many of us are advocating allowing victims of crime, or their families, to have a say in the sentencing of the criminal, and to lay hold of the criminal's property by way of recompense. It has even got to the point where President Clinton is advocating a constitutional amendment that would guarantee certain rights to crime victims – a move that would utterly subvert the basic ideas behind our system of justice.

Criminal justice is not a vengeance-fest. There's a reason why a criminal case is called, say, The People of the State of Missouri *versus* Joe Blow. The reason is that the case is a matter of the people, as a unit, judging and sentencing a criminal in as cold and impartial a manner as possible. We have civil courts to deal with emotional factors such as the victim's pain and suffering. In a criminal court, such factors must sing mighty small if fairness is to be ensured.

Certainly, the victim ought to be recompensed if possible. Fines imposed on a defendant could go to restoring the victim's lost goods, or to salve emotional distress.

To ensure that the victim's suffering receives at least symbolic acknowledgement, we might empower a jury to levy civil damages on a defendant, as is done in several European countries.

There, the prosecution team often consists of public prosecutors, representing the state on the criminal matter, and private attorneys, pleading the victims' and their families' suits for civil damages.

(Of course, this could prove unworkable in the United States, in that civil and criminal cases here have very different rules concerning procedure, evidence, and burden of proof. For example, in the O.J. Simpson trial, had the civil and criminal matters been adjudicated by the same jury, Simpson would undoubtedly not have had a civil judgement entered against him.)

The victim impact statement, which has become a standard and well-publicized feature of many high-profile criminal cases, has no place in a court of law. It is simply tasteless, not to mention inflammatory, to allow anyone not an officer of the court to exhort the judge to impose a heavy penalty on the prisoner.

I favor imposition of sentence immediately following the verdict, with no additional pleading, as is often done in European courts. The judge, after all, doesn't need much information beyond the prisoner's prior criminal record, in order to determine a proper punishment. He already has the facts of the case before him, and will have formed an opinion as to the heinousness of the prisoner's crime. To my mind, there are few more imposing examples of the swiftness, sureness, and integrity of British justice than the bewigged judge – with no help from the prosecution or defense – giving the convicted defendant a brief but bitter scolding before imposing a sentence and intoning, "Take the prisoner down."

Much of the emphasis on allowing victims to speak in court, I suspect, has to do with the increase in televised court cases. Sure, the sob sisters and armchair psychologists will hold that it's important to let the victim speak in court for the sake of "closure." Supposedly, seeing the man who killed my wife being sentenced to death or imprisonment isn't sufficient to allow me to sleep properly. No, only a vengeful rant in open court will suffice.

I doubt this. I wonder how many crime victims truly feel that it's important for them to stand up in court and demand maximum punishment. I suspect, though of course I can't prove, that the great majority of them would just as soon stay home, if it weren't for the social pressure on them to climb onto a soapbox *pour épater la canaille.* Closure, my hind foot! Especially in a high-profile case, the role of the victim or his family is to provide grist for Geraldo, Oprah, Sally Jessy, and their ilk. The victim impact statement is often demanded simply for the sake of drama.

Some of the best drama on TV, these days, is found on truTV (formerly Court TV), which televises actual trials. For consistency of product, it's untouchable: certainly far more gripping than *All My Children* could ever have hoped to be. Never let it be said that we don't get any good murders anymore. truTV brings us at least three or four humdingers each year, in addition to equally scintillating trials for non-capital crimes the like of which some of us didn't even know existed till we started watching these delightful real-life dramas.

Much though I enjoy the entertainment, I wonder whether our judicial system is uplifted by these televised trials. If, as is painfully obvious, the viewing public watches truTV for the drama rather than for the legal education, drama is what they will get – and might that not come, from time to time, at the expense of justice?

One of the most titillating murder cases ever shown on American TV was that of Air Force cadet David Graham, who was convicted of murder in a Texas courtroom for the December 1995 shooting death of a former high school mate, Adrianne Jones. Mr. Graham's girlfriend, former Annapolis cadet Diane Zamora, had been convicted of the same crime a few months before; both are now serving sentences of life imprisonment with no chance of parole for 40 years.

According to the two murderers' confessions (which both later repudiated) Ms. Zamora, outraged that Mr. Graham had had a fleeting affair with Ms. Jones, insisted that she be killed. The two of them abducted the victim, bashed her head in with a blunt instrument, and shot her.

To me, the most interesting legal point was the admissibility of Mr. Graham's confession. Written in the stilted style of an "Honorable Mention" entry in a Bad Bulwer-Lytton contest, it was full of cloying and circumlocutory references to Mr. Graham's and Ms. Zamora's sexual relationship, a nauseatingly lyric description of their conspiracy to murder Miss Jones, and an excessive use of the passive voice that betrayed the writer's military education. Mr. Graham subsequently disowned this confession, stating that it had been obtained under duress, but the judge ruled that despite its stylistic atrociousness, it could be introduced as evidence. Apparently, although his interrogators had used strong language in urging him to confess, they had not used physical torture or false threats, and he had been fully aware of his right to say nothing.

In terms of drama, the high point was the performance of Mr. Graham's attorney, Dan Cogdell. His client was lost from the get-go, but by the time the jury filed out to begin deliberations, many of the spectators felt that just possibly, Mr. Cogdell had clouded the issue enough to produce one or two votes for acquittal – which would have been all he needed. If the confession hadn't been in evidence, and with Ms. Zamora refusing to testify on Fifth Amendment grounds, the prosecution would have been hard put to place Mr. Graham at the crime scene. Mr. Cogdell managed to discredit several prosecution witnesses, and in his concluding *plaidoyer* he again raised doubts about Mr. Graham's confession. More important, for a TV viewer, was his frank and folksy performance in interviews outside the courtroom.

The most sickening point about the trial was the crime itself. The contemporaneous, equally celebrated, Peterson-Grossberg baby-killing case was a matter of two panicky fools who deserved, in my opinion, to get off lightly. The Graham-Zamora murder was a grossly deliberate crime committed by people who were fully aware of the heinousness of their offense, and who, in my opinion, deserved the gallows.

However, that does not excuse the vulgarity of the televised coverage of this trial and of other trials, which I suspect is slowly leading to a corruption of the criminal justice system.

Probably no more blatant example of this corruption can be brought forth, than the victim impact statement. These were not commonly allowed till a few years ago – coincidentally, right around the time Court TV went on the air. Is it possible that one purpose of these statements is not to promote justice, but to provide the spectators with a little more bang for the buck?

At the conclusion of the Graham trial, one of the Court TV commentators was burbling with positively epicurean delight about "the range of emotions displayed" in the several victim impact statements, as though Ms. Jones' relatives had been performing at a forensics tournament.

The Associated Press reported, "Several jurors wiped away tears when they listened to statements from the victim's family."

What if, one of these days, the sentencing judge is similarly affected, and in a moment of emotion gives the defendant double the sentence he'd planned to hand down?

This brings me to another recent development in criminal justice: the abolition or restriction of parole. Once again, this has coincided more or less with the growing popularity of televised trials. Could it be that this is because viewers of these trials tend to be punitive people, who enjoy seeing people severely sentenced, and demand satisfaction so loudly that their legislators oblige them with ever more draconian criminal penalties?

I'm opposed to the death penalty, but I'd not have shed any tears if Graham and Zamora had been executed. However, since they have been sentenced to prison, I feel that a minimum of 40 years is ridiculous. I say any prisoner serving a life sentence should have a chance at parole in 10 years – maybe not a very good chance, but a chance. Prisoners sentenced to a term of years should be able to apply for parole one-third into the sentence, and maybe even sooner. I can't get away from the notion that the purpose of prison is more to reform than to punish – and the sooner this can be accomplished, the better, even if it means springing a criminal before the vengeance-freaks have gotten their rocks off.

I can hear some readers saying, "See how you feel when someone you love is killed or raped."

As it happens, a very close friend of mine was murdered by a serial killer. And of course I wanted that son-of-a-bitch to be strung up. However, since I was attached to the victim, I would hardly be the person to go to for advice on what the sentence should be. And had I been given the opportunity, I would never have dreamed of standing up in court to urge the murderer's execution – no matter how richly he deserved it.

What are a victim's rights? Compassion, certainly. Civil damages when possible. Vengeance, or the right to demand it in a court of law? Never.

Shouts Of 'Fire,' And 'Fighting Words'

The United States Supreme Court has agreed to rule on whether a dead soldier's family can sue protesters who picketed near their son's burial service with signs that suggested that military casualties were God's punishment of the U.S. for tolerating homosexuality. A jury in Maryland had previously awarded Albert Snyder, the father of the dead soldier, $10 million in damages in his suit against the Rev. Fred Phelps and his Westboro Baptist Church on the grounds that by demonstrating near the burial service, the defendants had invaded the mourners' privacy and inflicted emotional distress. That judgement was thrown out last fall by a Federal Court of Appeals, on free-speech grounds.[*]

Now, it transpires, a judge has ordered Snyder to pay Phelps' legal bills – to the tune of about $16,000 – in view of the fact that the original verdict was overturned. This order has met with widespread outrage, and a number of people – most prominent among them is talk show host Bill O'Reilly – have stepped in to pay these bills on Snyder's behalf.

I submit that O'Reilly et al. are entirely within their rights, to contribute financially to Snyder's cause. However, I take the position that in these circumstances, Snyder should, indeed, be made to pay Phelps' bills.

It's clear to me that Snyder and his lawyers brought this

---

[*] The Supreme Court upheld the Court of Appeals' ruling, and the Westboro Baptist Church's right to free speech, in a decision announced in March, 2011.

suit not because the Snyder family suffered financial damages, or emotional damages that were worth more than one dollar. No: I submit that they brought this suit with the objective of financially ruining Phelps and his family. In my book, that's malicious prosecution, and should not be tolerated.

The suit amounted to an attempt to punish the defendant with bankruptcy for harshing the plaintiff's mellow. The plaintiff wanted to feel sad and solemn and was made to feel angry instead. That's unpleasant, but it's not actionable, in my opinion.

Are Phelps, et al., horrible people? I'd say so. But can we use the justice system to bankrupt someone – that being the obvious objective here – as punishment for extreme obnoxiousness? I'd say no. Our laws protecting freedom of speech do not exist to protect speech that most people approve of. Such speech needs no protection. The laws exist, rather, to protect speech that we abominate: speech that would be deeply offensive to most sensible people. The laws exist, you might almost say specifically, to protect the disgusting antics of Phelps and his odious posse.

What did Phelps, et al., do to Snyder? They carried signs, at some distance from the graveside, apparently. Did they interfere with the service? No. Did they threaten? No. Did they physically harm or assault or obstruct anyone? No.

Columnist Michael Smerconish, writing in the *Philadelphia Inquirer*, stated, "The lawyer in me hopes the court restricts Westboro's free-speech rights in the same way it has in the past with regards to defamation, obscenity, and so-called fighting words. It's a crime to yell 'Fire!' in the theater. It should be one to yell 'fag' at a fallen soldier's funeral as well."

I suggest that that's not the lawyer in Mr. Smerconish talking. It's the emotional idiot talking.

First of all, let's talk about "fighting words." The law does recognize that term; does recognize that some words, in some circumstances, are so offensive that the person who utters them can reasonably expect a blow in response. However, "fighting words" is an extenuating circumstance to be used on behalf of the person who threw the punch. It is *not* an excuse for prosecuting the speaker of those words, either civilly or criminally.

In other words, if I insult you in some unspeakable way, and you punch me in the face for it, the courts will take my provocation into account when deciding whether, and to what extent, you should be prosecuted for hitting me. However, the courts will not, should not, must not prosecute me for having uttered those words.

Now let's talk about the idea that Phelps' behavior was equivalent to shouting "fire" in a crowded theatre. I've heard that one from other commentators besides Smerconish, and it's a moronic argument whomever it comes from.

First of all, strictly speaking, it's *not* a crime to yell "fire" in the theatre, as Smerconish asserts. The consequences of that action – if a stampede results in injuries or property damage, for example – might be punishable. If no damage results, the worst charge that could be made to stick might be disorderly conduct: a civil offense, much like a traffic ticket. However, no sensible policeman would write the ticket, and no sensible theatre manager would demand that the cop do more than throw the offender out on the street.

Second, carrying signs (or yelling "fag," for that matter) does not constitute a potential danger to anyone but the carriers or the yellers themselves. To whom else were Phelps, et al., creating a hazard? Okay, so their conduct made people turn away in disgust – and well it might have. But I submit that the odium of their fellow man is the only punishment that can rightly be brought against them.

If Snyder's suit against Phelps is allowed to go forward, it will confirm the already prevalent (and horrifying) notion that you can break anyone you wish to break, merely by bringing suit against him – however frivolous that suit might be. He'll still have to defend himself against it, and pay astronomical legal costs.

That's a particularly pernicious danger in a situation like this one, where an emotion-based argument can persuade a jury to impose outrageous damages.

The calls for the reinstatement of those ridiculous damages – or even just the reinstatement of the suit – are, to me, more offensive than anything Phelps and his pals might have said. Phelps can be laughed off, on the grounds that he's ultimately powerless. A whole gang of imbeciles condoning the seizure of his assets: that constitutes a real danger.

An Easy Win In The Drug War

The increase of drug-testing in the workplace, the contemplation of drug-testing in the schools, and the ease with which most people seem to accept it, proves that we're getting our asses kicked in the "war on drugs." We are turning on ourselves, attacking our most basic right: the right to be left alone.

On TV the other day, in a "person-on-the-street" interview situation, a teenage girl said that random drug testing of high-school students would be a good thing, "Because then we would find drug-users we might not have known about." It's true that children, especially girls, have always tended to be contemptuous of civil liberties, but I'd never heard anything so extreme before. It's of a piece with the surprising percentage of young folks who say that "offensive" speech ought to be criminalized.

We've always loved minding other people's business, but the spirit of prohibitionism and officiousness that currently pervades this country is the most repulsive cultural trend I've seen in my 50-plus years. Drugs pose a much smaller threat.

We made a huge mistake, generations ago, by making many drugs illegal. We compounded that mistake when we started referring to "the war on drugs." By doing that, we made it impossible to change our direction. We must march forward, now, into the grave we've dug ourselves – or admit that we lost a war.

If, however, we truly wish to reduce the harm done by recreational drugs – as opposed to carrying on a "war" that any intellectually honest person will admit is unwinnable – there's one simple solution: LEGALIZE ALL DRUGS.

As of this minute, any and all drugs are entirely legal and unrestricted. Here's what will happen:

• Drug use in general rises temporarily; then drops steeply once the novelty wears off, staying at levels far below what we saw prior to legalization.

• Since you can now buy a joint or a vial of crack at your local Duane Reade or Walgreen's, prices plummet. Nobody buys drugs on the street anymore, because the street hoodlums don't guarantee their product, and can't compete on price. They're out of business!

• Since drugs are so cheap and easy to come by, the rate of violent crime drops dramatically. Hardly anybody, any longer, has to mug someone for a fix!

• The problem of prison overcrowding is solved almost overnight, as nobody is punished for sale or possession of drugs.

It should be pointed out that a certain element of our society *wants* to have a lot of people in prison, because it's good for the economy! The corrections industry is big and growing, and prisons are a significant sub-market of the real estate industry. There is even a real estate investment trust (REIT) that specializes in prisons. That's right: You can actually own stock in prisons. If we drastically reduced the prison population, Wall Street would lay an egg, and unemployment would kick up a point or two, and we sure can't have that!

You might ask, by making drugs legal and available, won't we encourage people to wreck their lives by abusing those drugs?

Do we encourage alcoholism by making alcohol legal? Do we encourage obesity by allowing Kentucky Fried Chicken and Pizza Hut to peddle their delicacies? No, we do not. We merely allow people to make their own choices. If I choose to clog my arteries with Big Macs, turn my brain to slosh with crack, turn my lungs into blackened golf balls with cigarettes, it is nobody else's goddam business.

Does that mean we have no recourse against drug abuse? Of course not! If a fellow's heroin habit is adversely affecting his job performance, his employer can sack him! If we're worried about people committing crimes under the influence of drugs, why not pass a law that makes drug use an aggravating circumstance in determining punishment? Or why not make a punishable offense of any intoxication that contributes to a crime? (We do that with traffic violations, after all. If you run a red light while sober, it's a little bitty fine; if you do it drunk, it sometimes means jail time.)

I also favor allowing the use of performance-enhancing drugs and steroids in athletic competition, instead of forcing athletes to go through a bunch of tests (which are easy to beat anyway). After all, how is the use of drugs or steroids different from the use of one diet in preference to another?

Look at it this way: I could win the 100-meter dash in the Olympics, and tell the press afterwards, "I owe my performance to eating a lot of pemmican," and immediately pemmican recipes would be flying about the Internet and the print media; Hormel and Oscar Mayer would start selling pemmican as fast as they could make it; then there'd be low-fat pemmican, turkey pemmican, and even tofummican. I'd get tens of millions of dollars to endorse the damn stuff. But if I say, "I owe my performance to anabolic steroids," my medals are stripped and I'm an international disgrace.

Why? I'll tell you. It's because everyone knows that anabolic steroids really do enhance performance, while anyone with half a brain knows that pemmican's benefits are marginal at best!

(Philip Roth confronts this issue in his book, *The Great American Novel*, in which a scientist feeds a baseball team "Jewish Wheaties," which causes them to go on an incredible winning streak. One of the players objects that it's not fair to win ballgames by eating Jewish Wheaties, since after all, *real* Wheaties – the "Breakfast of Champions" – don't enhance an athlete's performance at all. "That's what makes them real!" he argues.)

Here's the bottom line: If you're worried about someone beating you on the playing field, take better steroids. If you resent someone for having a better time than you're having, ask him where he buys his acid. If you object, on principle, to drug use, don't use drugs. Got it? Good.

The Nanny Trial*

I. American Justice Resurgent

The so-called "Nanny Trial," in Cambridge, Mass., in which testimony ended today and a verdict is likely tomorrow, is both reassuring and disturbing. Reassuring, because a defendant who many of us feared would be railroaded really is getting a fair trial; disturbing, for any number of reasons.

The case involves Louise Woodward, a teenaged English *au pair* accused of killing an eight-month-old baby, Matthew Eappen, by shaking him and smashing his skull against a solid surface. At the time of the alleged crime, Ms. Woodward was sensationalized as a monster, and her conviction on first-degree murder charges appeared certain. Tomorrow, she will almost surely be acquitted after a short deliberation – and rightly so.

The indictment for first-degree murder was preposterous, and it's hard to see why it was brought. The prosecution produced not one iota of evidence to indicate that she killed Matthew Eappen with malice, premeditation, or depraved indifference. At the outside, Ms. Woodward might have killed the baby by accident, and the prosecution couldn't even prove that!

---

* Joseph Dobrian wrote these two essays just before, and just after, the verdict in the murder trial of British *au pair* Louise Woodward in 1998.

Lacking evidence, the prosecution tried to convince the jury that Ms. Woodward was a strange, dislikable person, and therefore guilty. She evidently has her faults. She's immature, obsessive, perhaps selfish and lazy – but always within the realm of the normal. For instance, the prosecution tried to make a big thing of the fact that she went to see the musical *Rent* about 20 times in 10 weeks, and indeed that is pretty strange, but it becomes less so when you consider that she's a plain, dough-faced girl with a bad complexion and (evidently) poor social skills. People of that sort often develop limited lives, with a small circle of friends, going to the same places and doing the same things over and over – as you know if you've ever been to a *Star Trek* convention. That doesn't make her a killer.

The correspondents covering the trial for Court TV also got into the act, implying to the viewers that her lack of emotion on the witness stand might be indicative of her guilt. She was, apparently, supposed to have cried more. These correspondents seemed to hold her poise – which I considered commendable – against her, as though she should have resorted to histrionics in order to show us how innocent she was. If that is what our jurors look for, in weighing evidence, I promise you I'll opt to be tried by ordeal if I'm ever up on criminal charges. Fortunately, as stupid as I think most people are, the average juror is far more intelligent than the average Court TV correspondent.

Ms. Woodward's brief (and quickly aborted) attempt at tears on the witness stand appeared to have been rehearsed; it was perfectly on cue, and even her examining counsel pretended to choke up, at one point employing a fake tremor in his voice that must have set the judge to racking his brain for a way to cite him for contempt.

On the other hand, Ms. Woodward would sometimes smile, or even giggle, when recounting the most painful parts of her story. One Court TV reporter referred to her expression as a "smirk," which was unfair. Many of us will smile or giggle when relating terrible news, through sheer nervousness.

The parents of the deceased infant, both practicing physicians, also came in for some criticism – not from counsel, but from people following the case – on the grounds that they were neglectful of their children, leaving them with a teenaged girl for 45 hours per week. Dr. Deborah Eappen in particular was criticized, presumably on the grounds that the mother ought to be the primary care-giver. The Drs. Eappen did appear, from their conduct on the witness stand, to be rather unpleasant people – prim, rigid, stuffy, unbearably conceited yuppie scum – but their conduct as parents probably does not deserve reproach. Less wealthy parents, if both of them have jobs, leave their kids in a day-care center – where the caregivers could be anyone from Mary Poppins to John Wayne Gacy – and we consider this no more than a regrettable necessity. What's going on here, I think, is social envy: We resent a family that can afford to hire an *au pair*, and have a spare bedroom to give her.

It's lucky for Ms. Woodward that her defense is being paid for by the insurance company that covers her *au pair* agency. Hers is clearly a first-rate team of lawyers. With one exception (a bungled motion for a directed acquittal midway through the trial), their preparation has been impeccable. At one point, they astonished the courtroom by establishing that a prosecution witness was likely just a flaky woman who wanted to get her name in the papers. It must have taken them a good deal of detective work to dig up all the dirt they brought in about her financial situation, her employment history, and her personal life. She'd come into the courtroom a key witness; she left a laughingstock. In examining witnesses, whether their own or the prosecution's, her attorneys were flawless. They never stumbled, never asked a question they didn't know the answer to, never bullied. They went through their case as smoothly as a taut wire through cheese.

If Ms. Woodward – clearly not from a wealthy background – had had to pay for her own defense, or had pleaded poverty and used a public defender, she could not possibly have got this kind of representation. It makes you wonder how many people have been convicted on doubtful evidence, just because they lacked the resources to retain first-rate counsel.

That's as may be. Ms. Woodward, anyway, has had a fair trial, in a case that was televised in Great Britain, and followed closely by the British people. It's nice to see our justice system hit a home run when other folks are watching.

II. Fair Trial, Unconscionable Verdict

The conviction of Louise Woodward on a charge of second-degree murder, last night, was a far worse case of jury nullification than was the O.J. Simpson verdict. In the Simpson case, a great deal of incriminating evidence, to which the general public was privy, was kept from the jury. Going strictly on the evidence that was presented to them, it's possible to understand how the Simpson jury could have arrived at an acquittal. In the Woodward case, the jury appears to have willfully ignored both the prosecution's lack of a case, and the judge's instructions, in order to ensure punishment of a defendant they evidently felt was guilty of *something*.

A client of mine, a mother of three, once posited, "All baby killings are manslaughter." I won't go so far as to say that, but this was clearly a case where no charge stronger than manslaughter could be considered proper.

Second-degree murder, in the state of Massachusetts, means intentional killing with malice, but without premeditation. The prosecution could not, and did not, prove premeditation. It gave us some evidence that Ms. Woodward caused the death of Matthew Eappen – *maybe* enough evidence to prove that point beyond a reasonable doubt, although I would not concede even that. On the questions of malice and intent, the most that the prosecution proved was that it was *possible* that she acted with malice and with depraved indifference.

At the prosecution's press conference last night, head prosecutor Gerard Leone looked positively stunned – and not just stunned, but horrified, as though he knew full well that he'd let the matter get out of hand, and had secured a conviction on a greater charge than was warranted. He looked, in fact, the way he might have looked if he'd impatiently given a squalling baby a good shake, and suddenly noticed that it wasn't moving anymore.

It may well be that it was Mr. Leone's closing argument that won the murder conviction. Before he got up to speak, the prosecution's case appeared to be a rather meager collection of conjectures and possibilities. Mr. Leone, in his final plea, brought all these scraps together into a brilliant, dramatic and extremely picturesque oration. The scenario that he presented to the jury as the likely sequence of events was vivid, convincing – and, just possibly, correct – but what he described was manslaughter!

Apparently the jury felt that Ms. Woodward had to be found guilty of something, possibly in order to assuage the largely media-induced hysteria that had been in full howl since the day she was arrested, and which had succeeded in utterly demonizing a young woman who was, at worst, a bit of a brat.

Unless the presiding judge, Hon. Hiller Zobel, sets aside the verdict or reduces the charge to manslaughter*, Ms. Woodward will serve a sentence of life imprisonment. This is the mandatory sentence for second-degree murder in Massachusetts, and it brings up a recent development that I consider a dreadful blot on American justice: the concept of mandatory sentences for non-capital crimes.

---

* He did, a few days later, and Ms. Woodward was set free.

This case is a classic example of why mandatory sentencing is unjust. Setting aside the question of Ms. Woodward's guilt for the moment, it's still pretty clear that she is no danger to society. She's not going to ever repeat the offense. A long term of imprisonment would serve no purpose whatever, other than to satisfy some people's desire to see punishment inflicted, to destroy her life, and to devastate her family. Even on a conviction of second-degree murder – in a case such as this, with a defendant such as this – the possibility of parole in about five years would be far more just.

"Yeah, sure," I can hear some of you saying sarcastically, "she's bright, white and polite. How'd you feel if this were some uneducated, drug-taking, inner-city Negro or Hispanic welfare mother who'd done the same thing to her kid?"

Okay, that's a fair question. And the answer is, I would *not* feel the same way. Louise Woodward clearly is not the dregs of society; she's an ordinary girl who got in over her head and made a mess of it. She had a clean slate going into this case, and I'll stake my kilt she'll have a clean slate when – if – she comes out. If indeed she did kill Matthew Eappen, then public disgrace and the reproaches of her own conscience will have a much stronger effect on her than they would on someone of a different background.

(In the case of the uneducated, drug-using mother, I'd just sterilize her and turn her loose, and let her kill herself with crack.)

One remark that got my blood boiling came from a Court TV anchorperson, who said something to the effect of, "Why all this sympathy for Louise Woodward? What about sympathy for poor Matthew Eappen who's lying in the ground?" So, to avenge Matthew Eappen who's lying in the ground, we're supposed to lock Louise Woodward up for life, just so's we can see someone being punished?

It may be that Louise Woodward caused the death of Matthew Eappen, and if so, that's a bad thing. Far worse, in my opinion, is a team of prosecutors asking a jury to convict on a charge they must have known they had failed to prove. Far worse is a jury of 12 persons sworn to uphold the law, subverting the law so that vengeance, not justice, might be served.

Perhaps, after a case such as this, it's proper to simply cry, "God bless Captain Vere." But that slogan sticks in my throat.

L'Affaire Lewinsky[*]

I. Will Clinton Plead 'Testosteria'?

As I knew would happen, people are now talking about President Clinton suffering from a "disease," an "addiction."

Liz Smith, the syndicated gossip columnist, yesterday wrote that the President needs "an Oprah or Barbara Walters moment. ...his only chance...is to go on television and penitently fess up. He could speak directly to the American people with Hillary and Chelsea by his side in full support. He could say that he has long struggled with a sexual disorder, which...has repeatedly overcome his better judgement and behavior.

"He should offer restitution to Paula Jones and apologize to Monica Lewinsky for taking advantage of her youth. ...Then he could throw himself on the mercy of the American people...say he will go into treatment instantly for his neurotic disorder...then beg the American public to tell him what to do. 'Should I continue in office with this disorder while undergoing medical treatment?'"

This is the most hysterical (and I use that word carefully) version of these sentiments that I've heard so far this week, but other people have come up with comments in the same vein, all based on the idea that President Clinton's philandering is the result of a psychological disorder.

---

[*] Joseph Dobrian wrote these three essays at the time of the discovery of President W.J. Clinton's affair with Monica Lewinsky, and his subsequent impeachment and trial in Congress.

Yes, President Clinton has a severe disorder, possibly the worst that an American in this day and age can have. It's called having a working set of balls. If you listen to the right people, these days, you'll be convinced that to be a normal man is to be mentally ill, brutal, depraved, in need of psychological if not literal castration.

Apparently the President likes having sex with many different partners. So does about 95 percent of the male population, whether hetero or homo, and so it has always been. The only great differences among us men within that 95 percent is that some of us are more attractive than others, and some of us have more opportunity than others to fulfill our desire. To call this desire a disorder is something that would only occur to a woman who hates and fears (and probably secretly envies) male sexuality, or to a man who is painfully aware of his own shortcomings in that department.

Today, the mass media is dominated in great part by women like Liz Smith. In that same camp I might place Gloria Allred, Ann Landers, Shere Hite, and, yes, perhaps Oprah Winfrey: people who miss no opportunity to characterize normal male behavior as something that must be trained out of a man. A Freudian might suggest that such people want to destroy the penis they wish they had, exactly like the child who spitefully smashes another kid's toys.

It's not just the Liz Smiths, the Gloria Allreds, and other people of that mindset, who are contributing to the notion that to be masculine is to be bad. Also feeding that idea are the censorious men of the religious right, who seek to suppress the sexuality of males who are better breeding specimens than they; the neurotic, chip-on-the-shoulder women who file harassment suits because some male co-worker read *Playboy* in the break room; even the millions of soccer moms who are afraid little Davy will get a boo-boo on his finger if he plays American football like a normal red-blooded boy.

I'm glad I'm not young anymore. This kind of thinking was beginning to surface when I was growing up, but not enough to completely cripple me. I worry about the kind of boys we're raising now. It can't be good for them to be told, by authority figure after authority figure, that they are naughty by definition, and that their basic drives must be not just controlled, but virtually eradicated.

President Clinton should get treatment for a neurotic disorder? Now we're calling a healthy libido a neurotic disorder, in effect treating the male genitals as though they were a morbid growth – exactly as some pseudoscientists, years ago, claimed that the uterus was a source of mental illness, and performed hysterectomies on women they deemed unstable! (Hence my only slightly sarcastic use of the word "hysterical" above.)

A certain pop artiste has a reputation for cruising the streets of Manhattan's Lower East Side in her chauffeured limousine, picking up good-looking Hispanic teenagers, and performing fellatio on them. Most of us gleefully remember the (utterly apocryphal) story about a gravel-voiced male recording star having to have his stomach pumped after an excess of that particular activity one night. We might regard these people as a bit extreme in their tastes, but no more than that. Let a man use his penis on too many women, though, and he's disordered.

President Clinton just might let himself be talked into doing the very thing Ms. Smith suggests. That might bring him forgiveness from the Oprah-watching segment of the American public, but would we then be able to face the rest of the world, with such a cringing milksop as our President?

Can you imagine Jack Kennedy so abasing himself? First of all, Kennedy would never have let himself get into such a situation. If one of his interns had come to him, revealing that she'd been asked to testify as to his sexual practices, he'd have replied, with that Kennedy grin, "Say whatever you damn well please," and let her figure out just what she would gain by revealing anything. And what would have happened if the press had asked him, "Did you do it?" He would have grinned again, and wagged his head wryly, and replied, "I'll let you fellows answer that one yourselves," and that would have been that.

Anyone who'd said anything about his sexuality being the result of a mental disorder would have been laughed out of court, and quite right too.

II. Lewinsky Discredits Freud's Assertion

Every time I resolve to write nothing more about the Bill Clinton-Monica Lewinsky relationship, another development comes along that forces me to go back on my word.

If nothing else, according to the latest rumor, the two of them managed to prove that sometimes a cigar is *not* just a cigar. I'm not making a prediction, but it could well be that the story widely reported – that Ms. Lewinsky used one of the President's cigars as a dildo whilst Mr. Clinton appreciatively spanked the First Monkey, just prior to his official meeting with P.L.O. leader Yasir "That's My Baby" Arafat – will be the one item that the President won't be able to live down.

Otherwise solid citizens, plain folks with not much imagination or creativity in other areas of their lives, will sometimes perform weird and original acts in pursuit of sexual stimulation – acts far more bizarre than described above. There can be no condemnation of that practice, in and of itself, on moral grounds. About the worst adjective that one can justifiably apply to it is "decadent." (That is, I'm assuming it was a fairly high-quality, expensive cigar, because a cheap commercial cigar like a Dutch Mas-

ters or a Garcia y Vega would have disintegrated from such vigorous exercise, leaving Ms. Lewinsky with half a cigar swimming
around in her uterine canal.)

  This affair of the cigar isn't the kind of story that causes
righteous indignation, as the plain fact of marital infidelity will, in
some people. A President getting serviced by some floozy kneel-
ing under his desk, the public could stomach – just. But to envi-
sion Ms. Lewinsky with her panties off and her skirt hiked up, engaging in what might be called "performance art," while the President, staring at the action with cross-eyed intensity, brings out the
Executive Love-Thang and commences wagging it to attention...

  We can sum up the national reaction in one word:
"Eeeeeyew!" I mean, it would have been less an affront to the dignity of the Presidency if they'd been exchanging Golden Showers.

  The problem with certain sexual practices is not that
they're offensive-gross, but that they're funny-gross. And when we
discover that our President is just as embarrassingly kinky as any
of us, that discovery can knock a big hole in his ability to lead.

  I can't wait for "Stutterin' John" Melendez to crash the
next White House press briefing. If I were Howard Stern, I'd supply Stutterin' John with the following list of questions:

1. What brand and shape was the cigar?
2. Was it a natural, claro, or maduro wrapper?
3. What was its price?
4. What was its length and ring gauge?
5. Was it smoked afterwards? If so, by whom?
6. If not, did Ms. Lewinsky keep the cigar as a memento, or put it
back in the box? (I mean the humidor on his desk, of course;
not... oh, never mind!)
7. Did she take the band off first? Whether she did or not, did she
subsequently wear it on her finger as a proof of her love?

8. If the cigar was replaced in the humidor following this episode, was it subsequently offered to a visitor to the Oval Office?

9. Was that visitor Supreme Court Justice Clarence Thomas? If it was, did he ask, "Who put pubic hair on this cigar?"

(Just imagine some unsuspecting Friend Of Bill selecting that particular cigar and lighting it up as the President turns red from suppressed laughter:

"This is a fine cigar, Mr. President. A slight suggestion of sea air in the aroma; quite unusual, but I like it!")

Above all, what I want to know is, whose idea was it? And exactly how did the conversation go, when this particular sex act was brought up for discussion? Was it clinical? ("Here, Monica, I've got an idea that you'll find quite jolly. You take this, see, and drop your panties, and...") Or was it an embarrassingly spontaneous moment in which Ms. Lewinsky, overcome with animal lust while making like a Hoover on the Presidential Pants-Monster, suddenly stuck her hand into the humidor, selected a pleasuring implement, and began thrusting wildly while the president, horrified, cried, "God damn it, that's a 20-dollar Montecristo, there!"?

Mind you, I've always had an appreciation for the gross, but till I heard of this rumored episode, I never had the least interest in the details of the President's sex life. This put me over the edge. I don't have time, anymore, to be angry, indignant and disgusted with Kenneth Starr's efforts to seek out every sordid detail; I'm too busy laughing my ass off.

That, I'm pretty sure, has been Mr. Starr's strategy of late: Knowing that he can't get President Clinton on Whitewater, his objective is simple humiliation. And with regard to that objective, he's bowled a perfect score through nine frames. Now, we're all just waiting for a story that might gross us out even worse than the one about the cigar, and we're all pretty confident that we're going to hear one, and pretty soon at that.

I still say that Clinton should not be impeached, nor forced to resign – not over penny-ante foolishness like this. But oh, what foolishness! Apparently, his activities with Ms. Lewinsky included just about everything a person can think of, but *not* actual intercourse, on the grounds, one supposes, that Clinton felt that that act was reserved for his wife (at least while he was President). Now, we see how frustrating such a restriction must have been to him, that he was forced to resort to such bizarre and indelicate acts, as substitutes for good old-fashioned screwing!

Is this the guy we want paying a state visit to the Queen of England? (She'll probably send Princess Margaret to greet him in her place.) Will other heads of state ever be able to sit at the same table with him again, without snickering behind their hands? Might one of them offer him a cigar?

III. How I'd Have Handled It (So To Speak)

President Clinton may yet finish out his term of office despite his wandering weenie, but still, he has utterly botched his current predicament. It would have been so easy for him to have come out of *l'affaire* Lewinsky, if not smelling like a rose, at least in much better shape politically than he is today – but only if he'd been prepared to behave in a very un-Clintonesque manner, all along.

His brief TV appearance on Monday night was about what most of us expected, considering the idiocy and recklessness with which he'd put himself in that situation in the first place. For once, I suspect, he told the truth. He didn't come out and say "I'm sorry," because it was obvious that he was only sorry he'd been caught. He was correct that the matter of sexual infidelity is nobody's business but his and his family's. He was correct to point out that everyone's private life ought to be his or her own affair;

it's just too bad he hadn't learnt that little lesson back when he was pushing through the infamous Communications Decency Act.

The old maxim goes, "A conservative is a liberal who's just been mugged; a liberal is a conservative who's being investigated." We can only hope that this recent experience has opened President Clinton's eyes to what his own civil liberties policies have led to.

This whole business merely confirms what we've known all along: Whether or not he's performing his Presidential duties well, Mr. Clinton is a slime-doggie. Those who have supported him have done so in full knowledge of that fact. Several TV commentators have remarked that the people who have reason to feel betrayed are the President's aides and surrogates who in good faith defended him against charges of sexual misconduct, on the assumption that he was innocent. I say Nuts to that. If those people really were so delusional as to believe he was innocent, then they deserve the embarrassment they're feeling now. Experience keeps a dear school, but fools will learn in no other. And if, as I suspect, those aides and surrogates maintained that Clinton was innocent when they knew full well that he wasn't, then they were lying just as surely as their boss was, and any injury to their reputations is well-earned.

How could I have handled the whole mess better, if I'd been President?

First of all, when the Monica story first hit the streets, I would have said not a word, and my spokespeople would have said, "I haven't discussed that with the President; I don't expect to discuss it with him; I know nothing about it."

I'd not even have admitted that I was aware of the developing story, unless and until a reporter asked me about it point-blank. I'd then have said, "I have nothing to say about Ms. Lewinsky," and if I were specifically asked what kind of physical contact took place between us, I'd have frozen the reporter with a look and replied, "A gentleman neither asks nor answers such questions."

If I'd done that, a reporter could have made me look rather silly by asking, "Did you have sex with Sylvester Stallone, then?" if my response to that were "no," then it could be assumed that my previous answer, re Ms. Lewinsky, had been an implicit "yes." If I gave the same response as before – "A gentleman neither asks nor answers such questions" – I'd just sound silly. I'd be obliged to sit still and give the reporter my famous Stare. (If you have never experienced my Stare, thank God for it.) Or I suppose I could have said, "I can't remember. You'll have to ask Sly."

Asked about Ms. Lewinsky at the Paula Jones deposition – or, indeed, asked about my relationship with any other woman – I'd have refused to answer unless the only alternative were to be in contempt of court. If forced by law to answer, I would have answered truthfully, while disclosing as few facts and details as possible. Then, if details of my testimony leaked to the public, I'd be in a wonderful position to denounce Ms. Jones' counselors for being less interested in righting a possible wrong to Ms. Jones than in injuring the President of the United States.

(I have no doubt, by the way, that Clinton did invite Paula Jones up to his hotel room, back when he was Governor; I'm almost as certain that at some point during that interview, he did whip out the Gubernatorial Giggle-Stick and did exhort Ms. Jones to "kiss it." And just a notch below that is my strong suspicion (impossible to prove, of course) that Ms. Jones did drop to her knees and munch away like a champion, and only later decided to be bummed out about it – along the same lines of that old joke, "I didn't know I'd been raped till he never called me again.")

If I'd done all that, the question of whether or not I had asked anyone to lie on my behalf would probably never have arisen. I would probably not have had to appear before the grand jury at all. Instead of going on national TV and confessing that I'd done something naughty, I could have maintained a lofty silence. And it would have been far, far tougher for Kenneth Starr to pretend that my sex life had anything to do with his brief.

It is a funny paradox, that if you can play the gent, and play it with verve – even if it's common knowledge that you're the biggest whoremaster since Jack Kennedy – you can stand up to any assault on your moral character.

A final thought: I can't help suspecting that Dr. Starr's zeal, in this case, is fueled in part by the bitter knowledge that if he, himself, had ever approached a Monica, a Paula, or a Gennifer, she would not even have deigned to sneer at him.

Death

After I Croak

One of my on-line correspondents recently disagreed with my assertion that nobody asks to be born. She informed me that we *do* ask to be born: Each time we die, we are reincarnated in one way or another, and we each have some voice in selecting what our reincarnations will consist of. She was quite dogmatic about it, implying that whether I liked it or not, I was going to be reincarnated as *something*.

A lot of people believe this. Others profess to believe in some sort of afterlife – Heaven, Hell, Purgatory, Nirvana, whatever. I have no way of knowing what happens to people after they die, but I suspect that none of these ideas is very likely. I think it's more likely that when we die, we simply end.

At least, that is what I'm hoping. One life is quite enough for me, and even a never-ending Paradise might be a worse Hell than I'd care to deal with.

I was astonished at how furious I got (silently) at this woman's insistence that she *knew* I would be reincarnated, that it was inevitable. It was somehow more offensive than some Christian threatening me with eternal damnation for not having accepted Jesus Christ as my personal Saviour.

You can dismiss the threat of Hell by considering the source: You hear it from bitter, angry, mean-spirited, stupid people, who are painfully aware that you have a pretty nice life by comparison with theirs.

But I feel personally violated when some New-Ager lays her (invariably, her) beliefs on me in that manner. New-Agers, by and large, don't have the excuse of being stupid or vicious – and yet I couldn't help perceiving a strong tinge of malice behind this woman's insistence that I would be reincarnated. It was presumptuous and disrespectful: like, "Oh, you'll have children, all right, as soon as you meet the right woman!" – only worse.

Whether we believe in reincarnation, or in some sort of un-Earthly hereafter, it would appear that we have these beliefs because we're searching for some kind of purpose in life. Some would say that we live in order to gain enlightenment; others, that we live to glorify God; still others, that our purpose is to take care of our fellow creatures. In any case, to keep us going, most of us apparently need a purpose, or a reward at the end of it all – be it Heaven, or Nirvana, or what you will.

But what if each person's life is, in fact, ultimately pointless? What if you get nothing at the end? What if your existence and those of all your descendants are as insignificant as the blink of a mosquito's eye? In that case, we are on a journey to nowhere: Stuart Little looking for Margalo. And maybe – as turned out to be the case with Stuart Little – the journey, in and of itself, is the only point of the story.

That prospect does not upset me, and I don't understand why it would upset anyone. If what comes after this is utter blankness, so what? We're not likely to notice, are we?

You might ask, "Without some system of rewards or punishments, or without the need to strive for enlightenment, what would be the point of doing *anything*?" I can't speak for others, but I do whatever I do because, at the time, I figure it will make my life more pleasant if I do A rather than B. It makes a person feel good, when he's kind to someone else. It makes his life easier, if he learns more information. He'll be more comfortable in the long run, if he works harder.

We never do anything solely because we *should* do it. We weigh the consequences of our choices, and we choose what we believe to be the pleasantest – or the least unpleasant – alternative. In a sense, we always do what we want to do.

I've decided I'd prefer to die somewhere about 75, with the last thing to register on my mind being the woman lying beneath me suddenly looking over my shoulder and saying, "Raoul, put that shotgun down immediately!"

If I'm sent to Hell, I guess I won't have much to say about what eternity will be like. Were I permitted to design my own Heaven, it might be an enormous private estate – about as big as the old Russian Empire – occupied only by me and every cat I have ever lived with (plus a few new ones just for fun), with a huge state-of-the-art kitchen, an endless supply of food, booze, tobacco, good music, and books I want to read – and absolutely no people, unless I can invite them and kick them out as I please.

Many people talk of seeing all their friends and family in Heaven; a few even talk about meeting and making up with old enemies. That doesn't appeal to me, much. I have no interest in shaking hands with people who did me wrong. Even some people I did like, I never want to see again. I once had a friend who was particularly kind and helpful to me, at a time in my life when I didn't have a lot of friends. He was someone to whom I sometimes was embarrassingly ungrateful. When – not having seen him for nearly 20 years – I heard that he was dead, I felt positively relieved. There was one less person on Earth who knew what I was like at my worst. I would be mortified to meet him, or several other people like him, in the next world.

Heaven and Hell sound like similar places. Perhaps they are the same place. In Hell, you're pitched into an eternal fire; in Heaven, you spend eternity sitting around that fire, holding hands and singing "Kum Ba Ya." Both eventualities sound mighty unpleasant to me, but I suppose that in either case I'd become numb after a time.

I don't want to be reincarnated, because I see no benefit in it. As I understand it (and I admit that my understanding is imperfect), many people who believe in reincarnation hold that the reason for going through a great many lifetimes is that by so doing, you eventually hit a perfect level of spiritual enlightenment, which will enable you to utterly transcend the mundane. Other folks say that reincarnation is inevitable because your body and soul are not your own; they belong to the Universe, and must be re-cycled as a part thereof.

As to perfect spiritual enlightenment, what would I want with it? I can't buy anything with it; it won't do tricks for me; it won't even serve me a hot cup of coffee on a cold afternoon. It might get me laid, but if I were perfectly enlightened, I wouldn't be interested in such swinish pleasures, according to most people who claim to know about these things. You may have my share of spiritual enlightenment, if you want it. As for re-cycling myself, I have no objection to the Universe turning my dead body into compost, but if it puts its intrusive little hands on my psyche, I'm going to kick the Universe right in the nuts.

Whether you're assigned to an afterlife, or to a new life on Earth, doesn't it come down to the same thing? Isn't it a matter of having your past, present, and future evaluated by a gang of priggish Gods who bear comparison more with junior-high-school principals or prison guards than with anything else?

"No, Son, I'm afraid you're going to have to go back once again – and maybe this time you'll gain some understanding."

Do we never get away from schoolteachers, cops, bosses, and parents? *It never ends! It never ends! It never ends!*

My Favorite Star In The Sky

Joseph Dobrian, enough is enough. You are nothing but a festering boil on the hind end of Humanity. You are too horrible to be suffered to live. Accordingly, you will be shot. You will face a firing squad at sunrise, three days hence.

Okay, in reality, I don't expect to be killed by a firing squad, although a man can hope. But if this really were going to happen, I would arrange three symphonic concerts, one for each of the last three nights of my life, as my final request.

Never mind how. Conceivably, three different orchestras might be trucked into the prison, on successive evenings. More likely, I'd have to content myself with recorded music – preferably heard through a first-rate sound system, with video, but, since this is prison after all, probably heard through headphones, on a cheap personal machine.

But, screw it: this is fantasy. So, I'll imagine actual orchestras, led by dead conductors, performing in the prison yard or the gymnasium for the enjoyment of the general population.

*

The reason why I got to thinking about this scenario was that I was recently telling an acquaintance about a concert I'd attended, and I mentioned that the main work on the program had been Tchaikovsky's Symphony No. 6, the "*Pathétique*," which turned out to be the culminating work of his career, since he died a few days after its first performance.

"That's my favorite symphony of all time," I added. "I suppose most people would say Beethoven's Ninth was the greatest symphony ever, but not I."

Then, I asked the lady whether she had a very favorite piece of music, of any genre or form. She gave me a somewhat pitying look, and retorted, "What's your favorite star in the sky?"

I dared to tell her that if I knew anything about astronomy or astrology, it's likely I *would* pick out a favorite star – not what most people would do, I guess, but *me voilà* – but I did see her point. I'd asked her too broad a question. So, following that conversation, I re-phrased the question in my mind, and spent parts of the next several days attempting to answer it for myself.

I came up with this: If you knew it was going to be your last night on Earth, but you still had your faculties about you enough to enjoy music – if you were facing execution the next morning, let's say – what would you choose to listen to?

For me, it would have to be something orchestral. I like just about all kinds of music – classical, country/western, rock, various folk genres, you name it – but in the end, nothing beats classical. And while chamber music can be a real treat, for the end of my life, I require a full orchestra.

And, I concluded, one concert wouldn't do it. For some reason, the number three has always carried extra mojo, so three concerts, on three successive nights, it shall be.

The standard order of business for a classical music concert is to start with an overture (or some other short, lively piece), followed by a concerto or song cycle. Then intermission, and finally the major work of the concert: a symphony, tone poem, or orchestral suite. My concerts would follow that format, except that I'd try to pack in a little extra.

FIRST CONCERT (Eugen Jochum, conducting)

Ralph Vaughan Williams: English Folk Song Suite
George Frideric Handel: Music for the Royal Fireworks
Pyotr Ilyich Tchaikovsky: Serenade for Strings

(Intermission)

Arthur Sullivan: Overture to *Iolanthe*
Ludwig van Beethoven: Symphony No. 8

Do you notice how this first concert contains mostly lighter works? I have a sentimental attachment to the Tchaikovsky because as a young man I saw the Dance Theatre of Harlem performing a very formal, classical ballet to it – with the tutus and all – and can never hear the music without remembering that performance. As for the concluding work, it's generally conceded that Beethoven's Ninth was the "greater" work, but the Eighth was Beethoven's own favorite child. Beethoven's odd-numbered symphonies were all heavy and heroic, while his even-numbered symphonies were more fun and light-hearted – and of those, I enjoy the Eighth the most, by far.

SECOND CONCERT (Herbert von Karajan, conducting)

Elmer Bernstein: Overture to *The Magnificent Seven*
Edvard Grieg: *Peer Gynt* Suite (with vocals)
Maurice Ravel: Le Tombeau de Couperin

(Intermission)

Manuel de Falla: Dance #1 from *La Vida Breve*
Johann Strauss, Jr.: Roses from the South
Jean Sibelius: Symphony No. 2

Excepting the Strauss, these are not pieces one associates with von Karajan, but I'd be interested to see what he could do with them. Elmer Bernstein's work is seldom if ever heard in the concert hall, and I have no idea why. I've never heard a prettier dance tune than the Arabian Dance from *Peer Gynt*, nor been more awed by a single song than by Solveig's Song. And for a single musical moment, I can't think of anything that compares to that not-quite-resolved chord at the end of the minuet in the Ravel piece. It was hard to choose just one of Sibelius' symphonies, but I guess there's a reason why the Second is the best-known and most-played. The pulsing introduction draws you in immediately, and before you know it the rest of the piece has grabbed you by the throat. This is not a symphony. It's combat.

THIRD CONCERT (Leonard Bernstein, conducting)

Felix Mendelssohn: Overture to *A Midsummer Night's Dream*
Sergei Rachmaninoff: Piano Concerto No. 2 (Van Cliburn, piano)

(Intermission)

Maurice Ravel: La Valse
Pyotr Ilyich Tchaikovsky: Symphony No. 6 ("*Pathétique*")

If you want clear instruction in how an orchestra works together, you might do worse than to sit in the front row of the audience, when the Mendelssohn is being played. The Rachmaninoff is sometimes pooh-poohed by sophisticates, and indeed it is a little "poppy," a little redolent of figure-skating competitions. But, you love what you love, and that's one of mine. And I have never heard Cliburn take it on.

Ravel is my single favorite composer, and *La Valse*, with its dark, somewhat sinister tones, strikes me as an ideal piece to listen to on the eve of death.

Ditto the *Pathétique*. I have always believed that the *Pathétique* was all about death. Bernstein used to take that piece noticeably slower than did many conductors – particularly the first movement – and I believe he was correct. It's almost impossible to play that movement too slowly. I would take it at about the tempo I might use if I were enjoying my first kiss with a woman I'd dreamt of kissing for the past year and a half.

The second movement, which sounds like a waltz but isn't (it's in 5/4 time), has an almost mutant, or mongrel, quality to it, that gives it not the pathos of the first movement, but a sort of wistful hopefulness. That sentiment carries over into the third movement: a march that sounds more expectant than triumphant. The climax of that movement impresses me as somewhat vainglorious, defiantly so, as though covertly admitting that triumph will never be realized, and the movement seems to end with a feeling of false enthusiasm that's employed to conceal disappointment.

The adagio finale is perhaps the longest and the greatest anticlimax in musical history: a combination, it seems to me, of regret, despair, and, finally, resignation. Every time I've heard it performed live, the audience is sitting stunned at the end, and several seconds go by before the applause begins – and I have to pretend to believe that it's because they're so deeply moved, and not because they don't know that the piece is over, even though I know perfectly well that the latter is the more likely explanation.

I've heard it suggested that the *Pathétique* would have been more effective, more enjoyable, if the third and fourth movements had been switched and the piece had ended in a more traditional manner, with a big loud finale. If that had been done, the outcome would have been entirely different; the emotion of the piece would have been diluted to the point of ineffectiveness; the symphony would not have been *Pathétique*. To my mind, that unconventional adagio finale was one of the most brilliant creative decisions in the history of classical music.

As you can see from these three programs, my tastes run pretty heavily to the late romantics. Many years ago, I mentioned to a friend that that was the case, and she replied, "Don't worry: you'll outgrow it." My musical palate did become more eclectic with time, and I've learned to enjoy concert music from any era — even some that was composed during my lifetime. But if I knew I'd never hear any more music again in this world, I would stick with the kind of music that brung me to the dance in the first place.

Then, I suspect, I might be able to greet my final sunrise — and the 12 rifles — with equanimity. After three concerts like that, there doesn't need to be anything else.

My favorite star in the sky? I still don't know. But perhaps I'll pick one out, as I'm being marched down into the prison yard, and I'll keep it in my mind's eye as dawn pinks in the East and all the stars disappear from sight — and I'll remember the stars as I call out, "Shoot straight, you bastards; don't make a mess of it!"

CPSIA information can be obtained at www.ICGtesting.com
Printed in the USA
LVOW07s2027041213

363885LV00003B/938/P